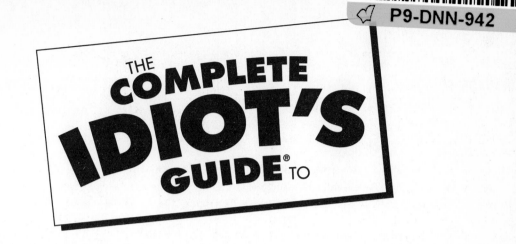

THE COMPLETE IDIOT'S GUIDE® TO

Vegan Cooking

by Beverly Lynn Bennett and Ray Sammartano

ALPHA

A member of Penguin Group (USA) Inc.

To those who are guided by the open heart and open mind of compassion.

ALPHA BOOKS

Published by the Penguin Group

Penguin Group (USA) Inc., 375 Hudson Street, New York, New York 10014, USA

Penguin Group (Canada), 90 Eglinton Avenue East, Suite 700, Toronto, Ontario M4P 2Y3, Canada (a division of Pearson Penguin Canada Inc.)

Penguin Books Ltd., 80 Strand, London WC2R 0RL, England

Penguin Ireland, 25 St. Stephen's Green, Dublin 2, Ireland (a division of Penguin Books Ltd.)

Penguin Group (Australia), 250 Camberwell Road, Camberwell, Victoria 3124, Australia (a division of Pearson Australia Group Pty. Ltd.)

Penguin Books India Pvt. Ltd., 11 Community Centre, Panchsheel Park, New Delhi—110 017, India

Penguin Group (NZ), 67 Apollo Drive, Rosedale, North Shore, Auckland 1311, New Zealand (a division of Pearson New Zealand Ltd.)

Penguin Books (South Africa) (Pty.) Ltd., 24 Sturdee Avenue, Rosebank, Johannesburg 2196, South Africa

Penguin Books Ltd., Registered Offices: 80 Strand, London WC2R 0RL, England

Copyright © 2008 by Beverly Lynn Bennett

THE COMPLETE IDIOT'S GUIDE TO and Design are registered trademarks of Penguin Group (USA) Inc.

International Standard Book Number: 978-1-59257-770-5
Library of Congress Catalog Card Number: 2008920992

10 09   8 7 6 5 4 3

Interpretation of the printing code: The rightmost number of the first series of numbers is the year of the book's printing; the rightmost number of the second series of numbers is the number of the book's printing. For example, a printing code of 08-1 shows that the first printing occurred in 2008.

Printed in the United States of America

Note: This publication contains the opinions and ideas of its authors. It is intended to provide helpful and informative material on the subject matter covered. It is sold with the understanding that the authors and publisher are not engaged in rendering professional services in the book. If the reader requires personal assistance or advice, a competent professional should be consulted.

The authors and publisher specifically disclaim any responsibility for any liability, loss, or risk, personal or otherwise, which is incurred as a consequence, directly or indirectly, of the use and application of any of the contents of this book.

Most Alpha books are available at special quantity discounts for bulk purchases for sales promotions, premiums, fundraising, or educational use. Special books, or book excerpts, can also be created to fit specific needs.

For details, write: Special Markets, Alpha Books, 375 Hudson Street, New York, NY 10014.

Publisher: *Marie Butler-Knight*
Editorial Director: *Mike Sanders*
Senior Managing Editor: *Billy Fields*
Acquisitions Editor: *Tom Stevens*
Senior Development Editor: *Christy Wagner*
Production Editor: *Megan Douglass*
Copy Editor: *Jan Zoya*

Cartoonist: *Steve Barr*
Cover Designer: *Becky Harmon*
Book Designer: *Trina Wurst*
Indexer: *Johnna Vanhoose Dinse*
Layout: *Ayanna Lacey*
Proofreader: *John Etchison*

Contents at a Glance

Contents

Appendixes

Foreword

Eating is the most basic function of human existence—so much so that we almost forget that our lives depend on it. In America today, the overwhelming cause of death is what we eat. This is bad enough, but now we are exporting our diet to the rest of the world.

Heart disease, cancer, and diabetes rates are climbing while most people believe they eat a healthy diet. In reality, these so-called "healthy" diets contribute to their illness. The problem starts from the very top of the education system. Bad advice is as common as Mom, baseball, and apple pie. Government, doctors, and family all are loaded with old wives' tales, false assumptions, and just plain bad advice. I must admit I spent the majority of my life in the camp of the clueless when it came to what was healthy to eat. When I look back, I must marvel at the fact that I survived the pain I inflicted on myself with my fork.

Most of us learn about our diet at our mother's table. We have no doubt that our mother loves us and, therefore, what she serves us must be the best. Wrong! When mothers eat bad diets, they pass along the problem to their children, and they pass it along to their own children. We must break this chain of bad eating habits before we destroy the thing we love the most—our families.

I was raised in rural America eating what we grew on the farm, and for the most part, our diet was very healthy. As we became more affluent, my mother brought into our diet what was available at the local grocery store, as it was the growing rage and it meant a lot less toil for her. White bread, canned meat, cheese, and ice cream were some of the modern marvels we started eating. Little did she know that we were on a very slippery slope toward future health problems. Over time, I added additional bad habits of my own to her advice and soon was a wreck just waiting to happen.

Overweight and with high blood pressure and a cholesterol level of over 300 finally got my attention before it was too late to correct problem. I wish when I was trying to reform my eating habits I would have had a book like *The Complete Idiot's Guide to Vegan Cooking*. The book you hold in your hands contains everything you need to make the transition from the standard American diet, which was killing me, to the vegan diet that saved my life. This book has the solution most Americans need right now, and it's as important as health insurance because a vegan diet can prevent most health problems.

The Complete Idiot's Guide to Vegan Cooking is easy to read, understand, and put into practice immediately. With this book, you can learn in weeks what it took me years to learn. Every family should read this book.

Howard F. Lyman, LL.D., is the president of Voice for a Viable Future, an educational nonprofit. He is a fourth-generation cattleman turned vegan and renowned public speaker. He has written two books, *Mad Cowboy* and *No More Bull!* His website is www.madcowboy.com.

Introduction

Whether you're new to the world of vegan cooking, or you're a seasoned cook who wants to pick up some additional pointers and add some exciting new recipes to your repertoire, this book is for you. In the following chapters, we guide you through all the aspects of preparing your own vegan food and share with you all the tricks of the trade that will soon have you cooking like a pro. Are you ready to begin? Then put on your vegan chef's hat and let's get started!

How to Use This Book

The book is organized into six distinct parts, each devoted to a different aspect of vegan cooking:

Part 1, "Vegan Cooking Basics," provides you with some essential information you need to have to get started. You learn about the health advantages of eating a balanced, plant-based diet and how to be sure your basic nutritional needs are being covered. We also walk you through the basics of substituting for animal ingredients and teach you how to veganize your favorite nonvegan recipes.

Part 2, "Morning Meal Options," gives you loads of vegan breakfast ideas from the quick and easy to the more time-consuming. We begin with fast and easy breakfast ideas, and move into breakfast and brunch recipes that require a little more time to prepare. And finally, you learn how to prepare some favorite vegan sweet and savory baked goods perfect for breakfast and other meals.

Part 3, "Teasers and Toppers," features recipes for appetizers, snacks, spreads, sauces, gravies, and dairy alternatives. We begin with appetizers and snacks and move on to versatile toppers and spreads. The next stop introduces you to a variety of exciting salsas, sauces, and gravies. Finally, you become proficient in mimicking a variety of dairy products like Parmesan, cheddar, pepper jack, and feta cheeses, in addition to a homemade nut milk, nondairy creamer, and tofu sour cream.

Part 4, "Let's Do Lunch," shows you how to make sensational vegan soups, chilis, chowders, and stews, as well as vegan versions of your favorite salad dressings, salads, and sandwiches. We begin with a variety of hot and cold soups and move on to learn how to prepare an assortment of classic salad dressings. Next comes a slew of classic and creative greens salads and slaws, followed by fruit-, veggie-, grain-, and pasta-based salads sure to impress at potlucks, picnics, and other gatherings. We finish by showing you how to prepare vegan versions of classic sandwiches.

Part 5, "What's for Dinner?" covers recipes for satisfying main dishes; veggie, bean, and grain side dishes; and versatile pasta and polenta. We thoroughly explore the realm of vegetable-, legume-, and grain-based side dishes that are as nutritious as they are delicious.

Part 6, "Sweet Endings," takes you to a very sweet place that focuses on cookies, bars, brownies, no-bake treats, and decadent desserts. You begin by learning how to make vegan versions of your favorite sweet baked goods, and you won't even need to turn on your oven for the no-bake goodies in store for you. For a sweet grand finale to the recipes in the book, we end with a series of decadent desserts sure to "wow" your family and friends—vegan or not.

After Part 6, we include some appendixes helpful to you as you further explore your vegan culinary talents. Appendix A contains a list of defined terms that are used in the book, and Appendix B features lists of vegan resources, like books, websites, and contact information for various related organizations.

Extras

In every chapter you'll find boxes that give you extra information, helpful tips, or just fun facts:

Soy What?

Soy What? boxes contain interesting or bet-you-didn't-know information relating to the ingredients, recipes, or other issues discussed in the book.

def•i•ni•tion

These boxes feature definitions that teach you the meanings of some terms you might not be familiar with.

Thyme-ly Tip

Thyme-ly Tip boxes offer timesaving hints and useful tips relating to the recipes or issues covered in the text.

Sour Grapes

Sour Grapes boxes alert you to potential problems or pitfalls.

Acknowledgments

We wish to express our heartfelt appreciation to everyone who helped make this book possible: to acquisitions editor Tom Stevens and senior development editor Christy Wagner; and to Howard Lyman for graciously agreeing to write the foreword. Howard has inspired countless people to go vegan through his tireless work as an activist, author, and documentary filmmaker. We would also like to thank our family and friends for their love and support, as well as vegan writers, cookbook authors, and activists everywhere who inspire us through their work and dedication to spreading the vegan message.

Special Thanks to the Technical Reviewer

The Complete Idiot's Guide to Vegan Cooking was reviewed by an expert who double-checked the accuracy of what you'll learn here, to help us ensure that this book gives you everything you need to know about making delicious vegan dishes at home. Special thanks are extended to Lisa Vislocky.

Trademarks

All terms mentioned in this book that are known to be or are suspected of being trademarks or service marks have been appropriately capitalized. Alpha Books and Penguin Group (USA) Inc. cannot attest to the accuracy of this information. Use of a term in this book should not be regarded as affecting the validity of any trademark or service mark.

Part 1

Vegan Cooking Basics

Part 1 is your crash course in vegan cooking and eating. Here we show you how to cover your nutritional bases, explain what constitutes healthy vegan eating, and offer advice on meal planning. And because knowing how to substitute for animal-based ingredients in your favorite recipes is essential to successful vegan cooking, Part 1 gives you all the necessary information for doing without eggs, dairy, meat, gelatin, and honey.

Vegan cooking is easy and can be a lot of fun when you're armed with the right information. So take a deep breath and get ready to dive right in!

Chapter 1

Healthful Vegan Cooking

In This Chapter

- The benefits of eating vegan
- Covering your nutritional bases
- A re-introduction to the food groups
- Planning good and good-for-you vegan meals

For those of you who might not be clear on what eating vegan entails, let's begin with the basics of vegan food philosophy. If you're eating vegan, you eat foods that come from plant-based sources like whole grains, beans and legumes, fruits, vegetables, and even the aquatically harvested sea vegetables. You avoid all animal-based foods and their rendered or processed byproducts, like meat, fish, fowl, eggs, all dairy products, and even honey and gelatin. It's all pretty simple: if it comes from or was once a plant, it's vegan, and if it once had a face, fins, wings, or feet, forget about it.

But don't worry about being deprived of good foods. You'll have plenty of delicious and satisfying plant-based options to fill your plate to overflowing. Although it may seem new to you at first, especially if you've been eating a diet based around meat, dairy, and eggs, you'll soon be pleasantly surprised by all the delicious and easy vegan meals you can prepare. You can even convert many of your favorite dishes to vegan. Get ready to satisfy and nourish yourself to the fullest!

Eating Vegan for Your Health

In addition to the environmental and animal welfare concerns behind the decision to begin cooking and eating vegan, the desire to be healthier might also factor in. Indeed, there are numerous health advantages to including more or all vegan meals in your diet.

Watch any evening newscast and you'll hear that scientists are discovering how many health issues and chronic diseases are diet-related, including obesity, diabetes, several forms of cancer, heart disease, hypertension, digestive disorders, and kidney and liver problems. The good news is that preparing and eating vegan meals can help you become leaner and lighter, reduce your chance of illness and disease, and as a result, help you live a longer, healthier life.

In comparison to animal-based foods, plant-based foods tend to be lower in fat, sodium, and calories, and they're completely cholesterol free. And because most are rich in dietary fiber, they help regulate and shorten transit time of food through the intestine and to lower cholesterol levels. Also, the greater fiber content of vegan foods makes them more satiating, which causes you to eat less and can lead to weight loss.

> ### Soy What?
>
> The Cornell-Oxford-China Diet and Health Project, or the China Study as it's more commonly known, is one of the most comprehensive and longest-running studies on the correlation between diet and disease. Dr. T. Colin Campbell, Professor Emeritus at Cornell University, and his son Thomas Campbell II published the findings of this health study in *The China Study* (BenBella Books, 2005). In it, they showed how changing to a vegan diet can drastically reduce your risk of obesity, diabetes, cancer, and heart disease.

Doctors also sometimes recommend plant-based foods for patients who suffer from food sensitivities to dairy, eggs, fish, and shellfish. If you count yourself among these special-diet devotees, you'll be thrilled by our tips for replacing animal-based products in Chapter 2, as well as the vast selections of recipes in the upcoming chapters.

We've also included alternate ingredient listings and variation suggestions for many recipes to accommodate for those who suffer from wheat, gluten, corn, and soy sensitivities.

Your Basic Nutritional Needs

To address any nutritional concerns you may have, as well as dispel a few myths commonly associated with a vegan diet, let's look at the nutritional aspects of eating vegan.

Follow the Rainbow

Following the food rainbow can lead to a pot of gold in terms of health benefits. If you consciously make a point of eating a colorful assortment of red, orange, yellow, green, blue, and purple fruits and vegetables, you'll easily supply yourself with a full range of vitamins and minerals, as well as antioxidants and *phytochemicals*. These substances can promote health and longevity, combat free radicals that attack your body's healthy cells, and help reduce your chances of developing cancer and other diseases.

Many of these vital nutrients are only naturally found in plant-based foods, and the ones present in animal-based foods are often the result of the animals eating plants or their feed being fortified with vitamins or minerals.

def•i•ni•tion

Phytochemicals (or *phytonutrients*) naturally occur in fruits, vegetables, and other edible plants and appear to have many beneficial health benefits for fighting and preventing illness and disease, lowering cholesterol levels, balancing hormones, and eliminating toxins.

Calcium Conundrum?

Undoubtedly, when you tell others you're eating vegan, you'll hear "You can't get enough calcium eating vegan," or "You need dairy products for calcium." Well, we're here to tell you that this is totally untrue. What is true is that the calcium in dairy products is the result of cows and other livestock consuming calcium-rich plant foods like grasses, cereal grains, and other vegetation. By directly eating these types of foods yourself, you can cut out the middleman (or animal), so to speak.

A healthy, well-balanced vegan diet—rich in a variety of fruits, vegetables, nuts, and whole grains—can more than adequately supply all the calcium needed for optimal bone health. Also, the fact that you don't consume animal protein also means your bones can actually end up being stronger than your dairy- and meat-consuming counterparts. Research has shown that vegans have higher rates of bone formation than people who consume meat and dairy, even if their calcium intake is lower.

In many other countries where people take in much lower amounts of calcium than we do, the levels within their bodies are higher, and osteoporosis (bone density loss) rates are lower, because they eat more plant-based foods on average than we do. This is due, in part, to the fact that the more acidic animal proteins our body takes in, in the form of meat and dairy products, the more it needs to compensate by releasing calcium from bones to balance out the pH level (the balance of acid and base substances) of our system.

To increase your calcium absorption capabilities, be sure you also get enough magnesium. These two minerals work best as a team in a ratio of 2:1, or 2 parts calcium to 1 part magnesium. You also need to have some vitamin D present in your system to hold on to calcium as well. Just 15 minutes of sunlight exposure per day stimulates the production of vitamin D by the body, and the sun is always your best source of vitamin D. Vegan dietary sources of vitamin D include fortified nondairy milks, cereals, and vegan margarine. For more information about meeting your nutritional needs as a vegan, see www.vrg.org/nutrition or www.pcrm.org.

Sour Grapes

Be aware of foods or supplements fortified with cholecalciferol, as it's a form of vitamin D that's only derived from animal sources. Choose supplemented vitamin D_2 (ergocalciferol) instead.

You can easily fulfill your calcium requirements by eating green leafy vegetables, legumes, seeds, nuts, and whole grains like quinoa. Interestingly enough, your body can more easily absorb the calcium from many plant-based foods when compared to dairy calcium. These include watercress, cauliflower, brussels sprouts, rutabaga, kale, mustard greens, bok choy, broccoli, and turnip greens. Many foods are fortified with calcium, magnesium, and vitamin D, such as soy-based products, cereals and grain products, orange juices and other beverages, and many prepackaged items.

Be Aware of B_{12}

As previously mentioned, vegan plant-based foods contain tons of vitamins, so you can easily fulfill these nutrient needs, especially if you eat a colorful assortment of fruits, vegetables, and whole grains. However, one that can be a bit more evasive on a vegan diet: B_{12}.

Sour Grapes

B_{12} deficiencies, although rare, can lead to anemia, fatigue, or permanent brain or nerve damage. The recommended dietary allowance for adults is 2.4 micrograms per day, with increased amounts recommended for women who are pregnant or breast-feeding, as well as the elderly.

B_{12} is made from fermenting bacteria and can be found in water and soil, which disperses it onto plants, but thorough washing removes most or all of it. It's also found in the gastrointestinal tract of host animals (us included), which is why meat-eaters usually get plenty of B_{12}. However, this vitamin is not contained in the flesh of animals until it comes into contact with gastrointestinal fluids during the slaughtering process.

Fortunately, humans need only a very small amount of B_{12} (which is measured in micrograms), and the human body can amply store a 3- to 5-year supply in the liver.

For an easy way to fulfill your B_{12} needs, you can take a vitamin supplement that meets the daily recommended value, or you can seek out B_{12} fortified foods like the following:

◆ Fortified orange and other fruit juices

◆ Enriched cereals and whole-grain products

◆ Fortified soy milk and other nondairy milks, and products made from them

◆ Fermented soy-based products (tempeh, miso, tamari, or shoyu)

◆ Nutritional yeast flakes sprinkled on or added to foods

> **Soy What?**
>
> Red Star Vegetarian Formula Nutrition Yeast has a nutty, almost cheeselike flavor, which is why it's used commonly as imitation cheese flavoring for foods and in nondairy cheese products. Red Star is available in both flake and powder forms. Flakes are recommended in this book, but you can substitute the powdered by using ⅓ of the amount called for.

Powerful Plant Protein

Proteins are found in all living things, including plants and animals. The building blocks of protein are known as *amino acids*, most of which our body makes naturally. The ones we cannot produce ourselves are called *essential amino acids* (*EAAs*), and we must obtain those through dietary sources.

You can easily meet your vegan protein needs by eating plenty of whole-grain products, beans, soy-based products, nuts and seeds, and leafy and dark green vegetables. And here's something to chew on: tofu, broccoli, and asparagus come in at more than 40 percent protein as a percentage of calories, which is higher than the amount found in eggs and ground beef (each 33 percent), and delicate watercress measures at a whopping 83 percent protein. These sources are all completely cholesterol free to boot.

> **def•i•ni•tion**
>
> **Essential amino acids (EAAs)** are the necessary protein-building blocks we must get through dietary sources to aid in the synthesis of body proteins when combined with the other amino acids our bodies are able to produce. Histidine, isoleucine, leucine, lysine, methionine, phenylalnine, threonine, trytophan, and valine are the EAAs.

You don't have to consciously combine vegan foods (commonly referred to as *protein combining*) to be sure you take in all the EAAs in exactly the amounts your body needs to produce proteins. Just eat a wide variety of these plant-based protein sources on a *regular* basis, and your body will do the matching up for you.

Crazy About Carbs

Even though the low-carb diet craze had many believing otherwise, carbohydrates—which are found in the sugars and starches of plant-based foods—are your friends. You need them to provide fuel and energy needs for all the parts of your body, especially your brain, which can only use glucose for energy. Also, the fiber that many carbohydrate-rich grains and fruits contain helps in the digestion and elimination process.

Many vegan foods are excellent sources of carbohydrates, most notably whole grains, rice, cereals, canned and dried beans, and fresh and frozen fruits and vegetables of all colors, shapes, and sizes. Just be sure to eat more complex carbohydrates and foods in their natural state. Those that have been overly processed and refined have been transformed into simple carbohydrates that can cause blood sugar levels to spike (rise quickly). This can trigger an increase in insulin production that will lead to your feeling hungry again sooner than you should.

Making Friends with Fats

Overall, plant-based foods tend to be lower in fat, especially saturated fats, than animal-based foods. Several plant-based foods contain healthy types of fats you need, known as *essential fatty acids* (*EFAs*), or omega-3 and -6.

def•i•ni•tion

> **Essential fatty acids** (EFAs) are fats the body is incapable of producing but that are required for health. Consequently, they're also necessary in the diet. The most important functions of the EFAs are to support normal growth and development (especially of the eyes and brain), serve as precursors of vital anti-inflammatory compounds, and potentially prevent heart disease.

Most people associate fish and seafood with EFAs, but they can also be found in some leafy greens, and most readily in nuts and seeds like walnuts, flaxseeds, pumpkin seeds, sunflower seeds, and hemp seeds (which contains them all), as well as the oils made from these ingredients. Many people feel that the omega oils are best enjoyed cold- or expeller-pressed or unrefined to preserve their beneficial nutrients, as heating some polyunsaturated oils to high temperatures can denature the oil and form harmful free radicals that cause cell damage. When choosing oils for cooking, seek out those that have the highest levels of monounsaturated fats like olive oil, safflower oil, sunflower oil, soybean oil, and peanut oil.

Vegetable-based margarines, which are often used in baked goods and as spreads, have been getting a lot of bad press lately. Many of the vegetable-based oils used to make these products are *hydrogenated* to make them solid or partially solid. These types of fats are commonly referred to as *trans fats* and have been associated with heart disease. Even though these cheaply made oils were popping up in prepackaged fried foods and baked goods of all sorts, the government has started cracking down on their use. We only recommend using nonhydrogenated vegan margarines in our recipes and discuss these options further in Chapter 2.

Fabulous Fiber

Most vegan foods also contain tremendous amounts of beneficial dietary fiber, something that's completely lacking in animal-based foods. Also, in several studies, increased fiber consumption has been reported to decrease the risk of certain cancers (like colorectal cancer) and lower cholesterol levels. So be sure to consume 25 to 35 grams fiber per day to optimize these health benefits.

Fibers are the structural components of plants. Two types of fiber are characterized by their solubility in water: insoluble and soluble. Many plant-based foods such as fruits and vegetables contain both types of fiber.

Insoluble fiber can be found in the skins of many fruits and vegetables, cruciferous vegetables, green beans, corn, and wheat and wheat-based products. These foods help regulate your bowel movements and shorten the transit time of undigested food through the intestine.

Soluble fiber is found in oats, barley, brown rice, flaxseeds, carrots, apples, and oranges. When they combine with water in the digestive tract, they gel, bind nutrients (including cholesterol), and escort them out of the body. In addition, because of the slow rate of digestion, fiber in general helps regulate blood sugar levels so you don't experience peaks and valleys in your energy levels throughout the day.

Eating fiber-rich foods also gives you a sense of fullness, so you eat less, which lowers your daily caloric intake, which helps you lose weight.

> **Soy What?**
>
> For every 14 grams of fiber you take in, your daily caloric intake is cut by 10 percent. The United States Department of Agriculture (USDA) says you should consume 25 to 35 grams of fiber, but 40 grams is the ideal amount and easily attainable when eating as a vegan.

So have we convinced you enough that with just a little effort on your part, plant-based vegan foods can easily supply you with all your basic nutritional needs? Just be sure to drink plenty of fluids, eat a colorful variety of plant-based foods, make wise food choices, and try to reduce the amount of excess fat, sugar, salt, and empty calories where you can. For those who are still in doubt or who rely a little too much on packaged food items, feel free to take the occasional multivitamin and mineral supplement.

Pyramid Schemes

When it comes to eating properly, portion size is important—and also one topic many people are confused about. Some of the confusion stems from misleading information and food manufacturers' packaging. Those of us over the age of 40 were taught in grade school that there were four basic food groups:

- Meats

- Dairy products

- Grains

- Fruits and veggies

This message came to us through educational films and colorful posters displayed on classroom walls. Many people don't realize it, but those were actually advertisements created and funded by meat and dairy special interests and, not surprising, were slanted toward promoting their products.

In 1992, the basic four food groups were kicked to the curb and replaced by a pyramid shape the USDA hoped would better illustrate our dietary needs and proper portion sizes. While the "base" of the pyramids was based on grains, it still was heavily weighted toward the promotion of meat and dairy.

The pyramid was updated in 2005 by flipping it on its side, reformatting the information a bit, and adding stairs to the design as a reminder to exercise. However, the latest pyramid recommendations don't work for vegans, even with some manipulating, and many people find the new design confusing.

The New Four Food Groups

Fortunately, in 1991, the Physician's Committee for Responsible Medicine (PCRM) developed a strictly plant-based set of dietary guidelines they aptly named the New

Four Food Groups. It is easy to follow and was specifically developed with vegans in mind. PCRM freely distributes copies of the Four Food Groups, and many of their brochures include easily recognizable food icons.

The New Four Food Groups consist of the following categories and serving suggestions:

Whole grains   Breads and breadlike products, hot and cold cereals, pasta, rice, and other grains. Need 5 or more servings daily. One serving can be $^1/_2$ cup cooked cereal, pasta, or grains; 1 cup cold cereal; or 1 slice of bread.

Legumes   Peas, lentils, beans, soy-based products, nuts, and seeds. Need 2 or more servings daily. One serving can be 1 tablespoon nut butter, 1 ounce vegan meat-less alternative product, $^1/_4$ cup nuts or seeds, $^1/_2$ cup cooked legumes, 4 ounces tofu or tempeh, or 1 cup soy milk.

Fruits   Whole fruits, fruit juices, frozen fruits, and dried fruits. Need 3 or more servings daily. One serving can be $^1/_4$ cup dried fruit, $^1/_2$ cup frozen or cooked fruit, $^1/_2$ cup fruit juice, or 1 whole piece of fruit.

Vegetables   Cruciferous, dark green leafy vegetables, dark yellow and orange vegetables, nightshades like potatoes and tomatoes, and other vegetables. Need 3 or more servings daily. One serving can be $^1/_2$ cup cooked or frozen vegetables or 1 cup raw vegetables.

Remember, these are the *minimum* daily requirements, so feel free to increase your number of servings in one or more categories as your appetite desires. If you didn't get to eat as well as you should one day, you can make up for it on the following day.

Also, you don't need to keep a food journal to be sure you fill all your quotas. Just be conscious of the ingredients you're using while preparing meals or when eating out. It can be very easy to consume several servings from each category at just one sitting or meal. For instance, by eating a bowl of soup or a large salad made with several types of vegetables, you can easily get in your 3 or more servings, or even 1 serving of whole grains, legumes, and fruit by having a simple PB&B (peanut butter and banana) sandwich.

Thyme-ly Tip

To learn more about PCRM and the New Four Food Groups for adults, as well as recommendations specifically for children, visit www.pcrm.org. This site also provides health and nutrition advice on a wide range of subjects, including cancer prevention, heart disease, and diabetes, plus recipes, vegetarian starter kits, and resource information.

Planning Healthful Meals

Now that you have the basic nutritional facts about vegan ingredients and understand how many and what size servings you need to strive for on a daily basis, we can now get into planning healthy vegan meals, whether you cook them all yourself or occasionally eat out. Doing a bit of planning when it comes to preparing vegan meals has several advantages, from ensuring a variety of tastes and textures in your ingredient selections to making shopping for these items a whole lot easier.

Some people are creatures of habit and like to eat the same thing day after day, such as a bowl of cereal for breakfast and a salad for lunch. This is probably fine for during the week to make things less hectic, but hopefully you'll change things up a bit on the weekend. If you don't, this pattern of eating can lead to falling into a dietary rut and becoming bored with your meals. Mealtime is much more exciting for you and your taste buds, as well as more nutritionally beneficial, if you eat a variety of foods.

Playing the Numbers

Even though most of us are still in the habit of only eating three large meals a day, nutritionists now recommend eating five to seven smaller meals and healthy snacks throughout the day. Eating smaller-size meals every few hours rather than three large plates or bowlfuls has several health advantages, including helping keep your blood sugar levels more even throughout the day.

Thyme-ly Tip

If you often find yourself feeling cranky, edgy, or yelling at others during the afternoon hours between 3 to 5 o'clock, eat a healthful snack. You're on edge because you're hungry and eagerly awaiting dinner.

For those trying to lose weight, eating more often can actually speed up your metabolism and aid in weight loss. Yes, that's right, it's a dieter's dream, eating more often and losing weight, and smaller portions are also more easily digested. But keep in mind that many of these extra meals are meant to be just nibbles and not an excuse for full-blown grazing on a bag of chips. Think small and be selective, make wise choices, and avoid grabbing for foods that contain tons of sugar, salt, and empty calories.

Sensible Suggestions

Start your day with a sensible breakfast, choosing foods that come from two or more of the new four food groups:

- Hot or cold cereal with some fresh fruit and soy milk

- Pancakes topped with fruit and syrup and a glass of fruit or vegetable juice

- A tofu scramble with veggies and slices of whole-grain toast or a muffin

A few hours later, around mid-morning, have a snack:

- A handful of nuts or seeds

- Some hummus or other dip with baby carrots or other cut fresh veggies

Have lunch a few hours after that:

- A salad with plenty of leafy greens and fresh veggies with maybe some garbanzo beans and a light dressing

- A veggie wrap with a small side salad

- A bowl of soup with a sandwich made on whole-grain bread with vegetarian deli-style slices (like Tofurky) and vegan cheese with lettuce, tomato, and sprouts

Thyme-ly Tip

Be an educated vegan consumer by diligently reading package ingredient lists. Hidden animal-derived ingredients can pop up in the most unusual places. Check this list of animal-derived ingredients before your next shopping trip: www. caringconsumer.com/resources_ ingredients_list.asp.

Mid-afternoon, have another snack:

- A piece of fruit or cut veggies

- A glass of juice or soy milk and an energy bar

- Whole-grain crackers with nut butter or vegan cheese

Follow this up with a dinner:

- A plate of pasta with marinara sauce and a side salad or cooked vegetables

- A veggie stir-fry over grains or noodles with a bowl of miso soup or baked tofu or tempeh

- A plate of beans, grains, and greens with a piece of cornbread

A couple hours after dinner, you can have another snack if you like:

- Popcorn or tortilla chips and salsa
- Whole-grain crackers with vegan cheese or a spread

If you didn't go overboard or if you want a special treat, have dessert:

- A scoop of nondairy ice cream topped with fruit or nuts
- A few vegan cookies or a vegan brownie
- A piece of vegan cake or pie

These are all just suggestions, so get creative and enjoy eating an assortment of healthy foods that appeal to you. In Parts 2 through 6 of this book, you learn to make, bake, and cook a wide variety of vegan recipes that will help in planning your meals. In Chapter 2, we share substitution ideas for replacing animal-based ingredients with vegan ones to make your meal preparations easier.

The Least You Need to Know

- Eating vegan doesn't have to leave you feeling deprived. There are lots of options available!
- Be aware of your vitamin B_{12} consumption and regularly eat fortified foods and/or take a supplement.
- Eat a wide variety of whole grains, fruits, legumes, and vegetables for maximum health benefits—and to lose weight!
- Use the new four food groups to guide your daily and weekly meal decisions.

Simple Substitutions

In This Chapter

- ◆ Substituting for meat, dairy, cheese, and eggs
- ◆ A look at vegan-suitable sweeteners
- ◆ Tips for veganizing your favorite recipes

Get ready to experience all the wonderful possibilities for replacing animal-based ingredients with plant-based ones. You could call this learning the art of substitution, because with a little sleight of hand, ingenuity, and creativity, you can easily replace just about any ingredient to make it vegan friendly.

In some instances—and with certain ingredients like soy milk, tofu, tempeh, and various prepackaged vegan alternatives—you and your guests may find it hard to believe that the dish is truly vegan. Other times, your substitutions might result in something that looks and tastes dramatically different from the original version but is still wonderfully delicious on its own merit.

Meatless Alternatives

Vegan alternatives to meat don't come with hidden strings attached like animal-based protein foods do, and they supply you with the lean, low-fat, cholesterol-free protein many doctors and dieticians recommend for fending off heart disease. Eating these meat alternatives also helps you avoid possible exposure to growth hormones, E. coli, salmonella, and other food-borne illnesses.

So many plant-based options are available for replacing meat in your vegan cooking. Basically, you can take one of two approaches: either utilize a few basic ingredients to make them yourself, or purchase prepackaged meatless alternatives to use in recipes and meal preparations. Whichever way you want to go is up to you, but to help you decide, we offer a brief rundown of a few of our favorite meat replacers and mimickers.

The Incredible, Edible Soybean

The soybean is a wonder food. It has so many uses—and is good for you! Soybeans can be ground up and used to make soy milk and many dairy replacement products, meatless loaves, and veggie burgers. But like a chameleon, these golden beans can also be transformed into tofu, tempeh, and a wide range of prepackaged meatless items.

Terrific Tofu

Tofu is one of the most versatile ingredients in a vegan's food arsenal. It can be used to replicate chicken, fish, and even ground beef in savory dishes; replace eggs in both cooking and baking; and replace dairy products in dressings, sauces, baked goods, and desserts. Tofu was once hard to find outside of Asian specialty markets, but its popularity has grown considerably over the last few decades and today you can find blocks of tofu in assorted sizes, flavors, varieties, and levels of firmness, either covered with water in packages or vacuumed packed, in most grocery and natural foods stores.

Tofu, or *bean curd*, is made in a manner similar to making cheese. A coagulant is added to soy milk; the curds and whey are separated; and the solids are shaped in molds, cut into blocks, and packaged for sale. At this point, the tofu still has soft texture so it's labeled *soft*, *silken*, or *silken-style* tofu. Soft tofu works well in puréed or blended preparations for making sauces, dressings, and desserts. For nonblended applications, if the tofu is packed in water, discard the water and then crumble it for use in tofu scrambles, mock egg salad, and vegan cheeses.

Many tofu manufacturers place heavy weights on the blocks of soft tofu to press out excess moisture to give them a firmer texture, and they're then labeled accordingly as *firm* or *extra firm*. These firmer blocks of tofu are better suited for savory preparations. They usually come packed in water, so gently squeeze out any excess water and then cut the block into cubes, strips, triangles, or cutlets as desired. Keep in mind that plain tofu is rather bland and that it has a spongelike quality, so if you squeeze out the excess moisture, it can then soak up more marinade or sauce, which will intensify its flavor.

The way you cut and season tofu can help it mimic meat in both appearance and flavor. You can add some nutritional yeast, seasonings, and tamari to give the tofu a chickenlike flavor, or cover it with bread-crumbs to make mock fried chicken or nug-gets. Seasoning it with a little kelp powder imparts a fishlike flavor. Thin strips of tofu marinated in tamari and maple syrup taste a little like pork or bacon. Crumbled tofu works well as a replacement for ground beef in chili, marinara sauce, and meatless burg-ers and loaves. Freezing and then thawing a block of tofu gives it a firm and chewy texture, rather than a tender one, which is desirable for some recipes.

Thyme-ly Tip

Tofu is typically packaged covered in water, which should be discarded prior to use. If you don't need the full block of tofu for a recipe, place the remainder in an airtight con-tainer, cover with fresh water, and store in the refrigerator. If you change the water daily, the tofu will stay fresh for up to five days.

Tantalized by Tempeh

As we said earlier, tofu is made like cheese. Well, the Indonesians came up with the idea of injecting a soybean mixture with a special beneficial mold and fermenting it, so you might say that the resulting *tempeh* is the blue cheese version of tofu. This fer-mentation procedure gives tempeh a rich, earthy flavor similar to mushrooms or beef, and it also concentrates the protein content and makes it more easily digestible than tofu for most people.

Tempeh has a marbled appearance and is sold as a solid, cakelike slab. Tempeh can be made with just soybeans alone or in combination with other ingredients like sun-flower seeds, sesame seeds, lentils, barley, millet, oats, quinoa, and rice. For the most flavorful tempeh, choose a multigrain or flavored variety. Steaming tempeh causes it to swell a bit, which increases not only its volume, but its ability to absorb marinades and sauces. Most tempeh is sold pre-steamed and ready for use.

Tempeh has a firmer texture than tofu and retains its shape better in recipes. You can thinly slice it; cut it into cubes, strips, or cutlets; or crumble it. Tempeh has a somewhat beeflike flavor, so try it crumbled or cut into strips to replace beef in stir-fries or sauces, or to make meatless burgers or sausages. Tempeh tastes especially delicious when combined with tamari, toasted sesame oil, balsamic vinegar, peanut butter, or ketchup. Also try it flavored with dried herbs like rosemary, basil, and oregano, or spicy curry powder, chili powder, or cayenne.

> ### Soy What?
>
> *Textured vegetable protein* (*TVP*) is a processed soy-based product made from defatted soy flour that's cooked under pressure and extruded through a machine. It's available in a dry form as granules, flakes, and chunks and needs to be rehydrated in hot liquid prior to use. The granules and flakes work well as a replacement for ground beef in chili, burgers, and tacos, and the strips can be used in stir-fries, casseroles, and stews.

Sensational Seitan

Ingenious monks are responsible for coming up with the idea of using water to rinse the starch out of wheat flour, leaving behind just the gluten, and then flavoring the gluten to make a tasty meat replacement. This traditional way of making *seitan* (also referred to as *gluten* or *wheat meat*) can take hours of rinsing and kneading, and many people still make it this way. Others use *vital wheat gluten* (also called *instant gluten flour*), which skips the rinsing step, requires minimal kneading, and enables you to make homemade seitan in less time.

Either way you approach making homemade seitan, how you cook it and the ingredients you combine and season it with greatly determine its final flavor and texture. Simmering it in a flavorful broth causes the raw, spongelike gluten dough to swell, become firm, and acquire a slightly chewy texture. Depending on what you add to the broth, you can give it a beef, chicken, pork, Asian, or Italian flavor. Commonly used flavoring ingredients include tamari, nutritional yeast flakes, tomato-based products, bay leaves, garlic, ginger, and fresh and dried herbs and spices.

> ### Soy What?
>
> If you want to try seitan without having to do so much work, you can buy pre-made seitan in most grocery and natural foods stores. It comes in various package sizes, shapes, flavors, and even covered in sauces, with the most popular varieties being chicken-style and teriyaki.

You can roll the seitan dough into logs and cut it into small chunks or large cutlets prior to simmering it. Afterward, you can thinly or thickly slice, cube, shred, or crumble it for use in soups, stews, stir-fries, or casseroles, or top slices with sauces or gravy, as well as use them on sandwiches. Besides simmering, you can also combine the seitan dough with other ingredients and bake it in a loaf pan as a roast, or cut it as desired, cover it with a sauce or gravy, and bake it as a casserole. (We use this last method to make a vegan version of barbecued short ribs in Chapter 15.) Seitan is also used as an ingredient in many meatless roasts, burgers, sausages, deli-style slices, and even imitation turkey roasts.

Other Plant-Based Options

Soybeans aren't the only protein-rich legumes you can use to bulk up recipes or replace meat. Black beans, pinto beans, garbanzo beans, red and brown lentils, peas, and even peanuts can be used to make veggie burgers and loaves, flavorful patties and sausages, and burrito and taco fillings. They can also add a chewy heartiness to sauces, chili, stews, and casseroles.

You can use finely ground, chopped, or whole nuts or seeds like walnuts, cashews, almonds, sunflower seeds, and pumpkin seeds in these same applications, for added texture and protein.

Mushrooms work well as a meat replacement, and they contain significant amounts of protein. They have a chewy texture; a rich, earthy, and somewhat beefy flavor; and can be made even more flavorful if marinated in tamari, balsamic vinegar, or wine with fresh or dried herbs and garlic. They can be finely ground, coarsely chopped, or sliced and added to recipes as a replacement for beef or pork in chili, sausages, and savory dishes. Large portobello mushroom caps can be eaten as meatless burgers or steaks.

Pre-Made Meatless Alternatives

In addition to the various ingredients you can use to make homemade meat replacements, several pre-made meatless products are available for you to use. Practically any type of meat or meat product you once enjoyed is now made in a meatless form. Check the refrigerated and freezer sections of your local grocery and natural foods stores to see what looks good. Asian specialty markets also sell many meat alternatives that are strikingly reminiscent in flavor and appearance to beef, pork, chicken, and even fish and seafood (even imitation shrimp with pink stripes).

Do a bit of browsing during your next shopping trip, and you're sure to find several of the following:

◆ Veggie burgers and hot dogs (even foot-long styles)

◆ Meatless sausage logs, patties, links, flavored large sausages, soyrizo, and brats

◆ Vegetarian bacon strips and Canadian bacon slices

◆ Vegetarian deli-style slices, such as ham, turkey, beef, bologna, salami, and pepperoni

◆ Meatless chunks, strips, meatballs, and crumbles

◆ Chicken-free patties and nuggets

> **Soy What?**
>
> The meatless alternatives market is a booming industry, as sales have increased tremendously and so has selection. Sample different products and brands to see which ones you like best, and compare sodium, fat, and ingredient contents as well as nutrition labels to assist you in the selection process.

Many of these products go far beyond anything you could whip up in your kitchen in terms of flavor, texture, and appearance.

Move Over, Milk

As we mentioned in Chapter 1, there's no need for you to drink cow's milk or any other animal-based milk to supply your body with calcium, because you can get plenty by eating plant-based foods. You also don't need cow's milk for use in your vegan cooking and baking recipes because, measure for measure, most nondairy milks substitute wonderfully in most instances. A few of the nondairy options you're sure to encounter include soy milk, rice milk, hemp milk, oat milk, multigrain milk, and nut milks like almond or hazelnut.

Most of these nondairy milks are available in a wide selection of various-size containers and as low-fat, plain, flavored, sweetened, and unsweetened varieties. Many are also fortified with vitamins, minerals, and calcium. Look for them in the refrigerated case or in aseptic containers on shelves in most grocery and natural foods stores.

You can also find vegan liquid nondairy creamers, plain and flavored soy-based yogurts in 6-ounce and 1-quart sizes (a rice yogurt recently hit the market, too), flavored soy yogurt-smoothie beverages, and tofu sour cream. Enjoy these on their own or use as substitutes in dips, dressings, soups, sauces, baked goods, and desserts to your heart's content. You'll also find recipes in Chapter 9 for making your own homemade nut milk, nondairy creamer, and herb-flavored sour cream.

Thyme-ly Tip

For those who like flavored nondairy milks, check the shelves of your local stores, where you're likely to find several varieties such as vanilla, chocolate, chocolate-banana, carob, banana, strawberry, strawberry-banana, chai, spiced, coffee, and horchata, and holiday flavors like pumpkin spice, eggless nog, and peppermint chocolate. Drink them by the glass; add them to coffee, tea, or hot chocolate; or use them in smoothies or alcoholic beverages as well as in your favorite recipes. Vegan liquid nondairy creamers also come in vanilla, hazelnut, and mocha flavors.

Better Than Butter

Cow's milk is also used to make butter, and so many Americans use copious amounts of it to cook or flavor their food and to make baked goods and desserts. Fortunately, you have several butter-replacement options in your vegan cooking and baking. Margarine is the logical choice for a spread, making frosting, and making cookies, but be sure to check the ingredients list carefully, as many whipped tubs and sticks contain whey and other dairy-based products.

When selecting margarine, sidestep those that contain unhealthy hydrogenated fats, also known as *trans fats*. Our favorite nonhydrogenated vegan margarines are Soy Garden, Earth Balance, and Spectrum Spreads. They work perfectly for all our vegan cooking and baking needs.

Many grandmothers and mothers swear by using lard or solid vegetable-based shortenings in their piecrusts for flakiness, but well-chilled margarine works well, as do palm-based shortenings that come in sticks and tubs. Many vegan bakers swear by these products for making piecrusts, pastries, cookies, cakes, and frostings. They can also be used for frying foods.

You can also use vegetable-based oils like olive, safflower, sunflower, and corn oil to flavor your cooked dishes, drizzle over breads and vegetables, and use for baking. Whenever possible, buy cold expeller-pressed oils, preferably organic, as they're less refined and have a better flavor. Coconut oil can also be used to flavor foods, in baked goods, to make delicious tasting frosting and confections, and even to moisturize your hair and skin.

Thyme-ly Tip

If you want to reduce the amount of fat in your meals, you can sauté or steam-fry ingredients with a little water, vegetable broth, or juice in place of all or part of the suggested oil.

Say Cheese

Cheese is often the one obstacle that keeps vegetarians from permanently going vegan. Fortunately, there's a vast array of vegan alternatives to dairy-based cheeses these days. Are you hankering for a hunk, need a slice to top your sandwich, or something to sprinkle on your soup or pasta? Then check the refrigerated case in your local grocery and natural foods store, and you're sure to find packages of vegan cheese blocks and pre-cut slices. The most commonly available brands are Vegan Rella, Soymage Vegan, Tofutti, and the highly acclaimed Follow Your Heart Vegan Gourmet Cheese Alternative.

Many people prefer the vegan cheese blocks, which can be sliced or shredded as needed for a topper for crackers or used in burritos, tacos, casseroles, salads, nachos, and even pizza. Although many vegan brands don't melt or get gooey, Follow Your Heart Vegan Gourmet Cheese Alternative actually does, and it comes in mozzarella, cheddar, nacho, and Monterey Jack flavors.

Thyme-ly Tip

Instead of using shredding or sliced vegan cheese when you want melted cheese, use a hot vegan cheese sauce. This especially works well for topping pizza, pasta, and nachos. In Chapter 9, we give you a recipe for Vegan Cheese Sauce Mix. By combining this dry mix with water or nondairy milk, you can whip up hot vegan cheese sauce in minutes.

In Chapter 9, we give you recipes for making your homemade vegan cheeses. These flavored cheeses have a relatively soft texture and can be easily spread, sliced, crumbled, or gently shredded for use in your favorite recipes and on sandwiches.

Nutritional yeast flakes are an easy way to give your food a cheesy flavor, and they're a key ingredient for making vegan cheeses and cheese sauces, including many of the recipes in Chapter 9. If you're looking for an alternative to Parmesan cheese for recipes and as a topping, you can use these cheesy-tasting flakes, purchase soy-based Parmesan cheese or a raw version called Parma, or try our Raw Parmesan Cheese (recipe in Chapter 9).

You can also use crumbled tofu combined with seasonings as replacements for ricotta, feta, and cottage cheese. Several brands of tofu cream cheese are available in both plain and flavored varieties. You can use these as spreads for bagels or sandwiches or to make dips, frostings, pastries and confections, and even vegan cheesecake.

Eggless and No Regrets

Eggs are high in fat and cholesterol, but you have several options to replace them in your vegan meal preparations—all of which are low fat and cholesterol free. The key to selecting which one to use and how to go about doing it often depends on the function eggs are performing in a recipe. Eggs are typically used to add moisture to recipes or to act as a binder, thickener, or leavening agent.

Here are some basic suggestions for replacing 1 egg in vegan recipes:

◆ 2 teaspoons baking powder whisked with 1 tablespoon vegetable oil and 2 tablespoons water

◆ 1 tablespoon cornstarch, arrowroot, soy flour, or other flour whisked with 1 tablespoon water or other liquid

◆ 1 tablespoon *Ener-G Egg Replacer* whisked vigorously with 2 tablespoons water (double package instructions)

◆ 1 tablespoon finely ground flaxseeds stirred or blended in a blender with 3 tablespoons water; allow to rest for 5 minutes or longer

def•i•ni•tion

Ener-G Egg Replacer is made with potato starch, tapioca flour, and leavening agents and can be substituted for eggs in many of your vegan baked goods. Look for boxes in most grocery and natural foods stores.

◆ 2 tablespoons tahini or nut butter, such as peanut butter or almond butter

◆ $\frac{1}{4}$ cup applesauce or mashed or puréed bananas, plus add $\frac{1}{2}$ teaspoon aluminum-free baking powder to recipe

◆ $\frac{1}{4}$ cup silken, firm, or extra-firm tofu blended until smooth with other wet ingredients in recipe

Replacing eggs is most challenging in baked goods and desserts. When it appears as though adding an egg or two was just needed for moisture and not for leavening, you can simply omit it with few ill effects, especially when making pancakes, cookies, and quick breads. If you're worried about the recipe being heavy or dry, add a tablespoon or two of water, nondairy milk, or fruit juice or purée, and add $\frac{1}{2}$ teaspoon aluminum-free baking powder for each egg that was needed. Leavening action is most needed when making vegan cakes, and to give them some lift, you can use one of these substitution suggestions like Ener-G Egg Replacer, blended tofu, or fruit purée, and also add an additional $\frac{1}{2}$ teaspoon baking powder.

When substituting for eggs in savory recipes in which eggs were being used as a binder or thickener, try adding 2 to 4 tablespoons flour, cornstarch, arrowroot, oats, breadcrumbs, ground nuts, tahini, peanut butter, tomato paste, or mashed potatoes or other vegetables as needed to achieve your desired results. If eggs were needed just for moisture, you can omit them and add a little additional water, vegetable juice, broth, purée, oil, or other liquid that's also used in the recipe. As we discussed earlier in this chapter, you can use crumbled tofu to make tofu scrambles, or blend it with other ingredients as the base for eggless quiches, as well as a binder in savory dishes.

Gelatin Alternatives

Another commonly used binder and thickener that's off-limits in vegan food preparation is animal-based gelatin. These innocent-looking ground powders; translucent sheets; and fine, stringlike shreds are obtained by boiling miscellaneous pieces and parts of animals in water until their natural collagen is released. Gelatin is commonly used to thicken candies, jellies and jams, sauces, marshmallows and other confections, desserts, and baked goods, and also to clarify soups, stocks, and even wine and other alcoholic beverages.

Many people are fond of the fruit-flavored jiggly desserts made from boxes filled with powdered gelatin, and if you miss these convenience items, check your local grocery and natural foods stores for vegetable-based plain and flavored gelatins made from starches, soy, and seaweed. Yes, we said *seaweed*. *Agar-agar*, also known simply as *agar* or *kanten* (also the name of a jelled dessert made with it; recipe in Chapter 22), is derived from seaweed and is odorless and tasteless. It's sold in sticks, flakes, and powders in most stores, and it's readily available and quite inexpensive in Asian specialty markets. Depending on which form and how much is used, it will slightly thicken or firmly gel the liquid or food it's used in.

Thyme-ly Tip

When thickening vegetable broth, gravy, sauce, pudding, or other such mixtures, use a starch or flour. For every 1 cup mixture you need to thicken, first dissolve 1 tablespoon starch or flour in 2 tablespoons cold water or other liquid. Whisk this mixture slowly into the other, and cook while whisking constantly for several minutes until desired thickness is achieved.

You can also use cornstarch, arrowroot, kudzu, tapioca flour, Ener-G Egg Replacer, or agar-agar combined with a little water or other liquid to gel and thicken your sauces, puddings, pie fillings, desserts, and nondairy cheese (see recipes in Chapter 9). Most of these ingredients need to be cooked or soaked to activate their gelling capabilities, while others can be simply mixed in and set aside or chilled.

Using flour and cornstarch results in a slightly cloudy, dull, creamy-looking mixture, while tapioca flour and arrowroot gives them a shiny gloss. Combining flaxseeds and water (see reference for replacing eggs earlier in this chapter) also makes a gummy, gel-like substance that can be used in similar food preparations.

How Sweet It Is

As far as sweeteners go, sugar is the one that many of us turn to most often. We sprinkle it on fruit, cereal, and toast; use it to lightly sweeten beverages, dressings, and sauces; and of course, rely on it to generously sweeten baked goods and desserts.

Sweet-tasting sugar comes in light- and dark-colored granules as well as in light and fluffy powdered form. Two of the most common forms of granulated sugar are made from sugar cane and sugar beets (commonly known as *beet sugar*). These two types of sugar are processed in similar ways, although sugar cane is more refined, often utilizing nonvegan bone char in the filtering process, and they do have slightly different tastes.

Unfortunately for those concerned about using all-vegan ingredients, the three largest U.S. sugar manufacturers all bleach their cane sugar to filter out impurities and to change its color from golden brown to bright white. Even brown and powdered sugar varieties go through this process. More than 50 percent of the time, this bleaching process is done using animal-based charcoal, referred to as bone char, thus making this type of sugar nonvegan.

def•i•ni•tion

Beet sugar is made from sugar beets—a light-colored, high-sugar-content variety of beets—and is processed much like cane sugar. Unlike cane sugar, it is never bleached with bone char. You can generally use beet sugar measure for measure to replace cane sugar. In most stores, you can find white, brown, and powdered beet sugars.

Finding vegan sugar is easier than you might think, though. Look for products such as unbleached cane sugar, evaporated cane juice, evaporated cane sugar, natural cane sugar, organic cane sugar (also light and dark brown sugar), turbinado sugar, raw sugar, demerara sugar, beet sugar, Sucanat, Muscavado, and dark brown molasses sugar. You can use these products measure for measure to replace their bleached counterparts. Florida Crystals, Wholesome Sweeteners, Billington's, Hain Pure Foods, and Rapadura manufacture many of these vegan sugar varieties. When in doubt as to whether a product is vegan, feel free to contact the company and ask.

In most grocery and natural foods stores, you can find maple sugar (made from dehydrated maple syrup) and date sugar (made from dried dates). These can both be used to sweeten your coffee or in your baking. Note that using either one of these may also effect your final product's texture and level of sweetness, but feel free to experiment with them, especially in muffins and cookies.

Honey Don't

Sugars aren't the only way to sweeten your beverages, foods, and baked goods; many liquid sweeteners can do the job as well. Honey, corn syrup, and maple syrup come to mind almost immediately. Although many people think of honey as a terrific pure and natural sweetener, the fact that it comes from bees, who work hard to collect nectar and regurgitate it as food for their colony, makes it a nonvegan product.

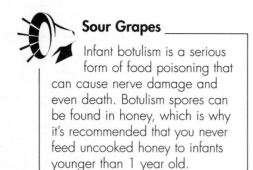

Sour Grapes

Infant botulism is a serious form of food poisoning that can cause nerve damage and even death. Botulism spores can be found in honey, which is why it's recommended that you never feed uncooked honey to infants younger than 1 year old.

Agave nectar and maple syrup are our two favorite liquid sweeteners, and both work well as replacements for honey. Agave nectar comes from the agave cactus, which is the same cactus used to make tequila. It has a mild flavor, comes in light- and amber-colored varieties, with most brands being minimally processed and considered suitable for use in raw food recipes as well as in cooked foods and baked goods. Golden maple syrup is terrific on pancakes and waffles, of course, but it's also delicious on sweet potatoes, winter squashes, and carrots and in muffins, scones, cookies, breads, and even frosting.

Other vegan liquid sweeteners include brown rice syrup, flavored brown rice syrup, frozen or bottled fruit juice concentrates, jarred apple juice concentrate, concentrated fruit juice syrup, molasses, sorghum syrup, and barley malt syrup. Use them to sweeten oatmeal or other hot cereals; in making granola, baked goods, and sweet and savory sauces; and to sweeten and flavor fruits, vegetables, and even beans.

Thyme-ly Tip

If you want to use a liquid sweetener in place of granulated sugar, you can often use less liquid sweetener, as their sweetness level is more concentrated. To replace 1 cup sugar, start by adding only ½ cup liquid sweetener, working up to 1 cup as desired. Also reduce the other liquid ingredients in the recipe by ¼ cup for each 1 cup liquid sweetener you've added.

Veganizing Tips

You can apply many of our substitution recommendations to make your favorite non-vegan recipes vegan—or "veganize" them, as we call it. Look over your recipes, and you might be able to see how easily they can be veganized by just swapping one ingredient for another. Try doing a switcheroo with olive oil or nonhydrogenated margarine for butter, and soy milk or rice milk for cow's milk in making a creamy sauce or luscious dessert. Or see how well tofu, seitan, or beans would work in making a soup, stew, or sandwich filling.

Other times you might be a little stumped, in which case you can try experimenting with different options. We suggest making a smaller-size batch of a recipe (to avoid wasting ingredients and money) until you get the new veganized version of the recipe tweaked just right to your liking.

When you first attempt to veganize recipes, start with something easy or recipes that already contain many vegan ingredients and only require changing one or two ingredients at the most. Remember, you have to crawl before you can walk, and the same can be said for vegan cooking. You need to know how to cook a tofu scramble before you can tackle a vegan spanakopita or lasagna roll-up. Then when you've had success with easy recipes, you can move on to more complex recipes that might entail making several changes or vegan substitutions.

Thyme-ly Tip

Not sure how to replace beef or chicken broth? It's simple! For beef broth, use an equal amount of vegetable broth and add some tamari and tomato paste (or ketchup) to darken its color and deepen its flavor. For a mock chicken-flavored broth, use a tiny amount of tamari and replace the tomato paste with nutritional yeast flakes and a little dried thyme and sage (or poultry seasoning).

Also, keep in mind that you might not be able to veganize some recipes, such as soufflés, meringues, and angel food cakes, because these items rely heavily on eggs and egg whites. You'll have to settle for tofu-based quiches (see recipe in Chapter 4) and vegan whipped toppings and cakes. Peruse Chapter 21 and 22 to find several recipe ideas to fill this void. And check out the other chapters in Parts 2 through 6 for inspirational vegan recipes to get you started on your path to cooking, baking, and enjoying vegan meals, and to give you even more ideas for veganizing recipes that you grew up eating or previously enjoyed preparing.

Better Vegan Baking

As a vegan baker, you'll be using leaveners and yeast to help your baked goods rise to great heights, and flours, starches, flaxseeds, agar-agar, and fruit purées to bind and thicken your creations. Vegan baking success and failure is intricately based on chemical reactions, which is why you need to be more precise, especially when it comes to measuring both wet and dry ingredients like leaveners and flours. Remember that the wet-to-dry ingredient ratio has tremendous impact on whether your baked goods come out dry and crumbly or moist and well formed.

With most recipes, you have some leeway for substituting one fruit or spice for another, as well as adding extra or different flavoring extracts to suit your tastes. Once you've had consistent success with a particular recipe, you can freely experiment with different flavor combinations. Just keep the wet-to-dry ingredient ratio the same or as close to the same as possible.

You can cut the fat content of your vegan baked goods by replacing some of the oil with other ingredients, like mashed or blended fruit purées. Often, from one quarter to one third of the oil or margarine called for can be replaced without altering the final product too significantly. Some of our favorite oil replacers include applesauce, mashed bananas, and canned sweet potato or pumpkin purée.

You can also blend dried fruit with water or fruit juices until it forms a smooth purée. Try this with whole pitted dates, figs, apricots, or raisins; prunes work especially well with chocolate-flavored baked goods. It helps to first soak the dried fruit for 20 to 30 minutes in liquid for easier blending. These fruit purées give your vegan baked goods extra moisture and sweetness. Fruit juices and fruit-juice concentrates can also be used in place of water to make your baked goods sweeter without adding extra sugars or liquid sweeteners.

And now, as you are about to venture forth into the recipe chapters, we offer you one final bit of advice: have patience, and remember, as with learning anything new, that practice makes perfect!

The Least You Need to Know

- With a little know-how, you can easily find vegan substitutions for the animal ingredients in many recipes.
- Soy-based products make it easy to substitute for meat, dairy, and eggs.
- Agave nectar is a great vegan substitute for honey.

Part 2

Morning Meal Options

Breakfast is the most important meal of the day, and that's true for vegans, too. The chapters in Part 2 show you how to prepare a wide assortment of breakfast favorites. It starts with a selection of vegan morning meal ideas that can all be prepared quickly or ahead of time, so you'll have no excuse for going without breakfast because you're running late or overslept.

We also offer a delicious assortment of vegan breakfast recipes to make on the weekends when you have more time, as well as a few elaborate dishes you can serve up for brunch or special occasions. Enjoy the sweet and savory baked goods in Part 2 at breakfast, brunch, or any other time of day.

Chapter 3

Fast and Easy Breakfasts

In This Chapter

- Rolling your own breakfast burritos
- Fruit- and fiber-filled breakfast cereals
- Soy-based protein in your skillet or on a bagel

Many consider breakfast the most important meal of the day, but many vegans might feel that the quick vegan breakfast options available are limited. To help you in your morning-sustenance mission, we've created a varied assortment of quick and easy, filling, and delicious vegan breakfast recipes—all of which can be prepared in less than 15 minutes.

Better Vegan Breakfasts

Many people can't even comprehend breakfast without including eggs or dairy in the preparation. However, with a little culinary creativity and substitution know-how, you can re-create and reinvent many of your old favorite breakfast offerings, often making them tastier and healthier using more nutritious ingredients.

Fortunately, many versatile soy-based ingredients and substitutes are available to help vegans in their meal preparations, especially at breakfast time. In this chapter, you learn how to use soy yogurt in a fruit-based breakfast burrito, add meatless crumbles to a potato and veggie hash, and top your favorite bagels or English muffins with slices of vegan cheese or a fruit and nut-enhanced tofu cream cheese spread.

Even though vegans leave behind egg-based dishes, you can still enjoy a mock scramble, thanks to tofu. This chapter gives you the lowdown on seasoning and cooking up a simple tofu scramble, including tips for creating a savory, Mexican-inspired breakfast burrito similar to the ones offered in restaurants.

Hopefully, these recipes and the others found in this chapter will inspire you to make the time and effort for a fast and easy vegan breakfast!

Purple People Pleaser Smoothie

This delicious smoothie, made with a blend of antioxidant-rich blue and red fruits along with some soy milk for a creamy texture, is guaranteed to give you energy and a healthy glow.

1½ cups fresh or frozen mixed berries such as blueberries, strawberries, and raspberries

1 cup soy milk or other non-dairy milk of choice

½ cup fresh or frozen cherries, pitted

½ cup pomegranate juice or cranberry juice

1 TB. ground flaxseeds

½ cup ice cubes (optional)

Yield: 2 smoothies
Prep time: 2 minutes
Serving size: 1 smoothie

1. Place berries, soy milk, cherries, pomegranate juice, and flaxseeds in a blender and blend for 1 minute or until completely smooth.

2. If you're using fresh fruit and would like a frozen smoothie, add ice cubes and blend for 1 minute or until completely smooth.

3. Divide mixture between 2 tall glasses and serve.

Variation: Add some soy yogurt, protein powder, or a little sugar or other sweetener, if desired.

Thyme-ly Tip

Fill your belly fast and satisfy your cravings for sweets naturally by including a smoothie in your daily diet. Smoothies are a great way to get several servings of a variety of fruits, beneficial dietary fiber, and extra protein (by adding nuts, seeds, and soy or nut milk) all at the same time.

Green Power Smoothie

Unusual combinations of fruits and veggies with nutrient boosters have become the "coolest" new trend in smoothie making, and this one is a great way to sneak broccoli and green leafy veggies by finicky eaters.

Yield: 2 smoothies
Prep time: 5 to 7 minutes
Serving size: 1 smoothie

2 leaves green kale or lacinato kale (also known as dinosaur kale), stems removed, and torn into small pieces

1 large banana, peeled and cut into 2-in. pieces

1 cup water or fruit juice

1 cup fresh or frozen broccoli florets

½ cup ice cubes

4 dried dates, pitted

4 whole raw almonds

1 TB. fresh ginger, coarsely chopped

1 TB. raw hemp seeds

1 TB. ground flaxseeds

2 tsp. *green food powder*

1. Place kale, banana, water, broccoli, ice cubes, dates, almonds, ginger, hemp seeds, flaxseeds, and green food powder in a blender and blend for 2 minutes or until completely smooth.

2. Divide mixture between 2 tall glasses and serve.

Variation: Substitute other varieties of greens like spinach or Swiss chard and other types of fruit, nuts, or seeds to suit your tastes.

def•i•ni•tion

Green food powders are made from a mixture of green plant-based foods, such as barley grass, wheat grass, alfalfa, spinach, kale, lettuce, broccoli, and parsley, as well as sea vegetables or algae like spirulina, chlorella, and kelp. Find them in most natural foods stores and online at sites such as www. mountainroseherbs.com.

Baja Breakfast Burrito

Breakfast burritos have become a popular restaurant take-out item, and this Mexican-inspired vegan version will get your day off to a spicy start.

8 oz. firm or extra-firm tofu

2 tsp. olive oil

⅓ cup onion, diced

⅓ cup green bell pepper, ribs and seeds removed, and diced

½ jalapeño pepper, ribs and seeds removed, and finely diced

1 green onion, thinly sliced

⅓ cup canned black or red beans, drained and rinsed

2 tsp. nutritional yeast flakes

1 tsp. chili powder

½ tsp. garlic granules or garlic powder

Sea salt and freshly ground black pepper

2 (8-in.) flour tortillas, variety of choice

2 TB. salsa of choice

¼ cup shredded vegan cheddar cheese

¼ medium Hass avocado, peeled and diced

Yield: 2 burritos
Prep time: 5 to 10 minutes
Cook time: 7 to 10 minutes
Serving size: 1 burrito

1. Crumble tofu into a large nonstick skillet using your fingers. Add olive oil, and sauté over medium heat, stirring often, for 2 minutes. Add diced onion, green bell pepper, jalapeño pepper, and green onion, and continue to sauté for 3 or 4 minutes longer or until tofu is slightly browned.

2. Stir in beans, nutritional yeast flakes, chili powder, and garlic granules, and cook for 1 more minute. Remove from heat and season mixture with salt and black pepper.

3. For easier rolling, warm each tortilla in a large skillet over medium heat for 1 or 2 minutes per side, or in a microwave oven for 20 to 30 seconds.

4. To assemble burritos, place tortillas flat on a large cutting board or work surface. Spoon ½ tofu mixture horizontally in center of each tortilla. Dividing evenly, place salsa, shredded cheese, and avocado on top of tofu mixture.

5. To finish rolling each burrito, fold bottom half of tortilla over filling, fold sides of tortilla toward center, and roll up from the bottom edge to enclose filling. Serve immediately, or wrap burritos in plastic wrap or place them in an airtight container and store in the refrigerator.

Variation: Serve these burritos on plates with shredded lettuce and cooked grains for a hearty breakfast or dinner meal.

Soy What?

Flour tortillas are great for making handheld wrap sandwiches, burritos, soft tacos, and baked casserole-style dishes. They come in a variety of colors and flavors, from wheat and other types of flour and even sprouted grains.

Fruit and Soy Yogurt Breakfast Burrito

Breakfast burritos can be sweet as well as savory, and this sweet-tasting one is filled with a creamy mixture of soy yogurt and an assortment of fresh fruit and berries, nuts, and seeds.

Yield: 2 burritos

Prep time: 5 to 10 minutes

Serving size: 1 burrito

---

1 apple of choice, diced

1 medium banana, peeled and thinly sliced

1 kiwi, peeled, cut in ½ lengthwise and thinly sliced

¼ cup strawberries, thinly sliced

¼ cup fresh or frozen blueberries, thawed if frozen

½ tsp. ground cinnamon

2 (6-oz.) pkg. plain or vanilla soy yogurt

¼ cup raw walnuts or other nuts of choice, coarsely chopped

2 TB. raisins

1 TB. raw sunflower seeds

2 (8-in.) flour tortillas, variety of choice

1. Combine apple, banana, kiwi, strawberries, blueberries, and cinnamon in a small bowl. Add soy yogurt, walnuts, raisins, and sunflower seeds, and stir gently to combine.

2. For easier rolling, warm each tortilla in a large skillet over medium heat for 1 or 2 minutes per side, or in a microwave oven for 20 to 30 seconds. To assemble burritos, place tortillas flat on a large cutting board or work surface. Spoon ½ of fruit mixture horizontally in center of each tortilla.

3. To finish rolling each burrito, fold bottom half of tortilla over filling ingredients, fold sides of tortilla toward center, and roll up from the bottom edge to enclose filling. Serve immediately.

Variation: Spread 1 or 2 tablespoons peanut butter or other nut butter on the tortillas before adding the filling.

Thyme-ly Tip _____

These fruit and soy yogurt-filled tortillas are delicious topped with a warm banana sauce. Simply combine 1 medium diced banana, ½ cup water or apple juice, 1 teaspoon agave nectar or sugar, and a dash of cinnamon. Cook over medium heat until banana is soft and mushy. Warm filled tortillas in the microwave for 1 minute and top with sauce as desired.

Bagels with Dried Fruit-n-Nut Spread

A bagel and a spread are a great fast and easy breakfast treat, but with a little effort and a handful of assorted dried fruit and nuts, you can dress up this humble combination.

1 or more bagels of choice, split

½ cup (4-oz.) tofu cream cheese

2 TB. raw walnuts, finely chopped

1 TB. raw sliced almonds

1 TB. date pieces coated in oat flour

1 TB. dried cranberries

1 TB. dried currants

1 TB. maple syrup

¼ tsp. pure vanilla extract

¼ tsp. ground cinnamon

Yield: ¾ cup
Prep time: 5 minutes
Cook time: 2 or 3 minutes
Serving size: 1 bagel plus 2 tablespoons spread

1. Toast bagel as desired.

2. In a small bowl, combine cream cheese, walnuts, almonds, date pieces, cranberries, currants, maple syrup, vanilla extract, and cinnamon.

3. Spread mixture on toasted bagels and serve. Store spread in an airtight container in the refrigerator.

Variation: Try these delicious dried fruit and nut combinations: raisin-dried cherry-pecan, dried apricot-cashew-sunflower seed, and dried mango-dried pineapple-coconut-macadamia nut. Or use toasted bread slices or English muffins instead of bagels.

Thyme-ly Tip _____

Several brands of vegan tofu cream cheese are available in the refrigerator case of many grocery and most natural foods stores. These tend to be lower in fat and calories than their dairy-based cream cheeses, and work well as nondairy substitutes in most sweet and savory recipes.

Avocado and Tomato Bagel Sandwich

Choose whole-grain or sprouted-grain bagels for this tasty veggie and cheese bagel sandwich that's a cinch to make for breakfast, lunch, or as a snack.

Yield: 2 sandwiches
Prep time: 5 minutes
Cook time: 2 minutes
Serving size: 1 sandwich

2 bagels of choice, split

Dijon mustard

1 medium plum tomato, cut into 4 slices

¼ medium Hass avocado, peeled and thinly sliced

2 slices vegan cheese of choice

1. Toast bagels and place on a large plate or work surface. Spread Dijon mustard on each bagel half.

2. Dividing them evenly, layer tomato, avocado, and cheese slices on bottom half of each bagel. Replace bagel tops and serve.

Variation: Add slices of cooked vegetarian Canadian bacon, a few meatless deli slices, greens, or other sliced vegetables.

Soy What?

Avocados get a bad rap. Sure, a medium-size avocado can supply you with nearly 55 percent of your recommended daily allowance of fat (mostly monounsaturated, heart-healthy fat), but they can also supply you with other nutrients you need, like folate, vitamins C and E, fiber, and potassium—almost twice as much as one banana.

Vanilla Nut Granola

Enjoy this crunchy and slightly sweet blend of oats, nuts, and coconut as a cold breakfast cereal, as a snack, or as a topping for nondairy ice cream or sorbet.

4 cups rolled oats

½ cup unsweetened shredded coconut

½ cup raw sliced almonds

½ cup raw pecans, coarsely chopped

½ cup oat bran

½ cup raw sunflower seeds

¼ cup raw hemp seeds or ground flaxseeds

1 tsp. ground cinnamon

½ tsp. ground cardamom

½ cup maple syrup

3 TB. water

3 TB. safflower oil

1 TB. pure vanilla extract

½ tsp. pure almond extract

Choice of one or more for individual servings:

Soy milk or other nondairy milk of choice

Soy yogurt of choice

Sliced fresh fruit or berries

Yield: 4 cups
Prep time: 5 to 10 minutes
Cook time: 30 to 40 minutes
Serving size: ¹/₂ cup dry granola

1. Preheat the oven to 325°F. Lightly oil a large cookie sheet.

2. In a large bowl, combine oats, coconut, almonds, pecans, oat bran, sunflower seeds, hemp seeds, cinnamon, and cardamom.

3. In a small bowl, combine maple syrup, water, safflower oil, vanilla extract, and almond extract. Pour wet ingredients over dry ingredients, and stir well to combine.

4. Transfer oat mixture to prepared cookie sheet and spread out into a single layer. Bake for 15 minutes.

5. Remove from the oven, stir granola with a spatula, spread out into a single layer, and bake for 15 more minutes. Stir granola again and bake for 15 to 20 minutes longer or until golden brown and dry.

6. Let cool completely and then transfer granola to an airtight container and store in a cool, dry place for up to a month. Enjoy bowlfuls of granola topped with your choice of soy milk, soy yogurt, and sliced fresh fruit or berries.

Variation: If you like your granola with big chunky pieces, only stir once, watching carefully and rotating trays to avoid burning. When granola is cool, break up into big pieces.

Sour Grapes

Granola often contains excessive amounts of fat, salt, and sweeteners, including the non-vegan honey. When purchasing granola, compare brands and carefully check nutritional labels and ingredients.

Hash in a Flash

Enjoy this hearty skillet-cooked mixture of seasoned veggies and meatless crumbles with toasted slices of bread or English muffins. Or if you need to eat on the run, roll it up in tortillas with some salsa and enjoy it as breakfast burritos.

Yield: **4 servings**	
Prep time: 5 to 7 minutes	
Cook time: 7 to 10 minutes	
Serving size: 1 cup	

3 cups red-skinned potatoes, finely diced

2 tsp. olive oil

½ cup refrigerated or frozen meatless crumbles

½ cup onion, finely diced

½ cup green bell pepper, ribs and seeds removed, and finely diced

1 TB. garlic, minced

2 tsp. nutritional yeast flakes (optional)

½ tsp. paprika or chili powder

½ tsp. dried thyme or Italian seasoning blend

Sea salt and freshly ground black pepper

1. In a large nonstick skillet, combine potatoes and olive oil and sauté over medium heat, stirring often, for 3 minutes.

2. Add meatless crumbles, onion, and green pepper, and continue to sauté for 3 or 4 minutes longer or until veggies are tender.

3. Add garlic, nutritional yeast (if using), paprika, and thyme, and season with salt and black pepper. Cook for 1 more minute. Serve hot.

Variation: You can replace potatoes with sweet potatoes and meatless crumbles with 3 or 4 diced vegetarian ham or Canadian bacon slices. For a soy-free version, replace meatless crumbles with coarsely chopped mushrooms.

Thyme-ly Tip _____

Breakfast hash dishes are typically made with leftover bits of chopped meat and veggies, so feel free to do the same by substituting any leftover veggies you may have. You can also make red flannel hash by replacing ½ the potatoes with finely diced beets.

Simple Scrambled Tofu

Here's a hot, fast, and delicious protein-rich breakfast. Just start the scramble cooking, drop some bread in the toaster, and you'll be eating within minutes!

8 oz. firm or extra-firm tofu

2 tsp. nutritional yeast flakes

½ tsp. garlic powder

½ tsp. onion powder

⅛ tsp. turmeric or curry powder

Sea salt and freshly ground black pepper

Yield: 2 servings
Prep time: 1 or 2 minutes
Cook time: 3 to 5 minutes
Serving size: ½ cup

1. Lightly oil a large nonstick skillet and place it over medium heat.

2. Crumble tofu into the skillet using your fingers. Sprinkle nutritional yeast flakes, garlic powder, onion powder, and turmeric over tofu, and stir well with a spatula.

3. Cook, stirring often, for 3 to 5 minutes or until desired doneness. Remove from heat, season with salt and black pepper, and serve.

Variation: If you prefer a soft-scrambled tofu, substitute 1 (12-ounce) package firm or extra-firm silken tofu. You can also add chopped veggies such as mushrooms, onions, green onions, peppers, tomatoes, or greens to your tofu mixture as it cooks, and add a little shredded vegan cheese at the end as desired.

Soy What?

It's recommended that the average American keep his or her dietary cholesterol consumption to 300 mg or less per day. A single egg contains about 212 mg cholesterol, so if you eat 2 scrambled or fried eggs per day, you've greatly exceeded this recommendation. In contrast, this scrambled tofu dish is totally cholesterol free.

Chapter 4

Weekend Breakfasts and Brunches

In This Chapter

- Experimenting with new flours and grains
- Eggless French toast and mini quiches
- Meatless sausage and bacon options

Now that you've mastered a few fast and easy vegan breakfast ideas, let's move on to recipes that require a little more time and effort to prepare. But don't worry—you won't be laboring for hours while your stomach is growling, as most of them can be prepared in under 30 minutes, perfect for weekends or on days when you may have more time in your morning schedule.

Breakfast Bonuses

Many of the recipes in this chapter can be made in larger batches and simply reheated, so feel free to cook up a storm on the weekend to ease your breakfast burden during the week ahead.

And instead of using the overly processed all-purpose flour many pancake houses rely on, use flours and grains high in fiber and flavor, like whole-wheat pastry, barley, oats, and corn. You, and those you share them with, will be pleasantly surprised by the light and fluffy results.

Ready to become a vegan breakfast short-order cook? Well, then tie on an apron and let's get mixing!

Rainbow Vegetable Hash Browns

You're sure to win rave reviews with this skillet side dish made with a sweet, savory, and colorful combination of assorted shredded and diced vegetables in addition to the traditional spuds.

1 large red-skinned potato, shredded

1 large sweet potato, shredded

1 large carrot, shredded

1 medium zucchini, shredded

1 medium yellow summer squash, shredded

½ cup red onion, finely diced

½ cup red bell pepper, ribs and seeds removed, and finely diced

2 tsp. nutritional yeast flakes

½ tsp. paprika

½ tsp. garlic granules or garlic powder

½ tsp. sea salt

¼ tsp. freshly ground black pepper

1 TB. olive oil

Yield: 4 servings
Prep time: 7 to 10 minutes
Cook time: 15 to 20 minutes
Serving size: 1 cup

1. Place shredded potato, sweet potato, carrot, zucchini, and summer squash into a colander and squeeze vegetables to remove excess moisture. Transfer mixture to a large bowl.

2. Add red onion, red bell pepper, nutritional yeast flakes, paprika, garlic granules, salt, and black pepper, and mix to combine.

3. Place olive oil in a large nonstick skillet. Add vegetable mixture and flatten firmly with a spatula to cover the bottom of the skillet. Cook over medium heat for 5 minutes without stirring. Stir mixture and flatten firmly again with the spatula. Cook for 5 more minutes without stirring. Stir and flatten again, and continue to cook for 5 to 10 minutes longer or until veggies are tender and golden brown. Serve hot.

Variation: Substitute other shredded vegetables such as beets or parsnips, or prepare hash browns with just potatoes and some green onions, if desired.

Thyme-ly Tip

You can also use the shredded vegetable mixture to make potato pancakes by blending ¼ cup flour of choice into the mixture. Place ¼ cup portions of the mixture into a skillet with olive oil, flatten each one with a spatula, and cook until brown and crispy on each side. Drain on paper towels and serve hot with applesauce and tofu sour cream.

Multigrain Waffles

Flaxseeds are used as an egg replacement in these fiber-rich waffles made with two types of flour and rolled oats, all of which give them a crisp and crunchy texture.

Yield: 4 (8-inch) waffles
Prep time: 7 to 10 minutes
Cook time: 15 to 20 minutes
Serving size: 1 waffle

1¼ cups water

2 TB. flaxseeds

¾ cup rolled oats

1¼ cup soy milk or other nondairy milk of choice

3 TB. safflower oil

½ tsp. pure vanilla extract

¾ cup whole-wheat pastry flour

½ cup barley flour

2 TB. turbinado sugar

2 tsp. aluminum-free baking powder

½ tsp. ground cinnamon

½ tsp. sea salt

1. Place ¼ cup water and flaxseeds into a blender, blend for 1 minute, and let sit for 5 minutes.

2. Combine remaining 1 cup water and oats in a small saucepan. Bring to a boil over medium heat, remove from heat, and set aside for 5 minutes.

3. Lightly oil a waffle iron and preheat iron according to manufacturer's instructions.

4. Add soy milk, safflower oil, and vanilla extract to the blender, and blend for 30 seconds.

5. Transfer oat mixture to a large bowl and combine with whole-wheat pastry flour, barley flour, sugar, baking powder, cinnamon, and salt. Pour in wet ingredients, and stir just until blended.

6. Depending on size of your waffle iron, ladle 1 cup batter onto iron and cook according to manufacturer's instructions or until golden brown. Repeat procedure for remaining batter. Serve hot with maple syrup, jam, or other toppings of choice.

Variation: You can use the batter to make pancakes by portioning ⅓ cup batter onto a hot, oiled skillet or griddle and cooking for 2 or 3 minutes per side or until golden brown.

 Sour Grapes

Flaxseeds, due to their high oil content, can become rancid. Store them in an airtight container, either in a cool, dark place, or preferably in the refrigerator, where they'll keep for several months. You can also grind up large batches of flaxseed and store them in an airtight container in the refrigerator.

Banana Chocolate-Chip Pancakes

These pancakes, filled with soft and gooey bananas and chocolate chips, are guaranteed to bring a smile to your face and have you coming back for seconds.

1⅓ cups whole-wheat pastry flour

1 TB. unbleached cane sugar or beet sugar

1 TB. aluminum-free baking powder

1 tsp. ground cinnamon

½ tsp. sea salt

1⅓ cups soy milk or other nondairy milk of choice

2 TB. safflower oil

1 tsp. pure vanilla extract

1 large banana, peeled and cut into quarters

¼ cup vegan chocolate or carob chips

Yield: 8 pancakes
Prep time: 7 minutes
Cook time: 15 to 20 minutes
Serving size: 2 pancakes

1. Place flour, sugar, baking powder, cinnamon, and salt in a medium bowl and whisk together. Add soy milk, safflower oil, and vanilla extract, and whisk well to combine. Set batter aside for 5 minutes.

2. Lightly oil a large nonstick skillet and place over medium heat (or use a griddle).

3. Pour ⅓ cup batter per pancake onto the hot skillet. For each pancake, thinly slice ¼ banana onto batter and sprinkle with 1 tablespoon chocolate chips.

4. Cook for 2 or 3 minutes or until edges of pancake are slightly dry and bubbles appear on top. Flip pancake over with a spatula and cook for 2 or 3 more minutes or until golden brown on the other side. Lightly oil the skillet again and repeat procedure for remaining batter, banana, and chocolate chips. Serve hot with maple syrup or other toppings of choice.

 Thyme-ly Tip

You can make larger batches of the pancake and waffle recipes in this book and freeze them in an airtight container or a zipper-lock bag. When you're ready to use them, simply thaw and reheat them in the microwave or toaster oven.

Variation: For an extra chocolaty-flavored version, replace ⅓ cup whole-wheat pastry flour with cocoa powder (or carob powder). To give them a mocha flavor, also replace ⅓ cup soy milk with brewed coffee.

Blueberry Corncakes

Cornmeal, which has a slightly sweet flavor, pairs nicely with plump, juicy blueberries as these simple breakfast corncakes deliciously illustrate.

Yield: 8 pancakes

Prep time: 3 to 5 minutes

Cook time: 15 to 20 minutes

Serving size: 2 pancakes

Thyme-ly Tip

When cooking large batches of pancakes or waffles, the ones cooked first often get cold before you're ready to serve. To solve this problem, put them on a large cookie sheet or oven-proof plate and place them in a 200°F oven to keep them warm while you cook the rest.

¾ **cup plus 4 tsp. whole-wheat pastry flour**

¾ **cup cornmeal**

1 tsp. aluminum-free baking powder

¼ **tsp. baking soda**

¼ **tsp. sea salt**

¾ **cup soy milk or other nondairy milk of choice**

¾ **cup water**

1 (10-oz.) pkg. frozen blueberries, unthawed

1. Place ³/₄ cup flour, cornmeal, baking powder, baking soda, and salt in a medium bowl and whisk together. Add soy milk and water, and whisk well to combine.

2. Place blueberries in a small bowl, sprinkle with remaining 4 teaspoons flour, and stir well to thoroughly coat berries with flour. Gently fold blueberry mixture into batter.

3. Lightly oil a large nonstick skillet and place over medium heat (or use a griddle).

4. Pour ¹/₃ cup batter per pancake onto the hot skillet.

5. Cook for 2 or 3 minutes or until the edges of pancake are slightly dry and bubbles appear on top. Flip pancake over with a spatula and cook for 2 or 3 more minutes or until golden brown on the other side. Lightly oil the skillet again and repeat procedure for remaining batter. Serve hot with maple syrup or other toppings of choice.

Variation: For a savory version, omit frozen mixed berries, add 1¹/₂ cups frozen or canned (drained) cut corn kernels or succotash, and ¹/₂ teaspoon chili powder, and serve with nonhydrogenated vegan margarine or salsa.

Quick and Easy Eggless French Toast

French toast is typically made with beaten eggs and milk, but this cholesterol-free vegan version shows that you don't have to raid the barnyard when you crave French toast.

2 cups soy milk or other nondairy milk of choice

¼ cup whole-wheat pastry flour

2 TB. nutritional yeast flakes

2 TB. maple syrup

2 tsp. pure vanilla extract

2 tsp. ground cinnamon

½ tsp. freshly grated nutmeg

8 slices whole-grain bread of choice

Yield: 8 slices	
Prep time: 5 to 7 minutes	
Cook time: 8 to 10 minutes	
Serving size: 2 slices	

1. In a large, shallow casserole dish, place soy milk, flour, nutritional yeast flakes, maple syrup, vanilla extract, cinnamon, and nutmeg, and whisk well to combine.

2. Place 4 bread slices into soy milk mixture, flip slices over to coat other side, and leave them to soak for 2 minutes.

3. Lightly oil a large nonstick skillet and place over medium heat (or use a griddle).

4. Using a fork, carefully remove bread slices from soy milk mixture and place them into the hot skillet.

5. Cook bread slices for 1 or 2 minutes or until golden brown on the bottom. Flip bread over with a spatula and cook for 1 or 2 more minutes or until golden brown.

6. While cooking first batch, repeat soaking procedure for remaining 4 slices of bread. Lightly oil the skillet again and repeat procedure for remaining bread slices. Serve hot with maple syrup, jam, or other toppings of choice. Give your French toast a light dusting of vegan powdered sugar before serving for an extra-special touch.

Variation: Instead of soy milk, try Soy Egg Nog or Horchata (a rice beverage), both of which can be found in most grocery and natural food stores. If you do so, add only 1 tablespoon maple syrup, 1 teaspoon vanilla, and ½ teaspoon cinnamon, and omit the nutmeg.

Thyme-ly Tip

For a fancy stuffed French toast, combine ½ cup tofu cream cheese, ½ cup sliced fruit or berries, 1 tablespoon soy milk, and 1 table-spoon maple syrup in a bowl. Divide mix-ture evenly to make 4 filled sandwiches. Soak and cook 2 sandwiches at a time, per recipe instructions, until golden brown on each side. Dust with vegan powdered sugar and serve with maple syrup.

Mini Spinach-Mushroom Quiches

Preparing these eggless tofu and vegetable quiches without a crust and baking them in muffin tins cuts down on your prep and baking times significantly.

Yield: 12 quiches
Prep time: 15 minutes
Cook time: 20 to 30 minutes
Serving size: 1 quiche

½ cup red onion, diced

½ cup crimini mushrooms or button mushrooms, cut in half and thinly sliced

1 tsp. olive oil

1 (10-oz.) pkg. frozen chopped spinach, thawed

⅓ cup sun-dried tomato pieces

1 TB. garlic, minced

1 TB. tamari or other soy sauce of choice

1 lb. firm or extra-firm tofu

½ cup soy milk or other nondairy milk of choice

¼ cup nutritional yeast flakes

1 tsp. Dijon mustard

½ tsp. turmeric

½ tsp. paprika

½ tsp. sea salt

½ tsp. freshly ground black pepper

Thyme-ly Tip

You can also use the tofu-veggie mixture to make a frittata by pouring it into an oiled 9-inch pie pan and baking for 30 to 40 minutes. For a classic quiche, prebake a 9-inch pre-made piecrust on a large cookie sheet for 10 minutes. Remove from the oven, pour in filling, and bake for 30 to 40 more minutes or until firm to the touch.

1. Preheat the oven to 375°F. Lightly oil 12 muffin cups and set aside.

2. In a large nonstick skillet, place onion, mushrooms, and olive oil, and sauté over medium heat, stirring often, for 2 minutes.

3. Place thawed spinach in a colander and squeeze spinach with your hands to remove excess moisture. Add spinach, sun-dried tomatoes, garlic, and tamari to the skillet and continue to sauté for 2 minutes longer. Remove from heat and transfer mixture to a medium bowl.

4. Crumble tofu into a blender using your fingers. Add soy milk, nutritional yeast flakes, Dijon mustard, turmeric, paprika, salt, and black pepper, and blend for 1 or 2 minutes or until completely smooth. Scrape down sides of the container with a rubber spatula and blend for 15 seconds longer. Add blended mixture to the bowl, and stir well with a rubber spatula to combine.

5. Fill prepared muffin cups ³/₄ full. Bake for 20 to 30 minutes or until a toothpick inserted in the center comes out clean. Let cool slightly before removing quiches from muffin cups. Serve warm or at room temperature.

Variation: Feel free to add additional ingredients such as slices or cubes of vegetarian Canadian bacon or sausages or a little shredded vegan cheese.

Savory Mushroom Sausages

Not only are these savory mushroom patties totally soy-free, they're also yeast-free, and if made with rice breadcrumbs, they're gluten-free as well.

8 oz. crimini mushrooms, thinly sliced

¾ cup onion, diced

2 tsp. plus 1 TB. olive oil

¼ cup raw walnuts or pecans, coarsely chopped

2 TB. raw sunflower seeds

3 large garlic cloves, thinly sliced

1 tsp. dried thyme

1 tsp. rubbed sage

½ tsp. sea salt

½ tsp. freshly ground black pepper

1 TB. balsamic vinegar

1 TB. maple syrup

1⅓ cups *rice breadcrumbs* or dry breadcrumbs

Yield: 8 patties
Prep time: 10 to 15 minutes
Cook time: 10 to 15 minutes
Serving size: 2 patties

1. In a large nonstick skillet, place mushrooms, onion, and 2 teaspoons olive oil, and sauté over medium heat, stirring often, for 3 or 4 minutes or until soft. Add walnuts, sunflower seeds, garlic, thyme, sage, salt, and black pepper, and sauté for 2 minutes longer. Remove from heat and set aside to cool for 2 minutes.

2. Transfer mushroom mixture into a food processor fitted with an S blade. Add vinegar and maple syrup, and process for 1 or 2 minutes or until completely smooth.

3. Transfer mushroom mixture to a medium bowl, add rice breadcrumbs, and stir well to combine.

4. Firmly flatten mushroom mixture into the bowl, and with a knife, cut mixture into 8 wedges. Place 1 wedge in your palm, form it into a patty, flatten it slightly with your hands, and place patty on a large plate. Repeat procedure to make a total of 8 patties.

5. Wash and dry skillet thoroughly. Place 1½ teaspoons olive oil into skillet, add patties, and cook over medium heat for 2 or 3 minutes or until golden brown on the bottom. Flip patties over with a spatula, add an additional 1½ teaspoons olive oil to skillet, and cook for 2 or 3 minutes longer or until golden brown on the other side.

def•i•ni•tion

Rice breadcrumbs are made from cooked or baked rice and nothing else. They have a slightly coarser texture than the traditionally used wheat-based breadcrumbs and can be used in recipes much like their counterpart, as a binder, thickener, breading, and topping. Find them prepackaged in most natural foods stores.

6. Drain patties on a paper towel–covered plate and serve hot. Store sausage patties in an airtight container in the refrigerator for up to 1 week.

Variation: Instead of 8 patties, form 4 patties and enjoy them as meatless burgers on hamburger buns with your choice of toppings and condiments.

~⌐

Tempeh Un-Bacon

Here, thin slices of tempeh are marinated and then baked until golden brown. Enjoy these crispy slices for breakfast, on sandwiches, or added to other dishes.

1 (8-oz.) pkg. tempeh	2 tsp. maple syrup
2 TB. tamari	1 tsp. toasted sesame oil
1 TB. water	½ tsp. garlic powder
1 TB. apple cider vinegar	¼ tsp. chili powder

1. Thinly slice tempeh into strips 4 inches long × 1 inch wide × ¼ inch thick, and place them on a large plate.

2. Combine tamari, water, vinegar, maple syrup, toasted sesame oil, garlic powder, and chili powder in a small bowl. Drizzle ½ of marinade mixture over tempeh slices, flip over slices, and drizzle remaining marinade mixture over slices. Place tempeh in the refrigerator and leave to marinate for 1 hour or more as desired.

3. Preheat the oven to 400°F. Line a large cookie sheet with parchment paper.

4. Place tempeh slices on the prepared cooking sheet, and spoon any marinade that remains on the plate over tempeh slices. Bake for 15 minutes. Remove from the oven, flip over tempeh slices with a spatula, and bake for 10 to 15 more minutes or until golden brown and crisp around the edges. Serve hot. Store bacon slices in an airtight plastic container in the refrigerator for up to 1 week.

Variation: Add ¼ to ½ teaspoon liquid smoke flavoring to the marinade to give the bacon a smoky flavor. This recipe can also be prepared using 8 ounces firm or extra-firm tofu instead of tempeh.

Yield: 8 slices

Prep time: 5 minutes (plus 1 hour or more for marinating tempeh)

Cook time: 25 to 30 minutes

Serving size: 2 slices

Sour Grapes

Find liquid smoke flavoring in most grocery and natural food stores. Several brands are suitable for vegans, including Colgin and Wright's. There is some concern that liquid smoke flavoring is a carcinogen, and it's also very concentrated, so use this flavoring extract sparingly to season foods.

Country-Style Biscuits and Gravy

Get ready for a real down-home breakfast favorite with this recipe featuring hot, vegan soy buttermilk biscuits topped with creamy, pan gravy flavored with small chunks of premade meatless sausages.

1⅔ cups soy milk or other nondairy milk of choice

2 tsp. freshly squeezed lemon juice

1⅓ cups plus 3 TB. whole-wheat pastry flour or spelt flour

5 TB. nutritional yeast flakes

1½ tsp. baking powder

¼ tsp. baking soda

¼ tsp. sea salt plus more to taste

¼ cup safflower oil or olive oil

4 frozen meatless sausage patties

½ cup vegetable broth

1 tsp. tamari

1 TB. olive oil

Freshly ground black pepper

Yield: 8 biscuits and 1½ cups gravy		
Prep time: 15 to 20 minutes		
Cook time: 15 to 20 minutes		
Serving size: 2 biscuits and ⅓ cup gravy		

1. Preheat the oven to 450°F. Lightly oil a large cookie sheet.

2. For biscuits, combine ⅔ cup soy milk and lemon juice in a small bowl, and set aside for 5 minutes to thicken.

3. Place 1⅓ cups flour, 2 tablespoons nutritional yeast flakes, baking powder, baking soda, and ¼ teaspoon salt in a medium bowl and stir well to combine.

4. Add safflower oil to soy milk mixture.

5. Add soy milk mixture to dry ingredients, and stir just until blended.

6. Transfer biscuit dough to a lightly floured work surface. Knead briefly and pat into a ¾-inch-thick rectangle. Cut rectangle into 8 squares, and place biscuits on the prepared cookie sheet. Bake for 10 to 12 minutes or until light golden brown on top. Remove from the oven.

7. While biscuits are baking, for gravy, cut meatless sausages into small pieces and cook in a dry, large nonstick skillet over medium heat, stirring often, for 2 or 3 minutes or until golden brown.

Thyme-ly Tip

Serve these soy buttermilk–flavored biscuits with soups, stews, or main dishes, and feel free to add some shredded vegan cheddar cheese or herbs to the biscuit dough after mixing for even more flavor. The meatless sausage pan gravy can also be served on its own on top of cooked grains or baked or mashed potatoes.

8. Place remaining 1 cup soy milk, vegetable broth, remaining 3 tablespoons flour, remaining 1 tablespoon nutritional yeast flakes, and tamari in a small bowl and whisk well to combine.

9. Add olive oil to the skillet. When oil is hot, add soy milk mixture and cook, stirring constantly, for 2 or 3 minutes or until thickened. Taste and season with salt and black pepper. Remove from heat. To serve, split biscuits and top with hot gravy as desired.

Variation: For richer-tasting biscuits, replace the oil with non-hydrogenated vegan margarine, cut the margarine into the dry ingredients until mixture resembles coarse crumbs, and stir in the soy milk mixture.

Chapter 5

Sweet and Savory Baked Goods

In This Chapter

- ◆ Delightfully sweet coffeecake and turnovers
- ◆ Quick and easy loaves and biscuits
- ◆ Muffins and scones for your every mood

For vegans, finding suitable dairy, honey, and egg-free breakfast or brunch baked goods can be a challenge. Some vegans are fortunate enough to have local natural foods stores that carry vegan baked goods. Often, these items just barely make the vegan cut and are still made with nutrient and fiber-deficient white flour, margarines that contain unhealthy trans fats, and many other overly processed ingredients that can weigh heavily on the minds and waistlines of those dedicated to living a healthful vegan lifestyle. So what's a vegan longing for a muffin, a warm biscuit, or slice of coffeecake to do?

In this chapter, we offer help for those of you in need of some great sweet or savory treats. You'll be pleasantly surprised by the wonderful flavors and textures, not to mention how easy it is to prepare these vegan creations!

Cinnamon Streusel Coffeecake

The sweet and spicy streusel mixture, with just a hint of orange, is used both as a filling and topping for this exceptional coffeecake.

Yield: 1 (9-inch) pan
Prep time: 5 to 10 minutes
Cook time: 30 minutes
Serving size: 1 piece

½ cup plus ⅔ cup turbinado sugar

2⅓ cups whole-wheat pastry flour

3 tsp. orange *zest*

1 tsp. ground cinnamon

¼ tsp. freshly grated nutmeg

¼ cup plus 2 TB. nonhydrogenated vegan margarine

⅓ cup soy milk or other nondairy milk of choice

⅓ cup freshly squeezed orange juice

⅓ cup applesauce

½ tsp. pure vanilla extract

1 TB. aluminum-free baking powder

¼ tsp. sea salt

Vegan powdered sugar

def•i•ni•tion

Zest is the outer peel of citrus fruit. It adds extra flavor without adding excess moisture to foods and is easily obtained using a fine grater or zester. Preferably, use organic fruit to avoid pesticide residues.

1. Preheat the oven to 375°F. Lightly oil a 9-inch square baking pan.

2. For streusel topping, in a small bowl, combine ½ cup sugar, ⅓ cup flour, 1½ teaspoons orange zest, ½ teaspoon cinnamon, and nutmeg. Using your fingers, work ¼ cup margarine into dry ingredients until mixture resembles coarse crumbs.

3. For batter, in a medium bowl, stir together remaining ⅔ cup sugar, soy milk, orange juice, applesauce, remaining 2 tablespoons margarine, remaining 1½ teaspoons orange zest, and vanilla extract. Add remaining 2 cups flour, baking powder, remaining ½ teaspoon cinnamon, and salt, and stir until smooth.

4. Spread ½ of batter into the prepared pan. Sprinkle ½ of streusel mixture evenly over batter. Place spoonfuls of remaining batter over streusel filling, covering it completely, and sprinkle remaining streusel over the top.

5. Bake for 30 minutes or until a toothpick inserted in the center comes out clean. Let cool slightly, sprinkle top of coffeecake with a little powdered sugar, and cut into 9 pieces.

Variation: Feel free to add ⅓ cup finely chopped pecans or other nuts to the streusel mixture.

Apple Turnovers

Crisp triangles of phyllo dough are filled with a mixture of sweetened apples and dried fruit. Enjoy these tasty pastries for breakfast, dessert, or as a snack.

2 large Granny Smith apples, peeled and diced

¼ cup raisins

3 TB. unbleached cane sugar

1 TB. whole-wheat pastry flour

1 TB. freshly squeezed lemon juice

½ tsp. ground cinnamon

¼ tsp. freshly grated nutmeg

9 sheets *phyllo* dough, thawed if frozen

Safflower oil

Yield: 6 turnovers
Prep time: 15 to 20 minutes
Cook time: 15 to 20 minutes
Serving size: 1 turnover

1. Preheat the oven to 400°F. Lightly oil a large cookie sheet.

2. For filling, in a small bowl, combine apples, raisins, sugar, flour, lemon juice, cinnamon, and nutmeg.

3. Place 1 phyllo sheet on a large cutting board or work surface. Keep remaining phyllo sheets covered with a slightly damp cloth to prevent them from drying out and cracking. Lightly brush safflower oil on phyllo sheet. Top with another phyllo sheet, lightly brush with safflower oil again, and place another phyllo sheet on top. Cut phyllo sheets lengthwise into 3 (6-inch-wide) strips. Move strips apart.

4. Working with 1 strip at a time, place ¼ cup filling about 2 inches from the bottom edge of phyllo strip. Fold one bottom corner up diagonally over filling to form a triangle (bottom edge of phyllo strip should be aligned with side edge). Continue folding triangle in alternating directions, much as you would fold a flag, to the end of strip.

5. Transfer turnover to the prepared cookie sheet. Repeat procedure with remaining phyllo sheets and filling. Bake for 15 to 20 minutes or until golden brown. Serve warm or at room temperature. Once filled, the unbaked turnovers can also be frozen on a cookie sheet and stored in an airtight plastic container or a zipper-lock bag and baked unthawed as desired.

Variation: For a wheat-free version, replace whole-wheat pastry flour with whole-grain spelt flour, and use spelt phyllo dough.

def•i•ni•tion

Phyllo (or *filo* or *fillo*), derived from the Greek word *phyllon* for "leaf," are paper-thin sheets of pastry dough sold in several varieties made from wheat and spelt flours. They're used to prepare many Mediterranean and Middle Eastern pastries, baked goods, and casserole dishes. Find packages of phyllo dough in the refrigerated and frozen sections of most grocery and natural foods stores.

Orange Cranberry Loaf

Sweet, tart, and festive could best describe this quick bread made with ruby-red cranberries and orange juice and zest.

Yield: 1 loaf

Prep time: 5 to 7 minutes
Cook time: 30 to 35 minutes
Serving size: 1 slice

---

2 cups whole-wheat pastry flour	**¼ cup agave nectar**
2 tsp. baking powder	**¼ cup safflower oil**
¼ tsp. baking soda	**1¼ tsp. pure vanilla extract**
¼ tsp. sea salt	**1 cup fresh or frozen cranberries**
Juice and zest of 1 orange	**1 cup vegan powdered sugar**
⅓ cup plus 1 TB. soy milk or other nondairy milk of choice	

Thyme-ly Tip

Easily adapt this recipe to make a delicious zucchini bread. Simply replace the cranberries with 1¼ cups grated zucchini, substitute the juice and zest of 1 lemon, add an additional ¼ cup soy milk and 1 teaspoon each ground cinnamon and ginger. Feel free to also add ⅓ cup chopped walnuts and ¼ cup dried currants or raisins.

1. Preheat the oven to 375°F. Lightly oil a 8×4×2½-inch loaf pan.

2. In a medium bowl, combine flour, baking powder, baking soda, and salt. Add orange juice and zest, ⅓ cup soy milk, agave nectar, safflower oil, and ½ teaspoon vanilla extract, and stir gently to combine. Fold in cranberries.

3. Pour batter into the prepared pan. Bake for 30 to 35 minutes or until a toothpick inserted in the center comes out clean. Allow loaf to cool slightly in the pan and transfer to a rack to cool completely before topping with glaze.

4. For glaze, in a small bowl, whisk together powdered sugar, remaining 1 tablespoon soy milk, and remaining ¾ teaspoon vanilla extract. Add additional soy milk 1 teaspoon at a time, if necessary, to achieve desired consistency. Drizzle glaze over loaf and allow to harden slightly before slicing.

Variation: Omit the glaze altogether and simply dust the loaf lightly with vegan powdered sugar.

Spiced Pumpkin Pecan Loaf

The aroma of this delicious loaf as it bakes will remind you of pumpkin and pecan pie, so feel free to enjoy slices topped with nondairy ice cream for dessert rather than as a breakfast treat.

1½ cups whole-wheat pastry flour

⅔ cup plus 2 tsp. turbinado sugar

2 tsp. baking powder

¾ tsp. ground cinnamon

½ tsp. ground ginger

½ tsp. freshly grated nutmeg

½ tsp. sea salt

¼ tsp. ground cloves

¾ cup pumpkin purée

½ cup water

3 TB. safflower oil

½ tsp. pure vanilla extract

⅔ cup raw pecans, coarsely chopped

Yield: 1 loaf
Prep time: 5 to 7 minutes
Cook time: 30 to 35 minutes
Serving size: 1 slice

1. Preheat the oven to 375°F. Lightly oil a 8×4×2½-inch loaf pan.

2. In a medium bowl, combine flour, sugar, baking powder, cinnamon, ginger, nutmeg, salt, and cloves. Add pumpkin purée, water, safflower oil, and vanilla extract, and stir gently to combine. Fold in ⅓ cup chopped pecans.

3. Pour batter into the prepared pan, sprinkle remaining ⅓ cup chopped pecans over top, and press them in gently with your fingers. Sprinkle remaining 2 teaspoons turbinado sugar on top of pecans. Bake for 30 to 35 minutes or until a toothpick inserted in the center comes out clean. Serve warm or at room temperature.

Variation: Vary the flavor of your loaf by adding ⅓ cup dried cranberries, currants, or raisins, and 2 tablespoons chopped crystallized ginger pieces to the batter.

Soy What?

In the United States, the pumpkin is so beloved that many towns hold annual pumpkin festivals that include contests for baked goods, pumpkin carving, pumpkin chucking, and largest and heaviest weight competitions. As of September 2007, Joe Jutras of Rhode Island holds the world record for the largest pumpkin on record at 1,689 pounds.

Mixed Berry Corn Muffins

These wheat-free corn muffins are quick and easy to make and bake, chock-full of berries, and topped with sweet and crunchy turbinado sugar.

Yield: 8 muffins
Prep time: 5 to 7 minutes
Cook time: 18 to 22 minutes
Serving size: 1 muffin

1 cup whole-grain spelt flour or white spelt flour

½ cup cornmeal

3 TB. plus 2 tsp. turbinado sugar

1 TB. baking powder

1 TB. arrowroot or tapioca flour

¼ tsp. sea salt

¾ cup soy milk or other nondairy milk of choice

3 TB. safflower oil

½ tsp. pure vanilla extract

¾ cup fresh or frozen mixed berries such as blueberries, strawberries, and raspberries

1. Preheat the oven to 400°F. Lightly oil 8 muffin cups.

2. In a medium bowl, combine flour, cornmeal, 3 tablespoons sugar, baking powder, arrowroot, and salt. Add soy milk, safflower oil, and vanilla extract, and stir until just blended. Gently fold in berries.

3. Fill prepared muffin cups ¾ full and sprinkle tops with remaining 2 teaspoons turbinado sugar. Bake for 18 to 22 minutes or until lightly browned and a toothpick inserted in the center comes out clean. Serve warm or at room temperature. Store extra muffins in an airtight plastic container or a zipper-lock bag, either at room temperature or frozen.

Variation: For savory muffins, replace the berries with ⅔ cup frozen cut corn kernels and ¼ cup shredded vegan cheese, and omit the sugar topping.

Thyme-ly Tip

When using frozen berries in most baked goods, you don't need to thaw them first. Carefully mix them in, but avoid overstirring or your batter and finished product will have an odd color. Coating the frozen berries with a little flour prior to adding them to your batter helps prevent them from sinking in your baked goods.

Jungle Monkey Muffins

Enjoy these moist banana-flavored muffins with coconut, cashews, and chocolate chips for both breakfast and dessert.

1½ cups whole-wheat pastry flour

1½ tsp. aluminum-free baking powder

1 tsp. ground cinnamon

¼ tsp. ground ginger

¼ tsp. sea salt

2 medium bananas, peeled and cut into 2-in. pieces

¼ cup water

¼ cup agave nectar or maple syrup

3 TB. olive oil or safflower oil

1 tsp. pure vanilla extract

⅓ cup raw cashews, coarsely chopped

⅓ cup vegan chocolate or carob chips

¼ cup plus 3 TB. unsweetened shredded coconut

Yield: 8 muffins
Prep time: 5 to 7 minutes
Cook time: 18 to 22 minutes
Serving size: 1 muffin

1. Preheat the oven to 375°F. Lightly oil 8 muffin cups.

2. In a medium bowl, combine flour, baking powder, cinnamon, ginger, and salt.

3. Place bananas in a small bowl, and mash them with a fork until smooth. Stir in water, agave nectar, olive oil, and vanilla extract.

4. Pour wet ingredients into dry ingredients, and stir until just blended. Stir in cashews, chocolate chips, and ¼ cup shredded coconut.

5. Fill prepared muffin cups ¾ full, sprinkle tops with remaining 3 tablespoons shredded coconut, and press it in gently with your fingers. Bake for 18 to 22 minutes or until a toothpick inserted in the center comes out clean. Serve warm or at room temperature. Store extra muffins in an airtight plastic container or zipper-lock bag, either at room temperature or frozen.

Variation: You can replace the cashews, chocolate chips, and coconut with an equal amount of fresh or frozen berries, chopped fruit, or other nuts or seeds. Easily adapt this muffin recipe to prepare a banana bread by pouring the batter into an oiled 8×4×2½-inch loaf pan and baking for 30 to 35 minutes.

Soy What?

Bananas provide vitamins A, B_6, and C; potassium, and magnesium. You'll find them quite useful in vegan baking, too. Take advantage of their sweet flavor by using a lesser amount of sweeteners, their moisture content to replace up to half the amount of oil called for, and their binding properties by using them as an egg replacement.

Sunny Raisin Bran Muffins

These dark, moist, and chewy muffins are made with a healthy dose of wheat bran, molasses, raisins, and sunflower seeds.

Yield: 8 muffins
Prep time: 5 to 7 minutes
Cook time: 18 to 22 minutes
Serving size: 1 muffin

1 cup soy milk or other nondairy milk of choice

1 TB. apple cider vinegar

¼ cup maple syrup

3 TB. blackstrap molasses

3 TB. olive oil or safflower oil

¾ cup whole-wheat pastry flour

¾ cup wheat bran

½ tsp. ground cinnamon

½ tsp. baking soda

¼ tsp. baking powder

¼ tsp. ground ginger

¼ tsp. sea salt

½ cup raisins

3 TB. raw sunflower seeds

1. Preheat the oven to 375°F. Lightly oil 8 muffin cups.

2. In a small bowl, combine soy milk and vinegar, and set aside for 10 minutes to thicken. Stir in maple syrup, molasses, and olive oil.

3. In a medium bowl, combine flour, wheat bran, cinnamon, baking soda, baking powder, ginger, and salt.

4. Pour wet ingredients into dry ingredients, and stir until just blended. Stir in raisins and sunflower seeds.

5. Fill prepared muffin cups ¾ full. Bake for 18 to 22 minutes or until a toothpick inserted in the center comes out clean. Serve warm or at room temperature. Store extra muffins in an airtight plastic container or a zipper-lock bag, either at room temperature or frozen.

Variation: Vary the flavor of these bran muffins by substituting other types of dried fruit, seeds, or nuts. You can also add chopped fruit, berries, or even shredded carrots or zucchini.

Thyme-ly Tip

If you have wheat sensitivities, make these muffins wheat-free by replacing the wheat bran with oat bran and using either whole-grain spelt flour, barley flour, or a combination of barley and oat flour. You can quickly and easily make oat flour by pulverizing rolled oats in a blender or food processor fitted with an S blade until it achieves a fine, flour-like texture.

Dried Fruit-n-Nut Scones

These tasty scones feature dried apricots, dates, almonds, and the delightfully sweet zing of crystallized ginger.

2 cups whole-wheat pastry flour

¼ cup plus 1 TB. turbinado sugar

2 tsp. baking powder

1 tsp. ground cinnamon

½ tsp. baking soda

¼ tsp. sea salt

¼ cup nonhydrogenated vegan margarine

1 (6-oz.) pkg. plain or vanilla soy yogurt

⅓ cup soy milk or other nondairy milk of choice

1 tsp. pure vanilla extract

¼ tsp. pure almond extract

⅓ cup dried apricots, cut into small pieces

¼ cup date pieces coated in oat flour

3 TB. raw sliced almonds

2 TB. chopped crystallized ginger pieces

Yield: 8 scones	
Prep time: 5 to 7 minutes	
Cook time: 15 to 20 minutes	
Serving size: 1 scone	

1. Preheat the oven to 375°F. Line with parchment paper or lightly oil a large cookie sheet.

2. In a medium bowl, combine flour, ¼ cup sugar, baking powder, cinnamon, baking soda, and sea salt. Using a fork, work margarine into dry ingredients until mixture resembles coarse crumbs.

3. Add soy yogurt, soy milk, vanilla extract, and almond extract, and stir until mixture just comes together to form a soft dough. Gently fold in apricots, date pieces, almonds, and crystallized ginger.

4. Transfer dough to the prepared cookie sheet, and gently pat dough to form a 9-inch circle. Cut circle into 8 wedges using a sharp knife, but don't separate wedges. Sprinkle top with remaining 1 tablespoon turbinado sugar.

5. Bake for 15 to 20 minutes or until lightly browned around edges. Let cool slightly before cutting again to separate into 8 wedges. Serve warm or at room temperature, plain or with jam, jelly, or margarine. Store extra scones in an airtight plastic container or a zipper-lock bag, either at room temperature or frozen.

Variation: Create other scone flavors by substituting other types of dried fruit, nuts, seeds, in addition to using chopped fruit or berries, or even vegan chocolate or carob chips.

Thyme-ly Tip

You can find date pieces coated in oat flour available in bulk bins in most grocery and natural foods stores. If you can't find date pieces, here's a tip for cutting pitted dates: coat your knife with a little oil to help you easily cut them into small pieces and to make for easier cleaning of your knife.

Maple-Pecan Oatmeal Scones

Maple syrup provides sweetness to the batter, as well as a glaze for the tops of these wheat-free scones.

Yield: 8 scones
Prep time: 5 to 7 minutes
Cook time: 15 to 20 minutes
Serving size: 1 scone

¾ cup raw pecans

2 cups rolled oats (not instant oatmeal)

2 tsp. baking powder

1¼ tsp. ground cinnamon

¼ tsp. sea salt

¼ cup plus 4 tsp. maple syrup

¼ cup applesauce

2 TB. olive oil

1 tsp. pure vanilla extract

1. Preheat the oven to 375°F. Line with parchment paper or lightly oil a large cookie sheet.

2. Place pecans in a food processor fitted with an S blade and finely chop. Transfer chopped pecans to a small bowl.

3. Add 1¼ cups rolled oats and ¼ cup chopped pecans to the food processor and process until mixture resembles fine crumbs. Transfer mixture to a medium bowl and combine with remaining rolled oats, ¼ cup chopped pecans, baking powder, cinnamon, and salt.

4. Add ¼ cup maple syrup, applesauce, olive oil, and vanilla extract, and stir until mixture just comes together to form a soft dough.

5. Transfer dough to the prepared cookie sheet, and gently pat dough to form a 9-inch circle. Cut circle into 8 wedges using a sharp knife, but don't separate wedges. Drizzle remaining 4 teaspoons maple syrup and sprinkle remaining ¼ cup chopped pecans over top.

6. Bake for 15 to 20 minutes or until lightly browned around edges. Let cool slightly before cutting again to separate into 8 wedges. Serve warm or at room temperature. Store extra scones in an airtight plastic container or a zipper-lock bag, either at room temperature or frozen.

Variation: For a nut-free version, replace the pecans in the dough with an additional ¼ cup rolled oats or barley flour.

Soy What?

Oats contain beneficial dietary fiber that aids in elimination and helps lower your cholesterol. In fact, oat-containing products may state on the package that "diets low in saturated fat and cholesterol that include soluble fiber from oatmeal may reduce the risk of heart disease."

Sweet Potato Biscuits

Canned sweet potato purée gives these biscuits a golden orangey hue, and Sucanat, ground cinnamon, and ginger add some extra sweetness and spice.

2 cups whole-wheat pastry flour

2 TB. Sucanat or packed brown sugar

2 tsp. aluminum-free baking powder

¾ tsp. ground cinnamon

½ tsp. ground ginger

½ tsp. sea salt

⅓ cup nonhydrogenated vegan margarine

1 cup canned sweet potato purée

⅓ cup soy milk or other nondairy milk of choice

Yield: 16 biscuits
Prep time: 7 to 10 minutes
Cook time: 12 to 15 minutes
Serving size: 1 biscuit

1. Preheat the oven to 400°F. Line with parchment paper (or lightly oil) a large cookie sheet.

2. In a medium bowl, combine flour, Sucanat, baking powder, cinnamon, ginger, and salt.

3. Using your fingers or a fork, work margarine into dry ingredients until mixture resembles coarse crumbs.

4. In a small bowl, combine sweet potato purée and soy milk. Add sweet potato mixture to dry ingredients, and stir just until combined. Do not overmix.

5. Turn out dough onto a lightly floured work surface and knead lightly 5 times. Using a rolling pin, roll dough to a ¾-inch thickness and cut with a 2-inch biscuit cutter into 10 biscuits. Place biscuits on the prepared cookie sheet, either touching (for soft-sided biscuit) or 1 inch apart (for a biscuit with lightly browned sides).

6. Gather up scraps, roll out again to a ¾-inch thickness, cut out 6 more biscuits, and place them on cookie sheet. Discard any remaining scraps.

7. Bake for 12 to 15 minutes or until lightly browned. Remove from the oven. Let cool slightly. Serve warm or at room temperature, either plain or with margarine, jam, or jelly.

Thyme-ly Tip

When making biscuits, you want them to be light, so mix and handle the dough as little as possible. Ideally, only roll out the dough twice for cutting the biscuits; otherwise, they'll come out tough and hard after baking. For flaky biscuits, use a 2- to 2½-inch cookie cutter or a small, floured juice glass as a cutter.

Variation: Alternatively, pat the dough with your hands into a ¾-inch-thick 8×8-inch square and cut it into 16 (2-inch) squares using a sharp knife. For extra flavor, add ½ cup finely chopped pecans to the dough, brush the tops with a little maple syrup or melted margarine, and sprinkle lightly with Sucanat or brown sugar.

Herbed Drop Biscuits

These easy drop biscuits have a savory flavor, thanks to a little dried thyme, dill weed, and garlic powder.

Yield: 16 biscuits	
Prep time: 7 to 10 minutes	
Cook time: 10 to 12 minutes	
Serving size: 1 biscuit	

1 cup soy milk or other nondairy milk of choice

1 TB. apple cider vinegar or freshly squeezed lemon juice

2 cups whole-wheat pastry flour

2 tsp. baking powder

¾ tsp. dried dill weed

¾ tsp. dried thyme

¾ tsp. sea salt

½ tsp. garlic powder or garlic granules

½ tsp. baking soda

¼ cup nonhydrogenated vegan margarine

1. In a small bowl or measuring cup, combine soy milk and lemon juice. Set aside for 5 minutes to thicken.

2. Preheat the oven to 400°F. Line with parchment paper (or lightly oil) a large cookie sheet.

3. In a medium bowl, combine flour, baking powder, dill weed, thyme, salt, garlic powder, and baking soda.

4. Using your fingers or a fork, work margarine into dry ingredients until mixture resembles coarse crumbs. Pour soy milk mixture into dry ingredients, and stir until a soft, sticky dough forms.

5. Drop dough by heaping tablespoonfuls onto the prepared cookie sheet. Bake for 10 to 12 minutes or until golden brown around the edges and on the bottom. Remove from the oven. Serve warm or at room temperature, either plain, with margarine, or split in half and topped with gravy.

Variation: Feel free to replace the dried thyme and dill weed with dried basil, oregano, or rosemary.

Thyme-ly Tip

You can make a nondairy buttermilk replacement: *clabber* (sour and thicken) nondairy milk by combining it with something acidic like lemon juice or vinegar. For 1 cup nondairy buttermilk, mix 1 cup soy milk or other nondairy milk with 1 tablespoon lemon juice or apple cider vinegar. Allow it to sit for 5 to 10 minutes or until thickened before using.

Tex-Mex Cornbread

This slightly spicy and savory cornbread bakes up moist and delicious and is quite colorful, thanks to the corn, red bell pepper, green onions, jalapeño pepper, and vegan cheddar cheese.

2 cups cornmeal

2 cups whole-wheat pastry flour

¼ cup unbleached cane sugar or *Sucanat*

2 TB. aluminum-free baking powder

1½ tsp. chili powder

¾ tsp. sea salt

1¾ cups soy milk or other nondairy milk of choice

¼ cup safflower oil or corn oil

½ cup vegan cheddar cheese, shredded

½ cup frozen cut corn kernels

½ cup red bell pepper, ribs and seeds removed, and finely diced

¼ cup green onion, thinly sliced

1 jalapeño pepper, ribs and seeds removed, and finely diced

Yield: 1 (9×13-inch) pan
Prep time: 7 to 10 minutes
Cook time: 20 to 25 minutes
Serving size: 1 piece

1. Preheat the oven to 375°F. Lightly oil a 9×13-inch baking pan.

2. In a medium bowl, sift together cornmeal, flour, sugar, baking powder, chili powder, and salt. Add soy milk and oil, and stir until just combined. Add shredded cheese, corn, red bell pepper, green onion, and jalapeño pepper, and gently stir to combine.

3. Transfer batter to the prepared pan. Bake for 20 to 25 minutes or until a toothpick inserted in the center comes out clean. Remove from the oven. Let cool slightly, and cut into 12 squares. Serve warm or at room temperature.

Variation: For a wheat-free version, replace the whole-wheat pastry flour with barley flour or whole-grain or white spelt flour.

def•i•ni•tion

Sucanat, manufactured by Wholesome Sweeteners, is a sugar made by dehydrating and granulating sugar cane. It has a slightly coarse texture, golden brown color, and a high concentration of molasses, which makes it an excellent substitute for light and dark brown sugar in recipes.

Part 3

Teasers and Toppers

Are you ready to wake up your taste buds? In the mood for a snack but not quite sure what you're craving? Want to pump up the flavors of your meals? Feeling adventurous and wanting to impress your friends with some of your vegan creations? If you answered "yes" to one or more of these questions, Part 3 is for you, as it contains vegan recipes to entice your palate and enhance your culinary creations.

If you're thinking about throwing a party or get-together, the following chapters are sure to get your party planning off to a great start. We begin with delicious vegan appetizers and snack ideas that are sure to get people talking. Many of the sauces, spreads, and toppings that follow can spruce up your vegan meals. Finally, you learn how to make your own homemade cheese and dairy substitutes.

Chapter 6

Appealing Appetizers and Snacks

In This Chapter

◆ Party-worthy appetizers

◆ Veganized dips and dunkers

◆ Healthy baked nibbles and snacks

Often preceding a meal or feast, or perhaps as a first course at a more elaborate affair, bite-size morsels or a small plate of food are offered to whet your appetite—hence the name *appetizers*.

At most restaurants and sit-down functions, vegan appetizer options are usually hard to come by, as most either contain several animal-based products, are topped with them, or were deep-fried using the same oil. If you're lucky, the soirée you're attending has a buffet featuring a veggie or fruit platter for you to nibble on or, worse-case scenario, to build a meal around.

Nibble on This

If you're thinking of throwing a party or get-together that calls for some tasty and easy vegan appetizers, this chapter is for you. In the following pages, we offer several recipes for appetizer and snack ideas, sure to help you plan your party menu. You'll appreciate the versatility of using premade nondairy replacements and tofu to create sumptuous spreads, sauces, fillings, and hot and cold dips. We also share ideas for transforming humble tempeh, TVP (textured vegetable protein), and meatless hot dogs into fantastic finger foods.

Healthful appetizers or snacks can be especially handy to keep hungry kids and spouses content and out of the refrigerator while you finish dinner. To temporarily alleviate their hunger pangs, put out some cut fruit or veggies, raw nuts or seeds, or vegan cheese and crackers for a simple nosh and nibble. For those times when you're hungry for a little something but you're not sure exactly what for, or not really wanting to sit down and eat a full meal, try combining a few of our appetizer or snack ideas.

Many of us like to nibble on something while watching a movie or a favorite show on TV. Check out your local grocery and natural foods stores for a vast array of vegan snacking options of baked, fried, and flavored chips and crisps of all kinds, crackers, pretzels, and even dehydrated fruits and veggies, just to name a few.

Spiced Baked Garbanzo Beans

These spiced garbanzo beans make for a great fiber-packed snack and can be used on top of salads like croutons or added to grain or pasta dishes for extra flavor and texture.

2 (15-oz.) cans garbanzo beans, drained and rinsed

2 TB. curry powder

1 TB. *toasted sesame oil*

1 TB. ground cumin

1 tsp. ground ginger

1 tsp. sea salt

Yield: 3 cups
Prep time: 1 or 2 minutes
Cook time: 40 to 45 minutes
Serving size: ¼ cup

1. Preheat the oven to 400°F. Line a large cookie sheet with parchment paper.

2. Combine garbanzo beans, curry powder, toasted sesame oil, cumin, ginger, and salt in a medium bowl, and stir well to evenly coat garbanzo beans.

3. Transfer garbanzo beans to the prepared cookie sheet, spread them into a single layer, and bake for 20 minutes. Remove from the oven. Stir garbanzo beans, spread them into a single layer again, and bake for 20 to 25 more minutes or until golden brown and crunchy. Taste and add additional seasonings as desired. Serve at room temperature. Store garbanzo beans in an airtight container at room temperature.

Variation: Replace the toasted sesame oil with olive oil, and use other spices, such as chili powder, garlic powder, or cayenne, or use herbs instead, such as rosemary, thyme, or Italian seasoning blend.

def•i•ni•tion

Toasted sesame oil derives its flavor and color from the pressed, toasted sesame seeds used to produce it. It's very aromatic, with a slightly thick consistency and a dark brown color. Toasted sesame oil is a staple in Asian cuisine and is commonly used in marinades, sauces, salad dressings, and stir-fries.

Veggie Spring Rolls

Spring rolls are made with a wide assortment of cooked and raw ingredients encased in paper-thin sheets of rice paper. They're a delicious Asian finger-food often enjoyed as an appetizer, snack, or as part of meal.

Yield: 12 spring rolls
Prep time: 20 to 25 minutes
Cook time: 2 or 3 minutes
Serving size: 1 spring roll

2 oz. rice vermicelli or bean thread noodles

1¼ cups napa cabbage, finely shredded

1 cup mung bean sprouts

½ cup carrot, shredded

½ cup red bell pepper, ribs and seeds removed, and finely diced

⅓ cup green onions, thinly sliced

¼ cup chopped fresh cilantro

¼ cup chopped fresh mint or basil

¼ cup roasted peanuts, finely chopped

12 (8- or 9-in.) round rice papers

4 oz. baked seasoned tofu or 1 cup prepared Shanghai Tofu (recipe in Chapter 15), cut into ½-in. strips

Dipping sauce of choice, such as tamari, Teriyaki Stir-Frying and Dipping Sauce (recipe in Chapter 8), or Thai Peanut Sauce (recipe in Chapter 8)

Soy What?

Find rice papers, rice vermicelli, and bean thread noodles in many grocery and natural foods stores and Asian specialty markets. Explore your local Asian specialty market, where you'll not only find these ingredients, but a lot of other interesting and exotic vegan ingredients as well.

1. Cook or soak rice vermicelli according to the package instructions and drain well. Roughly chop rice vermicelli and place in a medium bowl.

2. Add cabbage, mung bean sprouts, carrot, red bell pepper, green onions, cilantro, mint, and peanuts, and toss gently to combine.

3. Fill a 9-inch-round pie pan with warm water. Working with 1 rice paper at a time, submerge it in water and leave for 10 to 20 seconds or until soft and pliable. Remove rice paper from water, and place on a large plate or work surface.

4. Place ¼ cup veggie mixture about 1 inch from bottom and side edges of rice paper and lay 4 or 5 strips of baked tofu on top.

5. Fold bottom edge of rice paper up over filling, fold side edges of rice paper toward center, and roll up from the bottom edge, as tightly as possible, to enclose filling. Place spring roll, seam side down, on a large plate. Fill and assemble remaining rice papers in the same fashion. For faster assembly, soak one rice paper while you fill and roll another.

6. Cut each spring roll in half lengthwise and serve with dipping sauce of choice. Store uncut spring rolls in the refrigerator in an airtight plastic container or individually wrapped in plastic wrap.

Variation: Vary the flavor of your spring rolls by replacing the tofu strips with strips of cooked tempeh, thin strips of peeled cucumber, or thin slices of avocado or mango.

Spanakopita

Layers of crisp phyllo dough are filled with spinach and a seasoned tofu mixture instead of the typically used feta in this veganized version of the popular Greek delicacy.

¾ **cup onion, diced**

2 tsp. olive oil, plus extra for oiling phyllo dough

1 (10-oz.) pkg. frozen chopped spinach, thawed

½ **cup green onions, thinly sliced**

1 TB. garlic, minced

2 TB. chopped fresh dill

1 (12-oz.) pkg. firm or extra-firm silken tofu

⅓ **cup nutritional yeast flakes**

4 tsp. freshly squeezed lemon juice

1 tsp. garlic powder

1 tsp. onion powder

1 tsp. dried oregano

½ **tsp. sea salt**

¼ **tsp. freshly ground black pepper**

¼ **tsp. freshly grated nutmeg**

8 sheets phyllo dough, thawed

Yield: 16 servings
Prep time: 15 to 20 minutes
Cook time: 25 to 30 minutes
Serving size: 1 piece

1. In a large nonstick skillet, combine diced onion and olive oil and sauté over medium heat, stirring often, for 3 or 4 minutes or until soft.

2. Place thawed spinach in a colander and squeeze with your hands to remove excess moisture. Add spinach, green onions, and garlic to the skillet, and continue to sauté for 2 more minutes. Remove from heat and stir in chopped dill.

3. Crumble tofu into a medium bowl using your fingers. Add nutritional yeast flakes, lemon juice, garlic powder, onion powder, dried oregano, salt, black pepper, and nutmeg, and mash with a fork until completely smooth. Add spinach mixture, and stir well to combine.

4. Preheat the oven to 375°F. Lightly oil a 9×13-inch baking pan.

5. Place 1 phyllo sheet on a large cutting board or work surface. Keep remaining phyllo sheets covered with a slightly damp cloth to prevent them from drying out and cracking. Lightly brush phyllo sheet with olive oil. Top with another phyllo sheet, lightly brush with olive oil again, and repeat procedure using a total of 4 sheets of phyllo dough. Fold sheets in half lengthwise, and place them in the bottom of the prepared pan. Assemble remaining 4 phyllo sheets in the same manner and cover them with a slightly damp cloth.

6. Spoon tofu mixture on top of phyllo layers. Place reserved phyllo sheets on top of filling. Using a sharp knife, cut 16 diamond-shape pieces, but cut through the top layer of phyllo dough only.

7. Bake for 25 to 30 minutes or until golden brown. Let cool slightly before cutting all the way through the pieces again. Serve warm or at room temperature.

Variation: You can also use fresh spinach or Swiss chard, lacinato kale, or a combination of greens in this recipe, but you'll need to use 2 pounds or 2 large bunches of greens.

Thyme-ly Tip

For a fancier version, make individual spanakopita triangles. Follow the procedure used for making Apple Turnovers (recipe in Chapter 5), but cut the phyllo sheets into either 2-inch-wide strips (for small ones using 2 teaspoons filling) or 4-inch-wide strips (for medium ones using 2 tablespoons filling) to assemble each triangle.

Tofu Dog Bites

These cute little oven-baked treats are based on the favorite "Pigs in a Blanket" appetizer commonly served at picnics and parties. This veganized version uses tofu hot dogs and homemade biscuit dough instead of the commonly used tube of refrigerated biscuit or crescent dough.

2 cups whole-wheat pastry flour

1 TB. aluminum-free baking powder

1 tsp. nutritional yeast flakes

½ tsp. sea salt

¼ cup nonhydrogenated vegan margarine

¾ cup soy milk or other nondairy milk of choice

6 tofu hot dogs

Yield: 18 pieces
Prep time: 10 to 15 minutes
Cook time: 12 to 15 minutes
Serving size: 2 pieces

1. Preheat the oven to 400°F. Line a large cookie sheet with parchment paper.

2. Combine flour, baking powder, nutritional yeast flakes, and salt in a medium bowl. Using your fingers, work margarine into dry ingredients until mixture resembles coarse crumbs. Add soy milk, and stir well until it forms a ball of dough.

3. Place dough on a floured work surface, and knead for 1 minute. Roll or pat dough into a 15×7-inch rectangle. Using a pizza cutter or sharp knife, cut the rectangle into thirds horizontally, and cut each section into thirds to form 9 rectangles. Cut each of the 9 rectangles in half diagonally to form 18 triangles.

4. Cut each tofu hot dog into three pieces. Working with one triangle at a time, place one hot dog piece at the long, base end of a dough triangle, and roll toward the triangle point to enclose hot dog piece. Place point-side down on the prepared cookie sheet. Repeat rolling procedure for the remaining hot dog pieces and dough triangles.

5. Bake for 12 to 15 minutes or until golden brown. Serve warm or at room temperature with ketchup, mustard, barbecue sauce, or other dipping sauce of choice.

Variation: For extra flavor, spread a little mustard or barbecue sauce on each of the dough triangles prior to rolling.

Thyme-ly Tip

For a fancier version, use sheets of phyllo dough instead. Lightly brush 3 sheets of phyllo dough with olive oil, and stack sheets on top of each other with oiled sides facing down. Cut the sheets lengthwise into 1-inch-wide strips, place a hot dog piece on each strip, and roll to enclose. Place them seam-side down on prepared cookie sheet, and bake for 12 to 15 minutes or until golden brown.

Chipotle Tempeh Diamoniques with Creamy Dipping Sauce

Enjoy these spicy baked tempeh diamoniques (small diamond-shape pieces) all on their own (or added to other dishes), or dip them into their accompanying ranchlike, creamy herb dipping sauce.

Yield: 8 servings

Prep time: 10 to 12 minutes

Cook time: 30 to 35 minutes

Serving size: 1/2 cup tempeh pieces and 3 tablespoons dipping sauce

---

2 (8-oz.) pkg. tempeh

1/2 cup water

2 TB. tamari

1 TB. olive oil

1 TB. freshly squeezed lime juice

1/2 tsp. chili powder

1/2 tsp. *chipotle chile powder*

1/2 tsp. plus 1/4 tsp. garlic powder

1/2 tsp. dried oregano

2/3 cup Tofu Mayonnaise (recipe in Chapter 12)

2/3 cup soy milk or other nondairy milk of choice

1/4 cup green onions, thinly sliced

3 TB. chopped fresh parsley or dill

1 tsp. apple cider vinegar

1/4 tsp. sea salt

1/4 tsp. freshly ground black pepper

def•i•ni•tion

Chipotle chile powder (also known as *ground chipotle powder*) is made from finely ground, dried chipotle chiles. It can be used in place of, or along with, regular chili powder in your favorite recipes. Chipotle chiles are actually roasted or smoked jalapeño peppers, which explains their very spicy and smoky flavor.

1. Preheat the oven to 375°F. Lightly oil a large cookie sheet.

2. Cut each block of tempeh into 1/2-inch-wide strips vertically, turn strips 1/4 turn (strips should now be horizontal), and slice diagonally through strips to form 1-inch-wide diamond-shape pieces (or diamoniques).

3. Place tempeh pieces, water, tamari, olive oil, and lime juice in a medium bowl, and stir well to combine.

4. In a small bowl, combine chili powder, chipotle chile powder, 1/2 teaspoon garlic powder, and dried oregano.

5. Pour seasonings over tempeh mixture, and toss well to combine. Transfer tempeh mixture to the prepared cookie sheet, and spread out into a single layer.

6. Bake for 15 minutes. Remove from the oven. Stir tempeh with a spatula, spread out into a single layer, and bake for 15 to 20 more minutes or until golden brown around the edges.

7. While tempeh bakes, make dipping sauce. For dipping sauce, in a small bowl, place Tofu Mayonnaise, soy milk, green onions, parsley, vinegar, remaining 1/4 teaspoon garlic powder, salt, and black pepper, and stir well to combine. Place in the refrigerator to chill and allow flavors to blend.

8. Transfer cooked tempeh diamoniques to a large plate, and serve with dipping sauce.

Variation: If you prefer, cut the tempeh into 2-inch-long strips. You can also serve the baked tempeh pieces with Creamy Agave Dijon Dressing (recipe in Chapter 12).

Warm Artichoke and Spinach Dip

Prepare this warm, dairy-free dip made with tofu, artichokes, and spinach for parties or special occasions. Its rich and savory flavor is sure to impress your guests and have them begging you for the recipe.

1 (14-oz.) can artichoke hearts packed in water, drained	1 TB. Dijon mustard
	1 TB. freshly squeezed lemon juice
1/4 cup green onions, thinly sliced	1 tsp. dried basil or dill weed
2 TB. garlic, minced	1/2 tsp. sea salt
2 tsp. olive oil	1/4 tsp. freshly ground black pepper
1 (12-oz.) pkg. firm or extra-firm silken tofu	1/4 tsp. cayenne or hot pepper sauce
1/4 cup soy milk or other non-dairy milk of choice	2 cups spinach, coarsely chopped
1/4 cup plus 2 TB. nutritional yeast flakes	Paprika

> *Yield: 8 servings*
> **Prep time:** 5 to 7 minutes
> **Cook time:** 15 to 20 minutes
> **Serving size:** 1/4 cup

1. Preheat the oven to 375°F. Lightly oil a 9-inch round or square baking pan.

2. Place artichoke hearts in a food processor fitted with an S blade and coarsely chop.

3. In a large nonstick skillet, combine chopped artichokes, green onions, garlic, and olive oil, and cook over medium heat, stirring often, for 2 or 3 minutes or until artichokes are soft. Remove from heat.

4. Crumble silken tofu into the food processor using your fingers. Add soy milk, ¼ cup nutritional yeast flakes, Dijon mustard, lemon juice, dried basil, salt, black pepper, and cayenne, and process for 1 or 2 minutes or until completely smooth. Scrape down the sides of the container with a rubber spatula and process for 15 more seconds. Add artichoke mixture and spinach, and process for 30 seconds.

5. Transfer mixture to the prepared baking dish. Bake immediately or chill in the refrigerator until needed. Prior to baking, sprinkle remaining 2 tablespoons nutritional yeast flakes and a little paprika on top. Bake for 15 to 20 minutes or until lightly browned on top. Serve dip hot with raw veggies, slices of bread, or crackers.

Variation: Omit the chopped spinach and just stir in the artichoke mixture along with ½ cup chopped red bell pepper and ½ cup chopped black olives.

Thyme-ly Tip _____

For an even richer-tasting baked artichoke dip, replace the silken tofu with 8 ounces tofu cream cheese and ½ cup Tofu Mayonnaise (recipe in Chapter 12), and also add ⅓ cup shredded vegan mozzarella cheese or other variety of choice. You can also forego the baking of this dip and simply chill it well to allow the flavors to blend before serving.

Nachos Supreme

No one will be able to resist these vegan nachos loaded up with the works: seasoned TVP, refried beans, melted cheese, and a colorful assortment of chopped veggies.

⅔ **cup water**

⅔ **cup** *TVP* **granules**

2 TB. tamari

1½ tsp. ketchup

1 tsp. chili powder

½ tsp. garlic powder

½ tsp. onion powder

½ tsp. ground cumin

½ tsp. dried oregano

6 cups tortilla chips of choice

1 cup canned vegetarian refried beans of choice

1 cup shredded vegan cheddar cheese or other flavor of choice

1 jalapeño pepper, thinly sliced

1 medium plum tomato, diced

½ medium Hass avocado, peeled and diced

¼ cup green onions, thinly sliced

¼ cup kalamata olives or other black olives of choice, pitted and roughly chopped

Tofu sour cream or Herbed Tofu Sour Cream (recipe in Chapter 9)

Salsa of choice

Yield: 8 servings
Prep time: 7 to 10 minutes
Cook time: 15 to 17 minutes
Serving size: 1½ cups

1. For TVP mixture, in a small saucepan, combine water, TVP, tamari, ketchup, chili powder, garlic powder, onion powder, cumin, and oregano. Bring to a boil, cover, remove from heat, and set aside to rehydrate for 10 minutes.

2. Preheat the oven to 375°F. Line a large cookie sheet with parchment paper.

3. Spread tortilla chips in a single layer on the prepared cookie sheet. Spoon seasoned TVP mixture evenly over tortilla chips. Evenly place spoonfuls of refried beans on top, followed by shredded vegan cheese and jalapeño pepper slices.

4. Bake for 5 to 7 minutes or until cheese is melted. Remove from the oven. Carefully transfer tortilla chip mixture to 2 large plates. Dividing evenly between the plates, scatter tomato, avocado, green onions, and olives over the top. Place small dollops of tofu sour cream over the top, or serve in a small bowl along with salsa on the side, as desired.

Variation: Alternatively, assemble tortilla chips, seasoned TVP, refried beans, shredded cheese, and jalapeño pepper slices on 2 large microwaveable plates. Cook each plate in a microwave oven for 1 or 2 minutes or until hot and cheese is melted. Then top each plate with the remaining ingredients and serve as desired. And for chili and cheese nachos, replace the seasoned TVP mixture and refried beans with 1 cup canned vegetarian chili, bake, top with remaining ingredients, and serve.

def•i•ni•tion

TVP, or *textured vegetable protein,* may appear on prepackaged food labels also as *textured soy flour, textured soy protein,* or *hydrolyzed vegetable protein.* It's made from defatted soy flour that's been cooked, extruded, and dried. TVP is packed with fiber and protein, and is available prepackaged or from bulk bins in granules, chunks, and slices.

Tantalizing Toppers and Spreads

In This Chapter

◆ Middle Eastern favorites

◆ Mediterranean must-haves

◆ Sweet and savory nut-based spreads

Some of us rather enjoy "gilding the lily" or embellishing our vegan meals with a little extra something savory or sweet. These extra touches and additions often help heighten or brighten the flavors or visual appeal of both simply and elaborately prepared foods, as well as making them seem even more special.

The typical spreads most Americans use seem to rely heavily on dairy products and tons of fat. However, most vegan spreads and toppings have very concentrated flavors ranging from salty, spicy, pungent, rich, mellow, to even slightly sweet. We're sure you'll be pleased by the selections we've included in this chapter for enhancing your vegan meals and taking them to new gastronomic heights.

All these vegan toppings and spreads (with the exception of the guacamole) stay fresh for several days or longer in the refrigerator or can be made in larger batches and frozen for later use. Naturally, feel free to swap the ingredients and spices we've suggested to suit your tastes, as well as experiment with our variations of ideas to create your own versions.

Roasted Red Pepper Hummus

Rich and creamy hummus is a staple of Middle Eastern cuisine. Enjoy this version, made with freshly roasted red pepper, garbanzo beans, and other assorted ingredients, as a dip or as a filling for sandwiches.

1 red bell pepper, ribs and seeds removed, and cut into 1-in. pieces

1 tsp. plus 1 TB. olive oil

3 large garlic cloves

1 (15-oz.) can garbanzo beans, drained and rinsed

2 TB. freshly squeezed lemon juice

1 TB. raw *tahini*

1 TB. water

½ tsp. ground cumin

½ tsp. sea salt

½ tsp. paprika

⅛ tsp. cayenne

2 TB. chopped fresh parsley

Yield: 1½ cups	
Prep time: 5 to 7 minutes	
Cook time: 8 to 10 minutes	
Serving size: 2 tablespoons	

1. Preheat the oven to 450°F.

2. Place red bell pepper in a 9-inch round pie pan, drizzle with 1 teaspoon olive oil, and toss well to combine. Bake for 8 to 10 minutes or until soft and lightly browned around the edges. Remove from the oven and let cool for 5 minutes.

3. Meanwhile, place garlic in a food processor fitted with an S blade and finely chop. Add garbanzo beans, lemon juice, remaining 1 tablespoon olive oil, tahini, water, cumin, salt, paprika, and cayenne, and process for 1 or 2 minutes or until completely smooth. Scrape down the sides of the container with a rubber spatula. Add red pepper and parsley, and process for 1 or 2 more minutes or until completely smooth.

4. Transfer mixture to a medium bowl. Serve with raw veggies or pita breads. Store hummus in an airtight container in the refrigerator for up to 1 week or in the freezer for 6 months.

Variation: For ease, you can just use a chopped raw red pepper instead of roasting it in the oven, or use jarred roasted peppers.

def•i•ni•tion

Tahini is made from sesame seeds that are ground into a thick paste, and has a consistency similar to peanut butter. It is available in both raw and roasted varieties in most grocery and natural foods stores. If your tahini separates prior to opening, simply stir the oil back into it rather than draining it off.

Smoky Baba Ganoush

Enjoy this great Middle Eastern recipe as either a dip or spread. It has a slightly smoky flavor as the result of slow-roasting eggplant in the oven and using toasted sesame oil instead of the traditionally used olive oil.

Yield: 1½ cups
Prep time: 5 to 7 minutes
Cook time: 30 to 40 minutes
Serving size: 2 tablespoons

1 large or 2 medium eggplants (about 1¼ lb.)

2 large garlic cloves

2 TB. freshly squeezed lemon juice

1 TB. raw tahini

1 TB. toasted sesame oil

½ tsp. ground cumin

½ tsp. sea salt

¼ tsp. freshly ground black pepper

2 TB. chopped fresh parsley

1. Preheat the oven to 425°F. Lightly oil a large cookie sheet.

2. Cut eggplant in half lengthwise and cut several splits into flesh. Place cut side down on the prepared cookie sheet. Bake for 30 to 40 minutes or until very soft and eggplant begins to collapse. Remove from the oven and let cool slightly.

3. Meanwhile, place garlic in a food processor fitted with an S blade and finely chop. When eggplant is cool enough to handle, use a spoon to scoop out flesh and place in the food processor. Add lemon juice, tahini, toasted sesame oil, cumin, salt, and black pepper, and process for 1 or 2 minutes or until completely smooth. Add parsley and process for 1 more minute.

4. Transfer mixture to a medium bowl. Serve with raw veggies, crackers, or pita breads. Store baba ganoush in an airtight container in the refrigerator for up to 1 week or in the freezer for 6 months.

Variation: Alternatively, cook the eggplant on a grill, either whole or halved until soft. And for extra flavor, roast 1 seeded plum tomato along with the eggplant during the last 10 minutes of baking, and process it along with the other ingredients.

Soy What?

Depending on where you are, you might find alternate spellings for *hummus* and *baba ganoush*. Hummus might be called *houmus, hommos, humus,* or *hummus bi tahina.* Baba ganoush might be referred to as *baba ghanouj, baba ganouj, baba ghanoush,* or simply as *baba.*

Black Olive and Sun-Dried Tomato Tapenade

Sun-dried tomatoes, kalamata olives, and capers all blend together to create the savory, rich flavors of this versatile spread that can be enjoyed all on its own or used much like pesto to add extra flavor to your favorite dishes.

½ **cup sun-dried tomato pieces**

¾ **cup water**

1 cup kalamata olives or other black olives of choice, pitted

¼ **cup olive oil**

2 large garlic cloves

1 TB. capers

1 TB. freshly squeezed lemon juice

1 tsp. dried basil or Italian seasoning blend

¼ **tsp. sea salt**

⅛ **tsp. freshly ground black pepper**

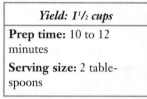

Yield: 1½ cups
Prep time: 10 to 12 minutes
Serving size: 2 table-spoons

1. Place sun-dried tomato pieces in a small bowl. Cover with water, and set aside for 5 to 10 minutes to rehydrate.

2. Drain off any excess water and transfer sun-dried tomato pieces into a food processor fitted with an S blade. Add olives, olive oil, and garlic, and roughly chop. Scrape down the sides of the container with a rubber spatula. Add capers, lemon juice, basil, salt, and black pepper, and process for 1 minute or until completely smooth.

3. Transfer mixture to a medium bowl. Serve on slices of bread or crackers; use as a filling for cherry tomatoes for an appetizer; or add to pasta, grains, or vegetable side dishes. Add a thin layer of olive oil to the top and store tapenade in an airtight container in the refrigerator for up to 1 week. Alternatively, freeze for up to 6 months in an airtight container or portion into ice cube trays and then transfer frozen cubes to an airtight container or a zipper-lock bag for use as individual servings.

Variation: For extra flavor, replace the lemon juice with balsamic vinegar. Or replace the sun-dried tomatoes with ½ cup green olives or other olives of choice.

 Sour Grapes

Even if the olives you're using are marked "pitted," it's best to double-check. Press down on each one or cut them in half. Otherwise, you or one of your guests may be in for quite a surprise while enjoying your creation—or even worse, crack a tooth!

Spinach-Walnut Pesto

This pesto recipe featuring spinach and parsley is much lower in fat than most pesto recipes and is a great way to sneak leafy greens into a finicky eater's diet.

Yield: 1½ cups

Prep time: 5 to 7 minutes
Serving size: 2 tablespoons

½ cup raw walnuts

3 large garlic cloves

2½ cups lightly packed fresh spinach, stems removed

½ cup lightly packed fresh Italian parsley, stems removed

¼ cup nutritional yeast flakes

2 TB. olive oil

1 tsp. lemon juice

½ tsp. sea salt

¼ tsp. freshly ground black pepper

1. Place walnuts and garlic in a food processor fitted with an S blade and finely chop. Add spinach, parsley, nutritional yeast flakes, olive oil, lemon juice, salt, and black pepper, and process for 1 or 2 minutes or until completely smooth. (For a thinner pesto, also add 1 or 2 tablespoons water during processing.)

2. Serve with slices of bread or crackers; use as a dip for raw veggies; use to flavor salad dressings, sauces, or mayonnaise; or add to pasta, grains, vegetables, or other dishes. Store pesto in an airtight container in the refrigerator for up to 1 week, with a thin layer of olive oil added to the top to reduce discoloration.

Variation: For a spicy arugula pesto, replace the spinach with 3 cups fresh arugula, use basil instead of parsley, and also add ¼ teaspoon or more crushed red pepper flakes.

 Sour Grapes

Spinach is high in oxalic acid, which, for some people, can contribute to developing kidney stones or gout. But don't let that deter you from enjoying this leafy green, which is also rich in beneficial folic acid; magnesium; and vitamins A, C, E, and K, as well as many antioxidants.

Holy Moly Guacamole

This spicy and colorful guacamole, flavored with two kinds of fresh chiles, will tingle your tongue and may even cause you to sweat a bit, so enjoy it with some refried beans and tortilla chips or as a topper for other dishes.

2 medium Hass avocados, peeled and diced

2 TB. freshly squeezed lime juice

1 TB. garlic, minced

1 medium plum tomato, seeded and diced

⅓ cup red onion, finely diced

⅓ cup red or orange bell pepper, ribs and seeds removed, and finely diced

¼ cup chopped fresh cilantro

1 jalapeño pepper, ribs and seeds removed, and finely diced

1 serrano pepper, ribs and seeds removed, and finely diced

¼ tsp. ground cumin

¼ tsp. chili powder or chipotle chile powder

Sea salt

Freshly ground black pepper

Yield: 2 cups	
Prep time: 5 to 7 minutes	
Serving size: ¹/₄ cup	

1. Using a potato masher or fork, mash avocadoes, lime juice, and garlic together in a medium bowl, as smooth or chunky as desired.

2. Add tomato, red onion, red bell pepper, cilantro, jalapeño pepper, serrano pepper, cumin, and chili powder, and stir well to combine. Taste and season with salt and black pepper as desired.

3. Serve with tortilla chips or raw veggies, or use as a spread on sandwiches or as a topping for your favorite Mexican dishes. Store guacamole, along with one pit (to limit discoloration), in an airtight container in the refrigerator for up to 3 days.

Variation: Alternatively, place avocados, lime juice, and garlic in a food processor fitted with an S blade and process until smooth. Add remaining ingredients and process until smooth or simply stir them in. And for ease and convenience, use ¹/₂ cup or more prepared salsa to replace the tomato, red onion, and peppers.

Thyme-ly Tip

To make lower-fat guacamole, replace part of the avocado with another vegetable. Try using 1 (10-ounce) package frozen peas that have been thawed or briefly cooked in the microwave, and purée them along with the avocado. You can also use 1 (15-ounce) can peas or white beans.

Carrot-Cashew Butter

In this recipe, carrots and cashews pair together beautifully to create a quick and easy spread you can use as an alternative to butter or margarine on your morning toast.

Yield: 1¹/₂ cups
Prep time: 5 to 7 minutes
Cook time: 7 to 10 minutes
Serving size: 1 tablespoon

2 cups carrots, thinly sliced (about 3 or 4 medium)

¹/₂ cup raw cashews

Sea salt (optional)

1. Place a steamer basket inside a large pot, and fill the pot with 1 or 2 inches water (water should not touch the steamer basket). Place carrots in the steamer basket, cover, and bring to a simmer over medium heat. Steam carrots for 7 to 10 minutes or until soft. Remove from heat and let cool slightly.

2. Transfer carrots to a food processor fitted with an S blade. Add cashews, and process for 1 or 2 minutes or until completely smooth. Scrape down the sides of the container with a rubber spatula and process for 15 more seconds. (For a thinner spread, add a few tablespoons water.) Taste, and add salt as desired.

3. Serve with slices of bread, crackers, or toasted bagels or English muffins, or use as a filling for celery stalks. Store the spread in an airtight container in the refrigerator for up to 5 days or in the freezer for up to 3 months.

Variation: Rather than steaming, boil the carrots in water until tender. For extra flavor, steam the carrots with a slice or two of fresh ginger, purée it along with the carrots, and add a little ground cinnamon.

Thyme-ly Tip _____

Feeling a little lazy, but want something yummy to slather on your toast? Instead of carrots, use 1 (14-ounce) can sweet potato purée. Process it in the same manner with 2 or 3 tablespoons nut butter of choice; 1 or 2 tablespoons maple syrup; and a little ground cinnamon, ginger, and nutmeg.

Raw Chocolate-Hazelnut Spread

This decadent, creamy spread made with hazelnuts and cacao nibs is so delicious you'll be tempted to eat it by the spoonful. You vegan raw foodists out there can eat this, too!

½ cup raw cacao nibs

1½ cups raw hazelnuts

2 TB. agave nectar

2 TB. unrefined coconut oil

Yield: 1½ cups
Prep time: 5 to 7 minutes
Serving size: 1 tablespoon

1. Place cacao nibs in a food processor fitted with an S blade and process for 1 minute or until finely ground. Add hazelnuts, and process for 1 or 2 minutes or until finely ground. Add agave nectar and coconut oil, and process for 1 or 2 more minutes or until completely smooth. (If mixture is too thick, also add 1 or 2 tablespoons water during processing.)

2. Use as a spread on apple or banana slices, celery stalks, or slices of bread or toasted bagels or English muffins. Store spread in an airtight container in the refrigerator for up to 1 week.

Variation: If you can't find cacao nibs, substitute 3 or 4 tablespoons cocoa powder or ¼ cup melted vegan chocolate chips.

def•i•ni•tion

Cacao nibs are the broken pieces of the shelled, raw cacao beans used to produce chocolate. They're dark brown with a slightly bittersweet, coffeelike flavor. Cacao nibs are rich in vitamins, minerals, and contain more antioxidants than blueberries, green tea, or red wine.

Chapter 8

Salsas, Sauces, and Gravies

In This Chapter

- ◆ Creamy vegan sauces and gravies
- ◆ Sauces for noodles and stir-fries
- ◆ Mexican-inspired salsas

Sauces often play a supporting role to the star attractions on your plate, and a good one can make even the humblest of meals memorable. Much like the toppers and spreads in Chapter 7, all the vegan salsas, sauces, and gravies in this chapter are designed to enhance and enrich the flavors of other dishes. Most can be used as an accompaniment or covering for raw or cooked vegetables, cooked pasta and grains, casseroles, and other main dishes.

One thing to remember is to not drown your foods in a sauce or gravy. A light covering is all you need. You can always add more, but it's often difficult, if not impossible, to take away. Following this line of reasoning, we suggest using a light drizzle when topping salads, vegetables, and side dishes and encourage being more generous on cooked grains, pasta, stir-fries, and casseroles.

Fresh Corn and Avocado Salsa

Make this all-raw salsa during the summer when corn, tomatoes, and peppers are at their ripest, and enjoy it with your favorite tortilla chips or Mexican or Southwestern dishes.

Yield: 2¹/₂ to 3 cups
Prep time: 5 to 7 minutes
Serving size: ¹/₄ cup

1 large tomato, cut into ¼-in. dice

1 ear sweet corn, shucked and cut off cob

1 Hass avocado, peeled and cut into ½-in. dice

½ cup red or orange bell pepper, ribs and seeds removed, and diced

¼ cup red onion, diced

⅓ cup green onions, thinly sliced

¼ cup chopped fresh cilantro

1 jalapeño pepper, ribs and seeds removed, and finely diced

1 TB. garlic, minced

Juice of 1 lime

2 TB. olive oil

Sea salt

Freshly ground black pepper

1. Place tomato, corn, avocado, red bell pepper, red onion, green onions, cilantro, jalapeño pepper, and garlic in a small glass bowl and toss gently to combine.

2. Add lime juice and olive oil, season with salt and black pepper, and toss gently again.

3. Serve as a dip for raw veggies or tortilla chips; as a topping for chili, tacos, tostadas, or other dishes; or as a filling for wraps or burritos along with other ingredients. Store salsa in an airtight container in the refrigerator for up to 3 days.

Variation: During the fall and winter months, you can substitute frozen corn and 1 (14-ounce) can diced tomatoes.

Soy What?
Most salsas are made from tomatoes, onion, and mild bell peppers, with added herbs and seasonings. Some even include fruits, beans, and chiles. They range in flavor from mild, medium, hot, to eye-watering hot and spicy.

Roasted Peach Salsa

When you're in the mood for a slightly sweet salsa with some kick, or you're having a party or just entertaining friends, whip up a batch of this oven-roasted salsa.

2 ripe peaches, cut in half

3 medium plum tomatoes, cut in half

1 green bell pepper, seeds and stems removed, and cut in half

1 red or orange bell pepper, seeds and stems removed, and cut in half

1 small red onion, cut in half

2 jalapeño or serrano peppers, ribs and seeds removed, and finely diced

4 garlic cloves

3 TB. olive oil

¼ cup chopped fresh cilantro

2 TB. agave nectar

2 TB. apple cider vinegar

½ tsp. chipotle chili powder or 1 tsp. chipotle in adobo sauce

Sea salt

Freshly ground black pepper

Yield: 3 to 3½ cups
Prep time: 5 to 7 minutes
Cook time: 5 to 7 minutes
Serving size: ¼ cup

1. Preheat the oven broiler. Lightly oil a large cooking sheet.

2. Place peaches, tomatoes, green bell pepper, red bell pepper, red onion, jalapeño peppers, and garlic cloves on the prepared cookie sheet. Drizzle olive oil over the top, toss well to thoroughly coat, and spread out into a single layer.

3. Place the cookie sheet under the broiler, and broil for 2 or 3 minutes or until mixture begins to blacken on top. Remove from the oven, stir, spread out into a single layer again, and broil for 2 or 3 more minutes or until tender. Remove from the oven and let cool slightly.

4. Transfer mixture into a food processor fitted with an S blade and coarsely chop. Add cilantro, agave nectar, vinegar, and chipotle chili powder, and pulse several times to combine. Taste and season with salt and black pepper.

5. Serve with tortilla chips or use as a topping for black beans, burgers, on with your favorite Mexican or Southwestern dishes. Store salsa in an airtight container in the refrigerator for up to 5 days.

Variation: Vary the flavor of your salsa by replacing the peaches with 2 mangoes or 4 or 5 fresh or canned pineapple rings.

Thyme-ly Tip

You can also prepare this salsa on the stovetop. Dice the peaches and vegetables, and place them, along with the remaining ingredients, in a medium saucepan. Cook over medium heat for 5 to 7 minutes or until tender. Let cool before serving.

Salsa Verde

Not all salsas are made with tomatoes; this spicy one features tomatillos and other green ingredients and is especially delicious paired with black beans or served with tortilla chips.

Yield: 2 cups
Prep time: 5 to 7 minutes
Cook time: 10 to 12 minutes
Serving size: 1/4 cup

12 oz. *tomatillos,* husked and cut into quarters

1/2 cup onion, diced

Water

3 large garlic cloves

1 cup chopped fresh cilantro

1/3 cup green onions, thinly sliced

2 jalapeño or serrano peppers, ribs and seeds removed, and finely diced

Juice of 1 lime

1/2 tsp. dried oregano

Sea salt

Freshly ground black pepper

def•i•ni•tion

Tomatillos are the small, round fruits of the tomatillo plant, a member of the nightshade family. The growing tomatillos are protected by a paperlike husk that often splits as they grow and is typically left intact when harvested and sold. Tomatillos are often mistaken for green, unripened tomatoes.

1. Place tomatillos, onion, and enough water to cover them in a medium saucepan. Bring to a boil, cover, reduce heat to low, and simmer for 10 to 12 minutes or until tomatillos are tender. Remove from the heat. Drain but reserve cooking liquid.

2. Transfer tomatillo mixture to a food processor fitted with an S blade. Add garlic cloves, and coarsely chop for 1 minute. Add cilantro, green onions, jalapeño peppers, lime juice, and oregano, and pulse several times or until as smooth or chunky as desired. (If you prefer a thinner version, add some reserved cooking liquid.)

3. Taste and season with salt and black pepper. Serve with tortilla chips or use as a sauce for black beans, tacos, burritos, or other Mexican dishes. Store salsa in an airtight container in the refrigerator for up to 5 days.

Variation: For extra flavor, roast the tomatillos, onion, and 2 whole jalapeño peppers on an oiled large cookie sheet at 425°F for 8 to 10 minutes or until soft and lightly browned around the edges.

Zesty Barbecue Sauce

This homemade barbecue sauce has zesty, robust flavor, thanks to a generous dose of apple cider vinegar, spices, garlic, and ginger.

¾ cup fire-roasted crushed tomatoes

⅓ cup apple cider vinegar

3 TB. tamari

2 TB. maple syrup

1 TB. blackstrap molasses

1 TB. olive oil

1 TB. spicy brown mustard or Dijon mustard

1 TB. garlic, minced

1 TB. fresh ginger, minced

1 tsp. chili powder

¼ tsp. freshly ground black pepper

¼ tsp. cayenne

Yield: 1½ cups
Prep time: 2 or 3 minutes
Serving size: ¼ cup

1. Place fire-roasted tomatoes, vinegar, tamari, maple syrup, molasses, olive oil, spicy brown mustard, garlic, ginger, chili powder, black pepper, and cayenne in a food processor fitted with an S blade (or a blender), and process for 1 or 2 minutes or until completely smooth.

2. Use as a condiment or sauce for sandwiches, baked beans, tofu, tempeh, seitan, or other dishes, as desired. Store sauce in an airtight container in the refrigerator for up to 1 week.

Variation: For a milder flavor, replace the fire-roasted tomatoes with 1 (6-ounce) can tomato paste and ⅓ cup water, omit the blackstrap molasses, and add 2 tablespoons turbinado sugar or additional maple syrup.

 Sour Grapes

On many varieties of bottled barbecue sauce, manufacturers list "natural flavors" or "natural flavorings" as an ingredient, and these could contain hidden animal-based ingredients. It's best to buy brands made by companies that only sell vegetarian and vegan products.

Thai Peanut Sauce

Spicy peanut sauce is a commonly used ingredient in Thai cuisine, and this one can be used as a salad dressing, a sauce for stir-fries and other dishes, and a dipping sauce for spring rolls or cubes or strips of baked tofu or tempeh.

Yield: 1¹/₂ cups
Prep time: 2 or 3 minutes
Serving size: 2 table- spoons

½ cup creamy peanut butter

½ cup water

¼ cup tamari

¼ cup lime juice

¼ cup peanut oil

2 TB. toasted sesame oil

1 TB. brown rice syrup or maple syrup

2 tsp. garlic, minced

2 tsp. fresh ginger, minced

¼ tsp. cayenne or crushed red pepper flakes

1. Place peanut butter, water, tamari, lime juice, peanut oil, toasted sesame oil, brown rice syrup, garlic, ginger, and cayenne in a food processor fitted with an S blade (or a blender), and process for 1 or 2 minutes or until completely smooth.

2. Use as a dressing or sauce for salads, pasta, or grains and with vegetable sides and main dishes. Store sauce in an airtight container in the refrigerator for up to 1 week.

Variation: For a lower-fat version, omit the peanut oil and add an additional ¹/₄ cup water and 1 tablespoon toasted sesame oil.

Soy What?
If you have peanut allergies, substitute cashew butter, soy nut butter, or tahini, and replace the peanut oil with safflower oil, or follow the variation suggestion for preparing a lower-fat version of the sauce. In general, substituting other nut butters or tahini works in your other favorite sweet and savory recipes as well.

Teriyaki Stir-Frying and Dipping Sauce

Teriyaki sauce is a Japanese soy-based sauce with a slightly sweet and sour flavor that's used to season dishes, as well as a marinade or basting sauce for stir-fried, baked, and grilled dishes.

⅓ cup tamari

¼ cup *brown rice vinegar* or *mirin*

¼ cup turbinado sugar

2 TB. toasted sesame oil

1 TB. garlic, minced

1 TB. fresh ginger, minced

½ tsp. dry mustard

¼ tsp. crushed red pepper flakes (optional)

Yield: 1 cup
Prep time: 2 or 3 minutes
Serving size: 2 table-spoons

1. In a small bowl, place tamari, vinegar, sugar, toasted sesame oil, garlic, ginger, dry mustard, and red pepper flakes (if using), and whisk well to combine.

2. Use as a dipping sauce for tofu, tempeh, vegetables, or spring rolls; add to stir-fries or toss with pasta or grains; or use as a marinade for baked or grilled pieces of tofu, tempeh, seitan, or vegetables. Store sauce in an airtight container in the refrigerator for up to 1 week.

Variation: For a thicker sauce, stir together 2 tablespoons cold water and 1 tablespoon cornstarch, add it to prepared sauce, and cook mixture in a small saucepan over medium heat, stirring occasionally, for 1 or 2 minutes or until thickened. And for extra flavor, add ¼ cup thinly sliced green onions or 2 tablespoons sesame seeds.

def•i•ni•tion

Brown rice vinegar is mild, mellow-flavored vinegar made from fermented rice (also sold in a seasoned variety). **Mirin** is a mildly sweet cooking wine also made from rice. It's similar to sake.

Béchamel Sauce

This vegan version of béchamel sauce, also known as white sauce, is an easy and versatile sauce all great cooks should have as part of their repertoire.

Yield: 2 cups
Prep time: 1 or 2 minutes
Cook time: 5 to 7 minutes
Serving size: ¹/₄ cup

¼ cup olive oil or safflower oil

¼ cup whole-wheat pastry flour or other flour of choice

2 cups soymilk or other non-dairy milk of choice

Freshly grated nutmeg

Sea salt

White pepper

1. Place olive oil and flour in a medium saucepan over medium heat, and cook, whisking occasionally, for 2 minutes or until lightly browned and fragrant. Slowly whisk in soy milk, and cook, whisking constantly, for 2 or 3 more minutes or until very thick.

2. Remove from heat and season with nutmeg, salt, and white pepper.

3. Sauce can be used as a base for other sauces such as vegan cheese sauce, as a topping for vegetables or other side dishes, as well as in casseroles and stews. Store sauce in an airtight container in the refrigerator for up to 1 week.

Variation: For a lighter sauce, replace 1 cup soy milk with vegetable broth.

Thyme-ly Tip _____

This béchamel sauce works equally well with other ingredients. Try it with roasted garlic, sliced mushrooms, vegetable purées, tomato sauce, white wine, shredded vegan cheese, or nutritional yeast flakes. Béchamel sauce also freezes rather well, so feel free to make up larger batches and freeze them.

Roasted Garlic and Shallot Gravy

Roasting garlic and shallots (a mild-flavored cousin of onions) brings out their natural sweetness and heightens their flavor. You're sure to find many delicious uses for this golden gravy.

3 oz. shallots (3 or 4 medium or 2 large), cut in ½

6 large garlic cloves

1½ tsp. olive oil

¼ cup whole-wheat pastry flour or other flour of choice

2 cups vegetable broth or water

2 TB. nutritional yeast flakes

½ tsp. dried thyme

½ tsp. sea salt

¼ tsp. freshly ground black pepper or white pepper

Yield: 2½ cups		
Prep time: 5 to 7 minutes		
Cook time: 25 to 30 minutes		
Serving size: ¼ cup		

1. Preheat the oven to 375°F.

2. Place shallots and garlic cloves in a piece of aluminum foil and drizzle olive oil over top. Gather up the corners of the foil, crimp to enclose shallots and garlic cloves, and place in a 9-inch round pie pan. Bake for 15 to 20 minutes or until shallots are soft when gently squeezed. Remove from the oven, and let cool for 5 minutes.

3. Meanwhile, place flour in a small saucepan and cook, stirring often, for 1 or 2 minutes to lightly brown flour. Remove from heat.

4. Transfer shallot mixture and flour into a food processor fitted with an S blade (or a blender), and process for 1 minute. Add vegetable broth, nutritional yeast flakes, thyme, salt, and black pepper, and process for 1 or 2 minutes or until completely smooth.

5. Transfer mixture back to the small saucepan, and cook over medium heat, whisking constantly, for 2 or 3 minutes or until thickened. Remove from heat.

6. Serve gravy over mashed potatoes, steamed or roasted vegetables, grains, and other dishes, or use as a sauce in casseroles. Store gravy in an airtight container in the refrigerator for up to 1 week or in the freezer for up to 6 months.

Thyme-ly Tip

Roasted garlic is a flavorful and versatile ingredient, and roasting a whole head of garlic is simple. Slice a little off the top of the head to expose some of the garlic cloves. Place garlic in foil and bake at 375°F for 30 minutes or until soft. Squeeze out the garlic cloves and enjoy it on slices of bread, or mash it and use it in recipes.

Variation: You could finely chop the roasted shallot and garlic and whisk them together with the flour and other ingredients and then cook mixture in a saucepan until thickened. Or if you prefer creamy, country-style gravy, stir in some soy milk or other nondairy milk, or the vanilla-free variation of Dairy-Free Creamer (recipe in Chapter 9).

Crimini Mushroom Gravy

No need to reach for beef broth to achieve a deep, rich-tasting gravy. Mushrooms, onions, and a little tamari give this easy vegan gravy a dark brown color, and if you prefer creamy country-style gravy, add some soy milk or other nondairy milk.

Yield: 2½ cups
Prep time: 5 minutes
Cook time: 8 to 10 minutes
Serving size: ¼ cup

2½ cups crimini mushrooms, cut in half and thinly sliced

½ cup onion, finely diced

1 TB. olive oil

½ tsp. dried thyme

⅛ tsp. freshly ground black pepper

¼ whole-wheat pastry flour or other flour of choice

2 cups vegetable broth or water

2 TB. tamari or Bragg Liquid Aminos

1. In a medium saucepan, combine mushrooms, onion, olive oil, thyme, and black pepper, and sauté over medium heat, stirring often, for 3 minutes or until soft.

2. Stir in flour and cook, stirring often, for 1 or 2 minutes to lightly brown flour.

3. Whisk in vegetable broth and tamari, and cook, whisking constantly, for 2 or 3 minutes or until thickened. Remove from the heat. Taste and add additional tamari or black pepper as desired.

4. Serve gravy over mashed potatoes, steamed or roasted vegetables, grains, and other dishes, or use as a sauce in casseroles. Store gravy in an airtight container in the refrigerator for up to 1 week or in the freezer for up to 6 months.

Variation: For a low-fat version, omit the olive oil and sauté the mushroom mixture in 2 to 4 tablespoons water. For extra flavor, add a little red wine and garlic to the mushroom mixture as it cooks.

> **Soy What?**
>
> Crimini mushrooms are actually baby portobello mushrooms, which is why crimini mushrooms are sometimes sold in packages as "baby bellas." When crimini mushrooms have grown to be 3 inches wide or larger, they're then referred to as portobellos.

Cheese and Dairy Alternatives

In This Chapter

◆ Creating creamy vegan cheeses

◆ Making your own dairy-free milk

◆ DIY vegan sour cream

For many people, the hardest part about adopting a vegan diet is giving up dairy products. If we had a dollar for every time we heard "I can't go vegan because I'd miss eating cheese," we would both be independently wealthy by now. It used to be tough for vegans to find good cheese and dairy alternatives, but variety and availability of products have greatly improved over the last 10 years.

Despite the availability of store-bought vegan products, learning how to create your own homemade cheese and dairy alternatives will save you money and ensure that the ingredients are wholesome, fresh, and healthy. This chapter starts you off in the right direction by providing you with some easy and versatile recipes for those times when you're craving something creamy or cheesy.

A Guide to Vegan Dairy Products

If you're looking for a block of cheese that will melt smoothly, stick with the commercially made vegan brands because homemade vegan cheeses generally don't have the stretching or melting capability their dairy counterparts do. They still get soft and gooey and will brown nicely if put under a broiler. A vegan cheese sauce can be put on a casserole or pizza as it's already premelted.

For vegan cheeses you can spread, slice, or crumble, try the spicy Almond Pepper Jack Cheese, Wine-n-Cheese Spread, or Tofu Feta. For topping your spuds and soups, try Herbed Tofu Sour Cream, as well as the Dairy-Free Creamer and Raw ABC Nut Milk, which can be used in beverages, on your morning cereal, or in recipes.

> **Soy What?**
>
> Homemade nondairy cheeses like those featured in this chapter are relatively low in fat compared to dairy cheeses and high in calcium, protein, and rich flavor.

If you're trying to include more raw foods in your diet, you're sure to enjoy the nut-based Raw Cheddar Cheese Spread on slices of apple or celery or your favorite crackers (dehydrated ones, for strict raw foodists), or the mock Raw Parmesan sprinkled on salads and savory dishes.

Raw Parmesan Cheese

You can easily and quickly whip up this cheesy, slightly nutty-tasting Parmesan-style seasoning with the help of a food processor.

¾ **cup whole raw almonds**   ¾ **cup *nutritional yeast* flakes**

3 TB. raw sesame seeds   **Pinch sea salt**

Yield: 1¹/₂ cups
Prep time: 2 minutes
Serving size: 1 tablespoon

1. Place almonds and sesame seeds in a food processor fitted with an S blade and process for 1 or 2 minutes or until finely ground. Scrape down the sides of the container with a rubber spatula.

2. Add nutritional yeast flakes and salt, and process for 1 more minute.

3. Use as a condiment and to add flavor to salad dressings, sauces, vegetables, pasta, and other dishes. Store Parmesan cheese in an airtight container in the refrigerator for up to 2 months.

Variation: You can substitute other varieties of nuts, such as walnuts, cashews, or pine nuts. For extra flavor, add 1 garlic clove and process along with the nuts.

def•i•ni•tion

Nutritional yeast is an inactive yeast, which differs greatly from the types of yeast used for brewing and baking, and has a surprisingly nutty, cheeselike flavor. It contains a wide assortment of minerals and B vitamins and can be a reliable dietary source of B_{12} for vegans. Look for it prepackaged and in bulk in grocery and natural foods stores.

Raw Cheddar Cheese Spread

This mock cheddar cheese spread made with raw cashews and sun-dried tomatoes requires no cooking.

Yield: 1½ cups
Prep time: 5 minutes plus 2 hours for soaking nuts
Serving size: 2 tablespoons

1½ cups plus ⅓ cup water

1½ cups raw cashews

1 TB. sun-dried tomato pieces

1 TB. raw tahini

2 tsp. freshly squeezed lemon juice

½ tsp. *Bragg Liquid Aminos*

½ tsp. garlic powder

¼ tsp. paprika

1. Combine 1½ cups water, cashews, and sun-dried tomatoes in a small bowl and set aside to soak for 2 hours. Drain off soaking water and discard.

2. Transfer cashew mixture to a food processor fitted with an S blade. Add remaining ⅓ cup water, tahini, lemon juice, Bragg Liquid Aminos, garlic powder, and paprika, and process for 2 minutes. Scrape down the sides of the container with a rubber spatula and process for 1 or 2 more minutes or until completely smooth. Transfer mixture to a small bowl.

3. Serve as a spread with raw veggies, fruit, crackers, slices of bread, or for sandwiches. Store spread in an airtight container in the refrigerator for up to 1 week.

Variation: Turn this spread into a mock cheddar cheese sauce by blending it with an additional ¼ cup water or more, and use it as a sauce or dip for raw or cooked vegetables. For extra flavor, add 1 tablespoon nutritional yeast flakes.

def•i•ni•tion

Bragg Liquid Aminos are a liquid protein concentrate that contains large amounts of dietary essential and nonessential amino acids. It's made from soybeans and water, but unlike its cousins tamari and shoyu, it hasn't been heated or fermented. Find Bragg Liquid Aminos alongside other soy sauces in most grocery and natural food stores.

Wine-n-Cheese Spread

Wine and cheese are commonly paired together as an offering at parties and special events, which was the inspiration for this wine-flavored vegan cheese spread.

8 oz. firm or extra-firm tofu

1 garlic clove

¼ cup nutritional yeast flakes

2 TB. raw tahini

1 TB. garbanzo bean or other light miso

1 tsp. Dijon mustard

½ tsp. paprika

½ tsp. sea salt

2 TB. or more red wine of choice

Yield: 1½ cups
Prep time: 5 minutes
Serving size: 2 tablespoons

1. Crumble tofu in a food processor using your fingers. Add garlic, and process for 1 minute. Add nutritional yeast flakes, tahini, miso, Dijon mustard, paprika, and salt, and process for 1 or 2 minutes or until completely smooth. Add red wine and process 15 more seconds.

2. Taste and add additional salt or red wine as desired. Transfer mixture to a small bowl.

3. Serve with crackers, slices of bread, or fruit, or use as a spread for sandwiches. Store spread in an airtight container in the refrigerator for up to 1 week.

Variation: For a nonalcoholic version, replace the wine with 2 tablespoons lemon juice. Or sprinkle finely chopped pecans or walnuts over the top of the spread.

 Sour Grapes

Some winemakers and other alcoholic beverage producers use animal-based clarifying agents like gelatin, egg whites, casein, and isinglass (a collagen derived from the swim-bladders of fish) to remove impurities. For more info, and to find listings of vegan-suitable alcoholic beverages and wines, visit www.vegans.frommars.org/wine/faq.php, www.tastebetter.com/features/booze, and www.vegparadise.com/news62.html.

Almond Pepper Jack Cheese

Enjoy this homemade, nondairy cheese made with almonds and flavored with red pepper, jalapeño pepper, and spices as a spread or sliced.

Yield: 1 (2-cup) block
Prep time: 5 to 7 minutes
Cook time: 3 to 5 minutes
Serving size: 2 table-spoons or 1 slice

⅔ cup sliced raw almonds

1½ cups water

3 TB. cornstarch

3 TB. freshly squeezed lemon juice

2 TB. olive oil

2 TB. nutritional yeast flakes

1 tsp. garlic powder

1 tsp. onion powder

¾ tsp. sea salt

¼ tsp. chili powder or paprika

⅓ cup red bell pepper, ribs and seeds removed, and finely diced

1 jalapeño pepper, ribs and seeds removed, and finely diced

1 tsp. Italian seasoning blend

½ tsp. crushed red pepper flakes

Soy What?

Almonds are a delicious source of protein and dietary fiber, as well as being rich in many vitamins and minerals. They're commonly ground for use in making flour (known as almond meal), nut butter, almond milk, and almond cheese. Almonds are also pressed to produce aromatic almond oil.

1. Place almonds in a blender fitted with an S blade, and process for 1 or 2 minutes until finely ground. Scrape down the sides of the container with a rubber spatula. Add water, cornstarch, lemon juice, olive oil, nutritional yeast flakes, garlic powder, onion powder, salt, and chili powder, and process for 1 or 2 minutes or until completely smooth.

2. Transfer mixture to a small saucepan and cook over medium heat, whisking often, for 3 to 5 minutes or until very thick. Remove from heat. Stir in red bell pepper, jalapeño pepper, Italian seasoning, and red pepper flakes, and let cool for 10 minutes.

3. Pour mixture into a 2-cup (16-ounce) plastic container, cover, and chill in the refrigerator for several hours or until firm. Unmold cheese for use. Serve as a spread with crackers or slices of bread or fruit, or cut into slices for sandwiches, or use in place of commercially made cheese in recipes. (This is a semi-soft style cheese, not a brick-style cheese, so it cannot be shredded.) Store cheese in an airtight container in the refrigerator for up to 1 week.

Variation: To make a firmer cheese, replace the cornstarch with 3 tablespoons agar-agar flakes.

Vegan Cheese Sauce Mix

Keeping this dry cheese sauce mix on hand makes it easy to whip up a batch of vegan cheese whenever you need to, in record time. It can be stored for up to 2 months in the refrigerator.

¾ **cup raw cashews or whole raw almonds**

½ **cup rolled oats**

¼ **cup raw sunflower seeds**

1 **cup nutritional yeast flakes**

2 **TB. arrowroot**

2 **tsp. dry mustard**

2 **tsp. garlic powder**

2 **tsp. onion powder**

2 **tsp. sea salt**

1 **tsp. paprika or chili powder**

Yield: 2 cups	
Prep time: 5 minutes	
Serving size: ¼ cup prepared sauce	

1. Place cashews, oats, and sunflower seeds in a food processor fitted with an S blade, and process for 2 or 3 minutes until finely ground. Scrape down the sides of the container with a rubber spatula. Add nutritional yeast flakes, arrowroot, dry mustard, garlic powder, onion powder, salt, and paprika, and process for 1 minute longer.

2. Transfer mixture to an airtight container and store in the refrigerator for up to 2 months.

3. To prepare cheese sauce from mix, whisk together ½ cup vegan cheese sauce mix and 1 cup water or soy milk in a small saucepan, and cook over medium heat, whisking often, for 2 or 3 minutes or until thickened. This makes 1 cup vegan cheese sauce. Serve as a sauce with raw or steamed vegetables, baked potatoes, pasta, or other dishes, or use dry mix to season and flavor sauces, soups, vegetables, or popcorn.

Variation: For a nut-free version, use an additional 1 cup rolled oats to replace the cashews and sunflower seeds. For a quick and easy preparation, replace cashews, rolled oats, and sunflower seeds with 1½ cups whole-wheat pastry flour or other flour of choice, and simply stir together with the remaining ingredients in a medium bowl.

Thyme-ly Tip

To make vegan fondue, cook together ⅔ cup Vegan Cheese Sauce Mix, 1¼ cups soy milk, 1½ teaspoons light miso or tamari, and a pinch of freshly grated nutmeg or black pepper. If you're in a festive mood, add a little red or white wine. Or use ⅔ cup Vegan Cheese Sauce Mix, a bottle of your favorite beer, and a little chili powder or hot pepper sauce.

Tofu Feta

Marinating tiny cubes of tofu in a simple vinaigrette infuses them with a slight tanginess and transforms them into a vegan replacement for Greek feta cheese.

Yield: 1¹/₄ to 1¹/₂ cups

Prep time: 2 or 3 minutes plus 30 minutes or more for marinating

Serving size: 2 tablespoons

---

8 oz. firm or extra-firm tofu

3 TB. olive oil

3 TB. water

1 TB. freshly squeezed lemon juice

1 TB. white wine vinegar or red wine vinegar

1 tsp. garlic, minced

¹/₂ tsp. sea salt

1. Squeeze tofu over the sink to remove any excess moisture. Cut tofu into ¹/₄-inch cubes.

2. Place olive oil, water, lemon juice, vinegar, garlic, and salt in a 2-cup airtight container, and whisk or cover and shake well to combine.

3. Add tofu cubes, and stir or cover and shake to thoroughly coat tofu. Let tofu marinate in mixture for 30 minutes or more before using on salads, sandwiches, or in recipes as desired. Excess marinade can be also used in recipes as desired. Store feta in an airtight container in the refrigerator for up to 1 week.

Variation: Instead of cutting tofu into cubes, crumble it with your fingers into large pieces and marinate in the same manner. For a low-fat version, replace olive oil with 1 tablespoon light miso and increase water to ¹/₄ cup.

Thyme-ly Tip

Much like the Greeks, Italians like to enjoy tiny balls or cubes of marinated mozzarella cheese, known as *bocconcini*, which translates as "little mouthfuls." To make a vegan version, cut vegan mozzarella cheese into ¹/₄-inch cubes and toss them with a little olive oil, dried basil and oregano, crushed red pepper flakes, and salt and black pepper as desired. Enjoy them as an appetizer or use in recipes.

Raw ABC Nut Milk

If you own a blender, you can easily make your own delicious raw nut milk like this one made with almonds, brazil nuts, and cashews. Enjoy it as a beverage, on cereal, or in recipes.

4 cups water

⅓ cup whole raw almonds

⅓ cup raw brazil nuts

⅓ cup raw cashews

2 dried dates, pitted (optional)

Yield: *3 cups*
Prep time: 5 minutes plus 2 hours or more if soaking nuts
Serving size: 1 cup

1. Combine 1 cup water, almonds, brazil nuts, and cashews in a small bowl and set aside to soak for several hours or overnight. (This helps make the nuts more easily digested, but you can skip this step if desired.) Drain off soaking water and discard.

2. Place 1½ cups water and nuts into a blender and blend for 1 minute. Add remaining 1½ cups water and dates (if using) and blend for 2 or 3 minutes or until completely smooth and creamy. Serve as is, or strain through a fine sieve, if desired. Store nut milk in an airtight container in the refrigerator for 3 or 4 days.

Variation: For a sweeter nut milk version, add a little agave nectar, a small amount of vanilla extract, or spices like ground cinnamon or cardamom. You can make flavored nut milks by also adding a small amount of sliced fruit or berries, or a little raw carob powder or cocoa powder.

Thyme-ly Tip

Nut milks are sold in most natural foods stores, but they can be expensive and are usually pasteurized. Make your own homemade raw nut milk for just a fraction of the cost.

Dairy-Free Creamer

You can use this slightly sweet, dairy-free creamer to flavor coffee, tea, or other beverages; to lighten up soups or stews; or to pour over berries or desserts.

Yield: 1 cup
Prep time: 2 or 3 minutes
Serving size: 2 table-spoons

½ **cup (4 oz.) firm or extra-firm silken tofu**

½ **cup soy milk or other nondairy milk of choice**

1 TB. *agave nectar*

½ **tsp. pure vanilla extract**

1. Crumble tofu in a blender using your fingers. Add soy milk, agave nectar, and vanilla extract, and process for 2 minutes or until completely smooth. Scrape down the sides of the container with a rubber spatula and process for an additional 15 seconds.

2. Use to flavor beverages and in recipes. Store creamer in an airtight container in the refrigerator for up to 1 week.

Variation: If you prefer, omit the vanilla to use this creamer in savory recipes. For a soy-free version, omit the tofu and soy milk and replace them with ¹/₄ cup raw cashews or almonds and ³/₄ cup rice milk or nut milk.

def•i•ni•tion

Agave nectar, also known as *agave syrup*, is a liquid sweetener derived from the Mexican agave cactus. It has a light, delicate flavor sweeter than honey, and is available in both light and amber-colored varieties. Use it as a replacement for honey, maple syrup, or other liquid sweeteners, either measure for measure or up to ⅓ less.

Herbed Tofu Sour Cream

Blending together silken tofu, soy milk, and lemon juice, plus a few seasonings and fresh parsley for extra flavor, produces a light and creamy mock sour cream that's delicious on baked potatoes, in chili, and in soups.

1 (12-oz.) pkg. firm or extra-firm silken tofu

2 TB. soy milk or other nondairy milk of choice

2 TB. freshly squeezed lemon juice

1 TB. olive oil or safflower oil

1 TB. nutritional yeast flakes

1 TB. agave nectar or unbleached cane sugar

½ tsp. sea salt

2 TB. chopped fresh parsley or dill

Yield: 2¹/₂ cups
Prep time: 2 or 3 minutes plus 30 minutes or more for chilling
Serving size: 2 table-spoons

1. Crumble tofu in a food processor fitted with an S blade using your fingers. Add soy milk, lemon juice, olive oil, nutritional yeast flakes, agave nectar, and salt, and process for 1 or 2 minutes or until completely smooth. Add parsley and process for 30 more seconds.

2. Transfer mixture to an airtight container and chill in the refrigerator for 30 minutes or more to allow flavors to blend. Serve as a dip or topping for baked potatoes, vegetables, salads, soups, stews, and other savory dishes, just as you would use sour cream. Store sour cream in an airtight container in the refrigerator for up to 1 week.

Variation: Feel free to substitute other fresh herbs, such as basil, cilantro, or mint. You can also omit the fresh herbs altogether and add other ingredients, such as garlic cloves, prepared horseradish, ground chipotle powder, or wasabi powder, or combine these ingredients with fresh herbs.

Thyme-ly Tip

You can adapt this recipe or its variations by thinning it with soy milk or water. Then, use it as a dressing for potato salads, leafy green salads, or tossed with grains or pasta to create creamy side dishes. It also makes a delicious sauce for steamed or roasted vegetables.

Part 4

Let's Do Lunch

It doesn't take much time to make your own delicious vegan lunch. Whether you're staying at home or brown-bagging it, Part 4 provides you with a vast array of options, including soups, chilis, and stews, salads of all sorts, and hot and cold sandwiches.

When you want something light and healthy for lunch, enjoy a pasta salad or one made with mixed greens and fresh veggies with a homemade vinaigrette or creamy dairy-free dressing, along with some crackers, a roll, or a slice of whole-grain bread. Better yet, mix and match recipes from several chapters to create the classic combo of a salad with a bowl of soup or sandwich. You also get ideas for replicating items from your favorite local restaurants using all vegan ingredients. All these recipe selections are easily portable.

Chapter 10

Soup's On

In This Chapter

◆ Chilled fruit- and vegetable-based soups for hot summer days

◆ Multicultural soup selections

◆ Vegan meat, cheese, and dairy soup ingredients

If you're just beginning to learn how to cook as a vegan, soups are a good place to start. If you're looking for an easy, quick, yet sustaining meal, try soup. Or if you don't like cooking on a daily basis, soup-making is for you. This chapter contains both hot and cold selections, so no matter what the season, you won't have to go without a bowlful of soup.

For those with hectic schedules, and for all the lazy and unmotivated cooks out there, keep in mind that making a pot of soup has an added bonus—leftovers! You can make it one day and enjoy it again the next, which is why all the soup recipes in this chapter were written to make enough for several servings or multiple meals. You can even make larger batches of any of the hot soup selections, freeze them in the desired portions for later use, and just thaw and reheat when you find yourself in the mood for soup.

And it's easy and fun to dress up your soups by garnishing individual servings with chopped herbs, shredded vegan cheese, a swirl of olive oil, or a dollop of tofu sour cream. Several of these soup recipes easily and deliciously illustrate how well vegan alternatives work as replacements for meat, cheese, and dairy. So what are you waiting for? Soup's on—vegan style!

Cold Cucumber, Soy Yogurt, and Dill Soup

This cool and creamy cucumber and soy yogurt soup is excellent served with curries and spicy dishes with some pita bread or, for a lighter meal, alongside a tossed salad with crisp crackers.

3 cups cucumber, seeded and diced

3 cups plain soy yogurt

2 cups soy milk or other nondairy milk of choice

¼ cup green onions, thinly sliced

2 TB. chopped fresh dill

1 TB. chopped fresh mint

1 tsp. garlic, minced

½ tsp. sea salt

¼ tsp. freshly ground black pepper or lemon pepper

Yield: 6 servings
Prep time: 5 to 7 minutes
Serving size: 1 cup

1. In a large glass bowl, place cucumber, soy yogurt, soy milk, green onions, dill, mint, garlic, salt, and black pepper, and stir well to combine.

2. Cover and chill in the refrigerator for 1 hour or more to allow flavors to blend.

3. Serve cold. For more visual appeal, sprinkle a little paprika on top of individual servings.

Variation: For extra flavor, add ½ cup chopped radishes and 1 teaspoon each lemon juice and zest.

Soy What?

You're sure to find several varieties of cucumbers at your local grocery store or farmers' market. Slicers are the most common and have firm, smooth skins with rather large seeds. Cucumbers grown for pickling are very small and often have bumpy skins. English cucumbers are slender with a thin skin and often contain very few small seeds.

Garden-Patch Gazpacho

This cool, colorful, and chunky gazpacho soup is perfect when your garden or farmers' market is overflowing with fresh veggies.

Yield: 6 servings
Prep time: 15 to 20 minutes
Serving size: 1 cup

4 cups tomatoes, diced

2 cups cucumber, cut into quarters lengthwise and diced

1 cup green bell pepper, ribs and seeds removed, and diced

1 cup red or orange bell pepper, ribs and seeds removed, and diced

3 TB. olive oil

2 TB. lemon juice or balsamic vinegar

1 jalapeño pepper, ribs and seeds removed, and finely diced

1 TB. garlic, minced

¼ tsp. ground cumin

¼ tsp. cayenne

¼ tsp. sea salt

¼ tsp. freshly ground black pepper

1 cup yellow cherry tomatoes, quartered

1 ear sweet corn, shucked and cut off cob

½ cup celery, diced

½ cup radishes, cut into quarters lengthwise and thinly sliced

⅓ cup green onions, thinly sliced

¼ cup chopped fresh cilantro

¼ cup chopped fresh parsley

1. In a large glass bowl, place tomatoes, cucumber, green bell pepper, red bell pepper, olive oil, lemon juice, jalapeño pepper, garlic, cumin, cayenne, salt, and black pepper, and stir well to combine. Transfer 2 cups mixture into a food processor fitted with an S blade, or a blender, and process for 1 or 2 minutes or until completely smooth.

2. Stir blended mixture back into the bowl. Add cherry tomatoes, corn, celery, radishes, green onions, cilantro, and parsley, and stir well to combine. Taste and adjust seasonings as desired.

3. Serve immediately, or cover and chill in the refrigerator for 1 hour or more.

Variation: Feel free to omit or substitute other varieties of tomatoes or vegetables as desired. You can also add 1 cup canned black beans or shelled edamame.

Soy What?

Gazpacho soup originated in the Andalusia region of Spain, and was originally a cold bread soup made with pieces of stale bread, olive oil, garlic, vinegar, and salt all mashed together in a mortar and pestle. Tomatoes and other vegetables were later added to the recipe.

Award-Winning French Onion Soup

This French onion soup won first prize in the Berea, Ohio, Onion Festival in 1999, edging out many traditionally prepared onion-based dishes, including a beef-based French onion soup and beer-battered onion rings!

2 lb. onions (3 or 4 medium), cut in half and thinly sliced	**¼ tsp. freshly ground black pepper**
2 tsp. olive oil	**4 cups water**
2 tsp. nonhydrogenated vegan margarine	**⅔ cup tamari**
1 TB. garlic, minced	**⅓ cup sherry (optional)**
1 tsp. dry mustard	**Vegan soy Parmesan cheese or Raw Parmesan Cheese (recipe in Chapter 9)**
¾ tsp. sea salt	

> *Yield: 8 servings*
>
> **Prep time:** 5 to 7 minutes
> **Cook time:** 25 to 35 minutes
> **Serving size:** 1 cup

1. In a large pot, combine onions, olive oil, and margarine. Cover and cook over medium heat, without stirring, for 5 to 7 minutes or until onions are soft.

2. Remove lid and stir onions. Add garlic, dry mustard, salt, and black pepper, and cook, stirring often, for 5 to 7 more minutes or until onions are lightly brown.

3. Add water and tamari. Bring to a boil, cover, reduce heat to low, and simmer for 15 to 20 minutes or until onions are very tender.

4. Remove from heat and stir in sherry (if using). Taste and add additional tamari or seasonings as desired. Top individual servings with a little vegan soy Parmesan cheese or Raw Parmesan Cheese as desired.

Variation: You can also add croutons to individual servings, or serve the traditional way by topping with a toasted slice of bread, sprinkle with shredded vegan mozzarella or other cheese, and either place under the broiler or in the microwave until cheese is melted.

 Sour Grapes

The sulfur-containing enzymes found in onions give them a strong odor and can cause eye irritation and even tears for some people. You can burn off some of the excess sulfur in the air by burning a candle while cutting them. Also, try rinsing them under cold water briefly, or chilling peeled onions in the refrigerator for a while prior to cutting.

Miso Noodle Soup

In Asia, miso soup is often enjoyed for breakfast, lunch, and dinner, and you can enjoy this light yet filling miso noodle soup, the final flavor and color of which is determined by the variety of miso you choose, in the same way.

Yield: 4 servings
Prep time: 5 minutes
Cook time: 6 to 8 minutes
Serving size: 1 cup

6 cups water

3 oz. udon noodles, broken in half

1 cup shiitake mushrooms, thinly sliced

½ cup green onions, thinly sliced

1 TB. garlic, minced

1 TB. fresh ginger, minced

3 TB. *miso* of choice

2 tsp. toasted sesame oil

2 tsp. sesame seeds

1. In a large pot, combine water, udon noodles, mushrooms, green onions, garlic, and ginger. Bring to a boil over high heat. Reduce heat to low, and simmer for 5 to 7 minutes or until noodles are tender.

2. In a small bowl, stir together 1 cup broth from the pot and miso, and add mixture back to the pot. Add toasted sesame oil and sesame seeds, and simmer for 1 more minute.

Variation: Vary the flavor by adding a piece of kombu to the simmering soup, or add a few nori flakes to the finished soup.

def•i•ni•tion

Miso is a thick paste made from fermenting soybeans with salt and koji (a beneficial type of mold), often along with other ingredients such as beans or grains. Choose a white, mellow, garbanzo bean, or barley miso variety for a light color and flavor. For a darker, stronger, and more robust final product, chose hatcho or red.

White Bean and Escarole Soup

This simple soup is a classic Italian comfort food packed with fiber, protein, calcium, and tons of flavor from the white beans and slightly bitter-tasting escarole.

1 (1- to 1½-lb.) head *escarole,* coarsely chopped

2 TB. garlic, minced

1 TB. olive oil

¾ tsp. dried basil

¾ tsp. dried oregano

½ tsp. crushed red pepper flakes

4 cups water or vegetable broth

1 (15-oz.) can cannellini or Great Northern beans, drained and rinsed

Sea salt

Freshly ground black pepper

Vegan soy Parmesan cheese or nutritional yeast flakes

Yield: 6 servings
Prep time: 5 to 7 minutes
Cook time: 10 to 15 minutes
Serving size: 1 cup

1. In a large pot, combine escarole, garlic, and olive oil, and sauté over medium heat, stirring often, for 2 or 3 minutes or until escarole begins to wilt. Add basil, oregano, and red pepper flakes, and sauté for 1 minute longer.

2. Stir in water and cannellini beans. Bring to a boil, cover, reduce heat to low, and simmer for 8 to 10 minutes or until escarole is tender. Taste and season with salt and black pepper. Top individual servings with vegan soy Parmesan cheese or nutritional yeast flakes as desired.

Variation: This soup can also be prepared using ⅔ cup dried white beans. Add an additional 2 cups water and simmer, covered, until beans are tender. For extra flavor, add ½ cup each diced onion, carrot, and celery, or 1 or 2 sliced vegetarian Italian-style sausages.

def•i•ni•tion

Escarole is a member of the endive family, which also includes curly endive and frisee, and is closely related to chicory and radicchio. It has dark green, broad, flat leaves, and like all endives, it has a slightly bitter flavor. Escarole is sometimes used in salads but is most often served sautéed, steamed, or added to soups or other cooked dishes.

Mediterranean Lentil Soup

Simple yet satisfying best describes this lentil soup made with dried brown lentils, some dried herbs, and fresh ingredients you probably have on hand: onion, carrot, celery, and garlic. A little red wine vinegar added at the end perks up the flavor.

Yield: 8 servings
Prep time: 5 to 7 minutes
Cook time: 40 to 50 minutes
Serving size: 1 cup

---

1 cup onion, diced

¾ cup carrot, diced

¾ cup celery, diced

1 TB. olive oil

1 TB. garlic, minced

6 cups water or vegetable broth

1 cup dried brown lentils, sorted and rinsed

½ tsp. dried basil

½ tsp. dried oregano

½ tsp. dried rosemary, crushed a bit with your fingers

½ tsp. dried thyme

1 bay leaf

1 TB. red wine vinegar or balsamic vinegar

¾ tsp. sea salt

½ tsp. freshly ground black pepper

Sour Grapes

When cooking with dried beans, always first sort or pick through them to look for any pieces of rock, dirt, or debris to avoid biting into something unpleasant—or worse yet, cracking a tooth!

1. In a large pot, combine onion, carrot, celery, and olive oil, and sauté over medium heat, stirring often, for 3 minutes to soften. Add garlic and sauté for 1 more minute.

2. Stir in water, lentils, basil, oregano, rosemary, thyme, and bay leaf. Bring to a boil, cover, reduce heat to low, and simmer for 30 minutes.

3. Stir in vinegar, salt, and black pepper, and simmer for 5 to 10 more minutes or until lentils are tender. Remove bay leaf and discard. Taste and adjust seasonings as desired.

Variation: For a French lentil soup, substitute French green lentils; omit the dried basil, oregano, and rosemary; add 1½ teaspoons dried tarragon; and increase dried thyme to 1 teaspoon.

Mighty Minestrone

This hearty Italian vegetarian vegetable soup contains a colorful assortment of fresh and frozen vegetables, beans, canned tomatoes, and pasta.

1 cup onion, diced

1 cup celery, diced

2 tsp. olive oil

2 TB. garlic, minced

1 (28-oz.) can crushed tomatoes

3 cups water or vegetable broth

3 cups green cabbage, coarsely chopped

2 cups red-skinned potatoes, cut into ½-inch cubes

1 (15-oz.) can mixed beans, drained and rinsed

1 (10-oz.) pkg. frozen mixed vegetable blend (carrots, green beans, corn, and peas)

1 cup zucchini, cut into quarters lengthwise, and thinly sliced

1 bay leaf

1½ tsp. Italian seasoning blend or ¾ tsp. each dried basil and oregano

¾ tsp. sea salt

½ tsp. freshly ground black pepper

¾ cup whole-grain elbow macaroni or other small shaped pasta of choice

Vegan soy Parmesan cheese or nutritional yeast flakes

Yield: 8 servings
Prep time: 10 to 15 minutes
Cook time: 40 to 45 minutes
Serving size: 1 cup

1. In a large pot, combine onion, celery, and olive oil, and sauté over medium heat, stirring often, for 3 minutes to soften. Add garlic and sauté for 1 more minute.

2. Stir in crushed tomatoes, water, cabbage, potatoes, canned beans, frozen vegetables, zucchini, bay leaf, Italian seasoning, salt, and black pepper. Bring to a boil, cover, reduce heat to low, and simmer for 25 to 30 minutes or until vegetables are tender.

3. Add elbow macaroni, and simmer for 8 to 10 more minutes or until macaroni is tender. Remove bay leaf and discard. Taste and adjust seasonings as desired. Top individual servings with vegan soy Parmesan cheese or nutritional yeast flakes as desired.

Variation: You can omit or substitute other fresh or frozen vegetables as well as use other canned beans as desired.

Thyme-ly Tip

Using frozen vegetables and canned beans and tomato products is a great way to save time in the kitchen. So for easier meal times, keep your pantry and freezer well stocked with the canned and frozen items you use most often.

Gingered Cashew-Carrot Soup

The combination of blended, freshly toasted cashews and our Raw ABC Nut Milk provides a velvety richness to this creamy and spicy carrot soup.

Yield: 6 servings
Prep time: 5 minutes
Cook time: 15 to 20 minutes
Serving size: 1 cup

⅓ cup raw cashews

⅓ red onion or shallot, finely diced

1 TB. fresh ginger, minced

1½ tsp. garlic, minced

1 tsp. toasted sesame oil

3 cups (about ¾ lb.) carrot, diced

4 cups water or vegetable broth

½ tsp. sea salt

¼ tsp. curry powder or ground cardamom

½ cup Raw ABC Nut Milk (recipe in Chapter 9) or other nondairy milk of choice

Thyme-ly Tip

Stay nearby when toasting nuts or seeds in a dry pan or roasting them in the oven, and stir if necessary to avoid burning them. Burned nuts and seeds have an unpleasant, somewhat bitter flavor, so if you do burn them, either discard or munch on them, and start over to avoid ruining the flavor of your final dish.

1. Place cashews in a large pot, and cook over medium heat, stirring often, for 2 or 3 minutes or until lightly toasted and fragrant. Transfer cashews to a small plate, and set aside.

2. Return the pot to medium heat. Add onion, ginger, garlic, and toasted sesame oil, and cook, stirring often, for 2 minutes or until soft.

3. Add carrot, 2 cups water, salt, and curry powder, and bring to a boil. Cover, reduce to low heat, and simmer for 10 to 12 minutes or until carrot is soft. Remove from heat and let cool slightly.

4. Transfer mixture and cashews to a food processor fitted with an S blade, or a blender, and process for 1 or 2 minutes or until completely smooth. Transfer blended mixture back into the pot. Stir in remaining 2 cups water and Raw ABC Nut Milk, cover, and simmer over low heat for 5 minutes. Remove from heat. Taste and adjust seasonings as needed.

Variation: For a richer-tasting soup, replace the Raw ABC Nut Milk with canned lite coconut milk.

Cheesy Broccoli Soup

Thick and creamy, this cheesy-tasting broccoli soup is thickened with a purée of vegetables instead of oil or flour.

2½ cups water or vegetable broth

1½ cups Yukon Gold potatoes, peeled and cut into ½-in. cubes

4 cups broccoli, coarsely chopped

½ cup onion, diced

½ cup carrot, diced

½ cup celery, diced

1 TB. garlic, minced

2 tsp. dried thyme

1 bay leaf

⅔ cup Vegan Cheese Sauce Mix (recipe in Chapter 10)

1 TB. Dijon mustard

½ tsp. sea salt

¼ tsp. freshly ground black pepper

2 cups soy milk or other nondairy milk of choice

Yield: 8 servings
Prep time: 5 to 7 minutes
Cook time: 25 to 35 minutes
Serving size: 1 cup

1. In a large pot, combine water, potatoes, 1 cup broccoli, onion, carrot, celery, garlic, thyme, and bay leaf. Bring to a boil, cover, reduce heat to low, and simmer for 20 to 25 minutes or until vegetables are tender. Remove from heat and let cool slightly. Remove and discard bay leaf.

2. Ladle ½ of mixture into a medium bowl. Transfer remaining mixture to a food processor fitted with an S blade, or blender; add Vegan Cheese Sauce Mix, Dijon mustard, salt, and black pepper; and process for 1 or 2 minutes or until completely smooth. Transfer blended mixture back into the pot. Process reserved mixture for 1 or 2 minutes or until completely smooth, and add back into the pot.

3. Stir in remaining 3 cups broccoli and soy milk, and simmer over low heat for 5 to 7 minutes or until broccoli is tender. Taste and adjust seasonings as desired.

Variation: Replace the fresh broccoli with 1 pound frozen broccoli or other frozen vegetables or vegetable blends.

 Sour Grapes

The steam resulting from blending hot foods or liquids in a blender can cause the lid to blow off, which could lead to serious injury. Always let the mixture cool slightly, and only fill the blender half full. For extra safety, place a towel on top, firmly hold down the lid with your hand, and begin blending on low speed.

Chapter 11

Hearty Chilis, Chowders, and Stews

In This Chapter

- ◆ Meatless chili-making fixin's
- ◆ Hearty East Coast chowders
- ◆ Stews from around the world

When the weather begins to turn colder, going into the fall and throughout the winter months, most of us hanker for something rich and hearty like a chili, chowder, or stew. These types of meals are both filling and satisfying all on their own, but even more so when paired with cooked grains or pasta. They can help take the chill off when you need it most.

Chowders have a consistency similar to a thick and hearty soup but often contain ingredients cut into medium or large pieces. Clam chowder usually comes to mind when one makes reference to having chowder, either the New England style, which has a cream or dairy base, or Manhattan style, which is tomato-based. We've included both styles in this chapter, but of course we've left the clams living happily in the ocean.

The vegan stews in this chapter are sure to intrigue and entice you and take your tongue on a mini vacation, with recipes hailing from Africa, Eastern Europe, and the southern, northern, and midwestern United States.

Many people think you can't make a good chili without having meat in it, known as chili con carne, but this just isn't so. However, if you want to imitate this style in a pot of vegan chili (like both of the recipes presented here do), you can use chopped mushrooms, crumbled tempeh, tofu, TVP (textured vegetable protein), or some of the packaged refrigerated or frozen meatless crumbles. Other great additions to chili include beans, corn, sweet potatoes, squashes, olives, and fresh herbs.

Smoky Mushroom Chili

Mushrooms have a meaty, chewy texture and take the place of ground beef, while a generous amount of spices and chipotle chiles in adobo sauce provide a smoky flavor and add a lot of heat to this all-veggie, soy-free chili.

1½ cups onion, diced

2 TB. olive oil

¾ cup green bell pepper, ribs and seeds removed, and diced

¾ cup red bell pepper, ribs and seeds removed, and diced

1 jalapeño pepper, ribs and seeds removed, and finely diced

12 oz. crimini mushrooms or other mushrooms of choice, coarsely chopped

2 TB. garlic, minced

2 tsp. chili powder

2 tsp. canned *chipotle chiles in adobo sauce*, puréed

1½ tsp. ground cumin

1½ tsp. dried oregano

1 (15-oz.) can black beans or black soybeans, drained and rinsed

1 (15-oz.) can pinto beans or kidney beans, drained and rinsed

1 (14-oz.) can fire-roasted crushed tomatoes

1 (14-oz.) can diced tomatoes with green chiles

¾ cup water

⅓ cup chopped fresh cilantro

¾ tsp. sea salt

½ tsp. freshly ground black pepper

Yield: 6 servings
Prep time: 10 to 15 minutes
Cook time: 25 to 30 minutes
Serving size: 1½ cups

1. In a large pot, combine onions and olive oil, and sauté over medium heat, stirring often, for 3 minutes or until soft. Add green bell pepper, red bell pepper, and jalapeño pepper, and sauté for 2 minutes.

2. Add mushrooms and garlic, and sauté for 3 to 5 more minutes or until vegetables are tender. Add chili powder, chipotle chiles in adobo sauce, cumin, and oregano, and sauté for 1 minute.

3. Stir in black beans, pinto beans, crushed tomatoes, diced tomatoes, water, cilantro, salt, and black pepper. Cover, reduce heat to low, and cook for 15 to 20 minutes or until tomatoes begin to break down. Taste and adjust seasonings. Serve with tortilla chips, crackers, or cornbread, if desired.

Variation: For a less-spicy chili, omit the chipotle chiles in adobo sauce and use 1 tablespoon chili powder instead.

def•i•ni•tion

Chipotle chiles in adobo sauce are smoked whole jalapeño peppers canned in a red sauce that typically contains tomatoes, onions, garlic, oil, vinegar, herbs and spices, and salt. The mixture has a hot, smoky flavor, and the chipotle chiles are usually finely minced or puréed prior to use.

Meatless-in-Cincinnati Chili

Cincinnati, Ohio, is world famous for its unique-tasting chili, which contains a surprising combination of spices that originated with several Greek and Middle Eastern immigrant restaurateurs.

Yield: 4 servings
Prep time: 5 to 10 minutes
Cook time: 20 to 25 minutes
Serving size: 1 cup

2½ cups water

2 TB. ketchup

1 TB. tamari

1 cup TVP granules

1½ cups onion, diced

2 tsp. olive oil

1 TB. garlic, minced

1 TB. chili powder

1 tsp. ground cinnamon

1 tsp. sea salt

½ tsp. ground cumin

½ tsp. dried oregano

½ tsp. paprika

½ tsp. freshly ground black pepper

¼ tsp. ground allspice

¼ tsp. ground cloves

¼ tsp. cayenne

1 (16-oz.) can tomato sauce

4 tsp. cocoa powder

1 TB. apple cider vinegar

1 bay leaf

Accompaniments of choice, such as cooked spaghetti, shredded vegan cheddar cheese, chopped onions, canned kidney beans or red beans, or tofu sour cream

Soy What?

Cincinnati chili is served in many ways: two way is spaghetti topped with chili; three way is spaghetti topped with chili and shredded cheddar cheese; four way is spaghetti topped with chili, cheese, and chopped onions; and five way is spaghetti topped with chili, cheese, chopped onions, and beans.

1. In a small saucepan, combine 1 cup water, ketchup, and tamari, and bring to a boil over high heat. Remove from heat, stir in TVP, cover, and set aside to rehydrate for 10 minutes.

2. Meanwhile, in a large pot, combine onions and olive oil, and sauté over medium heat, stirring often, for 3 to 5 minutes or until soft. Add garlic, chili powder, cinnamon, salt, cumin, oregano, paprika, black pepper, allspice, cloves, and cayenne, and sauté for 2 more minutes.

3. Stir in TVP mixture, remaining 1½ cups water, tomato sauce, cocoa powder, vinegar, and bay leaf. Cover, reduce heat to low, and cook for 10 to 15 minutes or until thickened.

4. Remove bay leaf and discard. Taste and adjust seasonings as desired. Serve individual servings with your choice of one or more accompaniments, or a combination of all of them.

Variation: You can replace the TVP with 1 (8-ounce) package tempeh, crumbled, or 2 cups chopped mushrooms, cooking them along with the water, ketchup, and tamari in the large pot first. Add the onions, and finish the chili as instructed.

Manhattan-Style Garbanzo Bean Chowder

Manhattan-style clam chowder is usually tomato based. Ours uses garbanzo beans instead of clams and dulse flakes (a sea vegetable) to give it a fresh-from-the-sea flavor.

⅔ cup red onion, diced

⅔ cup carrot, diced

⅔ cup celery, diced

⅔ cup red bell pepper, ribs and seeds removed, and diced

2 TB. olive oil

1 TB. garlic, minced

1 tsp. dried basil

1 tsp. dried oregano

1 tsp. dried marjoram

1 tsp. dried tarragon

6 cups water or vegetable broth

1½ cups red-skinned potatoes, cut into ½-in. cubes

1 (15-oz.) can garbanzo beans, drained and rinsed

1 (14-oz.) can crushed tomatoes

1 (10-oz.) pkg. frozen chopped spinach

2 TB. dulse flakes or ½ tsp. kelp powder

¾ tsp. sea salt

½ tsp. freshly ground black pepper

Yield: 6 servings
Prep time: 7 to 10 minutes
Cook time: 20 to 30 minutes
Serving size: 1½ cups

1. In a large pot, combine red onion, carrot, celery, red bell pepper, and olive oil, and sauté over medium heat, stirring often, for 5 to 7 minutes or until soft. Add garlic, basil, oregano, marjoram, and tarragon, and sauté for 1 more minute.

2. Stir in water, potatoes, garbanzo beans, crushed tomatoes, spinach, dulse flakes, salt, and black pepper. Bring to a boil, cover, reduce to low heat, and simmer for 15 to 20 minutes or until vegetables are tender. Taste and adjust seasonings.

Variation: Replace the canned garbanzo beans with 2 cups chopped mushrooms. For fun, use oyster mushrooms or lobster mushrooms if you can find them.

def•i•ni•tion

Sea vegetables are a valuable source of lignans, iodine, vitamin K, iron, magnesium, calcium, and several B vitamins. Some commonly used sea vegetables include hijiki, arame, wakame, dulse, nori, kelp, and kombu.

Chunky Corn Chowder

This hearty, low-fat chowder is bejeweled with flecks of color thanks to the corn, carrots, celery, and both red and green peppers. Instant mashed potato flakes and soy milk are used to create its thick and creamy consistency.

Yield: 6 servings	
Prep time: 7 to 10 minutes	
Cook time: 25 to 30 minutes	
Serving size: 1½ cups	

5 cups water

1½ cups red-skinned potatoes, cut into ½-in. cubes

⅔ cup red onion, diced

⅔ cup carrot, diced

⅔ cup celery, diced

1 TB. garlic, minced

1 tsp. dried basil

1 tsp. dried oregano

½ tsp. dried thyme

1 cup fresh or frozen cut corn kernels

⅔ cup green bell pepper, ribs and seeds removed, and diced

⅔ cup red bell pepper, ribs and seeds removed, and diced

½ cup green onions, thinly sliced

¾ tsp. sea salt

½ tsp. freshly ground black pepper or lemon pepper

1½ cups instant mashed potatoes flakes

1 cup soy milk or other nondairy milk of choice

¼ cup chopped fresh parsley

1 TB. freshly squeezed lemon juice

1. In a large pot, combine water, potatoes, red onion, carrot, celery, garlic, basil, oregano, and thyme. Bring to a boil, cover, reduce to low heat, and simmer for 10 minutes.

2. Stir in corn, green bell pepper, red bell pepper, green onions, salt, and black pepper, and simmer for 10 to 15 more minutes or until vegetables are tender. Slowly stir in mashed potato flakes, and simmer for 1 or 2 minutes or until thickened.

3. Remove from heat. Stir in soy milk, parsley, and lemon juice. Taste and adjust seasonings.

Variation: For extra flavor, add one or more of the following to the simmering soup: 2 cups cubed sweet potatoes or winter squash, ¼ cup chopped vegetarian Canadian bacon or ham, 1 finely diced jalapeño pepper, or 1 teaspoon chili powder or chipotle chili powder as desired.

Thyme-ly Tip

Instant mashed potato flakes work well as a fast and easy binder and thickener in recipes, such as soups, stews, sauces, casseroles, burgers, and loaves. Be sure to buy brands that are made with only dehydrated potatoes and don't contain any artificial preservatives or ingredients.

Mushroom-Barley Stew

This filling stew made with mushrooms and barley is great to make during the cold winter months.

1½ cups carrot, thinly sliced

1½ cups celery, thinly sliced

1 cup onion, diced

2 tsp. plus 2 TB. olive oil

8 oz. crimini mushrooms or other mushrooms of choice, thinly sliced

1 TB. garlic, minced

¾ tsp. dried basil

¾ tsp. dried oregano

½ tsp. dried thyme

½ tsp. rubbed sage

6 cups vegetable broth

⅓ cup hulled barley or pearl barley, rinsed

¼ cup tamari

2 TB. sherry (optional)

½ tsp. sea salt

½ tsp. freshly ground black pepper or lemon pepper

½ cup barley flour or spelt flour

¼ cup chopped fresh parsley

Yield: 6 servings
Prep time: 7 to 10 minutes
Cook time: 40 to 50 minutes
Serving size: 1½ cups

1. In a large pot over medium heat, combine carrot, celery, onion, and 2 teaspoons olive oil. Sauté, stirring often, for 5 minutes or until soft. Add mushrooms, garlic, basil, oregano, thyme, and rubbed sage, and sauté for 2 minutes.

2. Stir in 4 cups vegetable broth and bring to a boil. Add barley, cover, reduce heat to low, and simmer for 30 to 40 minutes or until barley is tender.

3. Meanwhile, in a small saucepan, combine remaining 2 cups vegetable broth, tamari, sherry (if using), salt, and black pepper.

4. In a small bowl, whisk together flour and remaining 2 tablespoons olive oil to form a smooth paste. Whisk paste into the saucepan mixture. Cook over low heat, whisking occasionally, for 2 or 3 minutes or until thickened. Remove from heat.

5. When barley is tender, stir thickened mixture into the pot along with parsley. Taste and adjust seasonings as desired.

Variation: You can also add 2 cups chopped spinach or other greens of choice, or replace the barley with an equal amount of mixed grain and wild rice blend.

> **Soy What?**
>
> You can purchase whole barley grains as hulled barley, which has the outer inedible hull removed but the grain's germ and bran are still intact, or as pearl (or pearled) barley, which is further processed to remove the bran and polished (known as pearling).

Green Gumbo

Green Gumbo is one of the many gumbo recipes commonly prepared in Louisiana, and this version contains soyrizo rather than the more traditionally used ham hock or andouille sausage.

Yield: 6 servings
Prep time: 20 to 25 minutes
Cook time: 45 to 55 minutes
Serving size: 1½ cups

1 bunch collard greens or 1 (10-oz.) pkg. frozen

1 bunch turnip greens or 1 (10-oz.) pkg. frozen

1 bunch kale or 1 (10-oz.) pkg. frozen

1 bunch spinach or 1 (10-oz.) pkg. frozen

1 (12-oz.) pkg. soyrizo

4 TB. olive oil

¼ cup whole-wheat flour or spelt flour

1½ cups onion, diced

1 cup celery, diced

1 cup green bell pepper, ribs and seeds removed, and diced

2 jalapeño peppers, ribs and seeds removed, and finely diced

2 TB. garlic, minced

6 cups water

3 cups green cabbage, shredded

1 bay leaf

½ tsp. sea salt

½ tsp. paprika

¼ tsp. garlic powder

¼ tsp. onion powder

¼ tsp. dried basil

¼ tsp. dried oregano

¼ tsp. dried thyme

¼ tsp. freshly ground black pepper

¼ tsp. cayenne or crushed red pepper flakes

⅛ tsp. white pepper

⅛ tsp. dry mustard

¼ cup nutritional yeast flakes

¼ cup chopped fresh Italian parsley

1. Remove stems from collard greens, coarsely chop greens, and set aside. Repeat with turnip greens, kale, and spinach.

2. Remove soyrizo from its casing, and place soyrizo and 1 tablespoon olive oil in a large pot over medium heat. Sauté, stirring often, for 3 to 5 minutes or until soyrizo is crispy. Using a slotted spoon, transfer soyrizo to a small plate and set aside.

3. Add remaining 3 tablespoons olive oil and flour to the pot, and stir together to form roux. Cook roux over medium heat, stirring often, for 10 to 15 minutes or until golden brown.

4. Stir in onion, celery, green bell pepper, jalapeño peppers, and garlic, and cook, stirring often, for 5 to 7 minutes or until vegetables are soft. Slowly stir in 1 cup water and then stir in remaining 5 cups water.

5. Add reserved soyrizo, collard greens, turnip greens, kale, spinach, green cabbage, bay leaf, salt, paprika, garlic powder, onion powder, basil, oregano, thyme, black pepper, cayenne, white pepper, and dry mustard. Bring to a boil, cover, reduce heat to low, and simmer for 20 to 25 minutes or until greens are tender.

6. Add nutritional yeast flakes and parsley, and simmer for 3 more minutes. Remove bay leaf and discard. Taste and adjust seasonings as desired.

7. Serve individual servings over cooked brown rice or other grains, with a little hot pepper sauce as desired.

Variation: You can substitute other fresh or frozen greens such as Swiss chard, mustard greens, beet greens, or escarole, or replace all the herbs and spices with 1 tablespoon Creole blend seasoning.

def•i•ni•tion

Roux (pronounced *rue*) is a French cooking term that refers to a mixture of fat (such as butter or oil) and flour, which is commonly used as a thickener for sauces, soups, and stews. The mixture is cooked while stirring often to remove the starchy taste of the flour. The longer the roux cooks, the deeper its color becomes.

African Groundnut Stew

In Africa, peanuts are also called groundnuts because they grow in the ground. This tempeh and vegetable stew, flavored with peanut butter, is our version of one of Africa's most famous dishes.

Yield: 6 servings
Prep time: 15 to 20 minutes
Cook time: 35 to 40 minutes
Serving size: 1½ cups

1 (8-oz.) pkg. tempeh, cut into ½-in. cubes

4 tsp. olive oil or peanut oil

1½ cups onion, diced

2 TB. garlic, minced

2 TB. fresh ginger, minced

1 tsp. ground cumin

1 tsp. ground coriander

½ tsp. cayenne

1 (28-oz.) can diced tomatoes

2 cups water or vegetable broth

1 (6-oz.) can tomato paste

4 cups Swiss chard or other green of choice, coarsely chopped

1 medium eggplant, cut into 1-in. cubes

1 large sweet potato, cut into 1-in. cubes

1 medium zucchini, cut into quarters lengthwise and thinly sliced

1 medium green bell pepper, ribs and seeds removed, and diced

½ cup creamy or crunchy peanut butter

Thyme-ly Tip

We really love Swiss chard and use it in raw salads as well as cooked dishes. It comes in a variety of colors: green with white stems; red (or rhubarb chard) with green leaves and red stems; ruby with deep red leaves and stems; and rainbow, which is brilliantly multicolored.

1. In a large pot over medium heat, combine tempeh and olive oil. Sauté, stirring often, for 5 minutes.

2. Add onion and sauté, stirring often, for 3 to 5 minutes or until onion is soft and tempeh is lightly browned. Add garlic, ginger, cumin, coriander, and cayenne, and sauté for 1 minute.

3. Add diced tomatoes, water, and tomato paste. Stir well to combine, and add Swiss chard, eggplant, sweet potato, zucchini, and green bell pepper. Bring to a boil, cover, reduce heat to low, and simmer for 20 to 25 minutes or until vegetables are tender.

4. Add peanut butter, and simmer for 3 more minutes. Taste and adjust seasonings as desired.

5. Serve individual servings over cooked millet, couscous, or other cooked grains as desired.

Variation: If you are sensitive to peanuts, you can substitute other varieties of nut butter.

Chapter 12

Dazzling Dressings and Mixed-Greens Salads

In This Chapter

◆ Whisk and blend your way to great dressings

◆ Vibrant leafy green salads

◆ Colorful, savory, and sweet slaws

Salads are often the only vegan-friendly option on restaurant menus. But when a restaurant has a salad bar, options expand tremendously! Bring the idea of the salad bar home—and save yourself a ton of money—by making your own fresh salads and dressings, chock-full of all the ingredients you like. This chapter shows you exactly how.

When it comes to dressings, sometimes you want something with a little more oomph and pizzazz than olive oil and vinegar or a light squeeze of lemon juice. This chapter offers recipes for several salad dressings to satisfy all tastes and needs, from simple whisked vinaigrettes to blended no-fat and low-fat dressings, a creamy tahini-based Goddess dressing, and even a vegan tofu-based mayonnaise.

After giving the salad dressing selections a whirl, we hope you try one (or more!) of the mixed-greens salads and slaws that follow. View the ingredient combinations for these salad recipes as suggestions, and feel free to replace or substitute any of the ingredients to accommodate for seasonal produce availability and to suit your tastes.

Salads are suitable for eating year-round and can be enjoyed for lunch as well as dinner. We try to eat some sort of salad made with fresh raw ingredients on a daily basis, and we hope these recipes will encourage you to do so as well.

Balsamic and Herb Vinaigrette

A classic vinaigrette is made with 1 part vinegar to 3 parts oil, while stronger versions use 1 part vinegar to 2 parts oil. This flavorful Italian-inspired vinaigrette contains a little water to make the final product much lower in fat.

⅓ cup *balsamic vinegar*

¼ cup water

1 TB. Dijon mustard

1 TB. garlic, minced

1½ tsp. Italian seasoning blend, or ½ tsp. each dried basil, oregano, and thyme

1 tsp. unbleached cane sugar or beet sugar

¼ tsp. sea salt

¼ tsp. freshly ground black pepper

⅔ cup olive oil

Yield: 1½ cups	
Prep time: 3 to 5 minutes	
Serving size: 2 table-spoons	

1. In a small bowl, whisk together balsamic vinegar, water, Dijon mustard, garlic, Italian seasoning blend, sugar, salt, and black pepper.

2. Slowly drizzle in olive oil, and continue to whisk vigorously. Taste and adjust seasonings as desired.

3. Serve with mixed greens, vegetable salads, or cooked pasta and grains, or use as a marinade for grilled vegetables, mushroom burgers, tempeh, or tofu. Store dressing in an airtight container in the refrigerator for up to 2 weeks.

Variation: Alternatively, place balsamic vinegar, water, Dijon mustard, garlic, Italian seasoning blend, sugar, salt, and pepper in a blender, and blend for 1 minute. With the blender running, slowly add olive oil and blend for 1 more minute. For extra flavor, replace Italian seasoning blend with 2 tablespoons each chopped fresh basil and parsley and also add 1½ teaspoons nutritional yeast flakes.

def•i•ni•tion

Balsamic vinegar is traditionally made from white Trebbiano grapes in Modena, Italy. It's aged in a successive number of casks made of various types of wood; most brands are aged for 3 to 12 years. The aging process is used to develop a rich, slightly sweet, and highly acidic flavor; dark brown color; and distinctive aroma.

Low-Fat Miso-Ginger Dressing

This light and creamy dressing, made with miso and fresh ginger, makes an excellent dip for raw veggies as well as a condiment for baked tofu sandwiches.

Yield: 1½ cups

Prep time: 5 minutes

Cook time: 2 minutes

Serving size: 2 tablespoons

---

1 cup water

1 TB. cornstarch

3 TB. apple cider vinegar

2 TB. fresh ginger, minced

2 TB. garbanzo bean miso or other light miso of choice

2 TB. toasted sesame oil

1 TB. agave nectar or apple juice concentrate

1. For oil replacer, in a small saucepan over medium heat, whisk together water and cornstarch, and cook, whisking often, for 1 or 2 minutes or until thickened. Remove from heat, and set aside to cool.

2. Transfer cooled water-and-cornstarch oil replacer to a food processor fitted with an S blade or a blender. Add vinegar, ginger, miso, toasted sesame oil, and agave nectar, and process for 1 or 2 minutes or until completely smooth. Scrape down the sides of the container with a rubber spatula, and process for 15 more seconds.

3. Serve with mixed greens, vegetable salads, fruit salads, and cooked grains. Store dressing in an airtight container in the refrigerator for up to 2 weeks.

Variation: For a spicy, orange-flavored dressing, replace the apple cider vinegar with orange juice and add ½ teaspoon curry powder.

Thyme-ly Tip

Apple juice concentrate is a great all-natural sweetener that has a slightly sweet apple flavor. You can use it much like you would other liquid sweeteners, such as maple syrup, brown rice syrup, or agave nectar in both sweet and savory dishes.

No-Fat Raspberry–Poppy Seed Dressing

This fat-free, raspberry-flavored dressing was inspired by the sweet-and-sour poppy seed dressing Beverly's great-grandmother was famous for serving at potlucks and family get-togethers.

1 cup water	⅓ cup frozen raspberries
1 TB. cornstarch	2 TB. red onion, finely diced
⅔ cup unbleached cane sugar or beet sugar	¾ tsp. dry mustard
⅓ cup apple cider vinegar	¾ tsp. sea salt
	1½ tsp. poppy seeds

Yield: 2 cups
Prep time: 5 minutes
Cook time: 2 minutes
Serving size: 2 table-spoons

1. For oil replacer, in a small saucepan, whisk together water and cornstarch, and cook over medium heat, whisking often, for 1 or 2 minutes or until thickened. Remove from heat, and set aside to cool.

2. Transfer cooled water-and-cornstarch oil replacer to a food processor fitted with an S blade or a blender. Add sugar, vinegar, raspberries, red onion, dry mustard, and salt, and process for 1 or 2 minutes or until completely smooth. Scrape down the sides of the container with a rubber spatula, and process for 15 more seconds.

3. Transfer mixture to an airtight container, and stir in poppy seeds. Use as a dressing with mixed greens, vegetable salads, fruit salads, and pasta salads. Store dressing in an airtight container in the refrigerator for up to 2 weeks.

Variation: For a thicker, frosty, pink-colored dressing, omit the water-and-cornstarch oil replacer and replace with ¾ cup olive oil and ¼ cup water.

Thyme-ly Tip

The water-and-cornstarch oil replacer used in both the Low-Fat Miso-Ginger Dressing and No-Fat Raspberry–Poppy Seed Dressing can also be used to make low-fat and no-fat versions of your other favorite dressings. Prepare it in larger amounts and keep it in an airtight container in the refrigerator for up to several weeks.

Goddess Dressing

This creamy and tangy dressing contains flaxseed oil and hemp seed oil, both of which are excellent sources of omega-3 and -6 essential fatty acids.

Yield: 2 cups
Prep time: 3 to 5 minutes
Serving size: 2 table-spoons

½ cup raw tahini

⅓ cup water

¼ cup flaxseed oil

¼ cup hemp seed oil or olive oil

3 TB. cup apple cider vinegar

2 TB. freshly squeezed lemon juice

2 TB. Bragg Liquid Aminos or tamari

1 TB. agave nectar

1 TB. garlic, minced

⅛ tsp. powdered kelp (optional)

⅛ tsp. cayenne (optional)

¼ cup green onions, thinly sliced

¼ cup chopped fresh parsley

2 TB. raw sesame seeds

1. Place tahini, water, flaxseed oil, hemp seed oil, vinegar, lemon juice, liquid aminos, agave nectar, garlic, powdered kelp (if using), and cayenne (if using) into a food processor fitted with an S blade or a blender. Process for 1 minute or until completely smooth.

2. Scrape down the sides of the container with a rubber spatula. Add green onions, parsley, and sesame seeds, and process for 1 more minute.

3. Use as a dressing or sauce for salads, cooked grains or pasta, and raw or steamed vegetables. Store dressing in an airtight container in the refrigerator for up to 2 weeks.

Variation: For a more prominent sesame flavor, replace the flaxseed oil with toasted sesame oil, and the hemp seed oil with raw sesame oil.

def•i•ni•tion

Essential fatty acids (EFAs), or omega-3 and -6, are fats required in the diet because the body either doesn't make or can't synthesize enough for use. You can easily obtain them through dietary plant-based sources such as vegetable oils, flaxseeds, hemp seeds, wheat germ, sunflower seeds, pumpkin seeds, walnuts, grains, fruits, and green leafy vegetables.

Creamy Agave Dijon Dressing

This slightly sweet and tangy tofu-based dressing, reminiscent of creamy honey mustard dressings, works equally as well as a replacement for vegan mayonnaise in your favorite recipes.

6 oz. firm or extra-firm silken tofu

2 large garlic cloves

½ cup soy milk or other non-dairy milk of choice

¼ cup agave nectar

2 TB. Dijon mustard

2 TB. whole-grain mustard or stone ground mustard

2 TB. olive oil

2 TB. apple cider vinegar

¼ tsp. sea salt

¼ tsp. freshly ground black pepper

¼ cup green onions, thinly sliced

¼ cup chopped fresh parsley

Yield: 2 cups
Prep time: 3 to 5 minutes
Serving size: 2 table-spoons

1. Crumble tofu into a blender using your fingers. Add garlic cloves, and process for 1 minute. Add soy milk, agave nectar, Dijon mustard, whole-grain mustard, olive oil, vinegar, salt, and black pepper, and process for 1 or 2 minutes or until completely smooth.

2. Scrape down the sides of the container with a rubber spatula. Add green onions and parsley, and process for 30 more seconds.

3. Use as condiment on wraps, sandwiches, and burgers; as a dressing for salads; as a dip for raw veggies or chips; and in your other favorite recipes as desired. Store dressing in an airtight container in the refrigerator for up to 2 weeks.

Variation: For a creamy peppercorn ranch dressing, omit the whole-grain mustard and green onions, use only 2 tablespoons chopped parsley, add 1 tablespoon chopped fresh dill, and substitute ½ teaspoon whole black peppercorns for the freshly ground pepper. But add the peppercorns at the end with the herbs, and only process briefly.

Soy What?

We only use raw, unpasteurized apple cider vinegar in our vegan recipes because we prefer its refreshing, tart flavor. We also commonly use it in the preparation of raw food dishes that we eat on a regular basis.

Tofu Mayonnaise

This creamy and versatile recipe is an inexpensive alternative to store-bought vegan mayonnaise.

Yield: 2 cups
Prep time: 2 or 3 minutes
Serving size: 1 tablespoon

8 oz. firm or extra-firm tofu

⅓ cup water

⅓ cup olive oil or safflower oil

1 TB. Dijon mustard

1½ tsp. unbleached cane sugar or maple syrup

1½ tsp. apple cider vinegar

1½ tsp. freshly squeezed lemon juice

1½ tsp. nutritional yeast flakes (optional)

¼ tsp. sea salt

1. Crumble tofu into a blender using your fingers. Add water, olive oil, Dijon mustard, sugar, vinegar, lemon juice, nutritional yeast flakes (if using), and salt, and process for 1 or 2 minutes or until completely smooth.

2. Scrape down the sides of the container with a rubber spatula and process for 15 more seconds.

3. Use as a condiment on wraps, sandwiches, and burgers; to make dressings and dips; and in your other favorite recipes. Store mayonnaise in an airtight container in the refrigerator for up to 2 weeks.

Variation: For a lighter tofu mayonnaise, use soft tofu instead, or substitute 1 (12-ounce) package firm or extra-firm silken tofu and only add 1 or 2 tablespoons water. For extra flavor, add 1 teaspoon each garlic powder and onion powder.

 Thyme-ly Tip

You can easily adapt this recipe to make flavored tofu mayonnaise by adding one or more of the following: wasabi powder, chipotle chiles in adobo sauce, cranberry sauce, garlic cloves, prepared horseradish, chopped fresh parsley, dill, basil, or other fresh herbs. Blend them along with the other ingredients.

Avocado and Citrus Spinach Salad

Serve this salad in the winter and spring when citrus fruits begin to flood the market. For more visual appeal and flavor, replace its simple citrus vinaigrette with No-Fat Raspberry–Poppy Seed Dressing (recipe earlier in this chapter).

1 (5-oz.) pkg. baby spinach	½ cup red onion, thinly sliced
2 medium Hass avocadoes, peeled, cut in half lengthwise, and thinly sliced	⅓ cup raw sliced almonds or raw pumpkin seeds (optional)
2 oranges, peeled and cut into segments	Juice and zest of 1 orange
1 ruby red grapefruit or other grapefruit of choice, peeled and cut into segments	Juice of ½ ruby red grapefruit or other grapefruit of choice
	¼ cup olive oil
	Sea salt
	Freshly ground black pepper

> *Yield: 6 servings*
>
> **Prep time:** 8 to 10 minutes
>
> **Serving size:** 1½ cups

1. In a large bowl, combine spinach, avocadoes, oranges, grapefruit, and onion. Sprinkle almonds (if using) over top of salad.

2. For dressing, in a small bowl, whisk together orange juice and zest, grapefruit juice, and olive oil. Taste, season with salt and black pepper, and whisk again. Drizzle dressing over salad and toss, or simply drizzle over individual servings.

Variation: For extra flavor and texture, replace ½ of baby spinach with baby arugula, and scatter alfalfa sprouts, radish sprouts, or micro-greens over the salad.

Thyme-ly Tip

Here's a tip to keep avocadoes from discoloring: after you've cut the segments from the oranges and grapefruit, firmly squeeze the remaining citrus fruit sections, as well as the extra grapefruit half that wasn't used in preparing the dressing, over the sliced avocadoes. Gently toss to evenly coat avocadoes with the juice, and add to spinach.

Hail Caesar Salad

Our veganized version of Caesar salad contains only a few basic ingredients, but its garlicky and tangy dressing will have you coming back for more.

Yield: 6 servings
Prep time: 10 to 12 minutes
Cook time: 10 to 15 minutes
Serving size: 1½ cups

2 slices whole-grain bread, cut into ½-in. cubes

1½ tsp. plus ⅓ cup water

1½ tsp. plus 3 TB. olive oil

½ tsp. Italian seasoning blend or ¼ tsp. each dried basil and dried oregano

½ tsp. garlic powder

¼ tsp. paprika

¼ tsp. plus ½ tsp. sea salt

2 TB. freshly squeezed lemon juice

3 large garlic cloves

4 tsp. mellow miso or garbanzo bean miso

4 tsp. nutritional yeast flakes

2 tsp. Dijon mustard

½ tsp. kelp powder

¼ tsp. freshly ground black pepper

1 head romaine lettuce, torn into bite-size pieces

3 TB. vegan Parmesan cheese or Raw Parmesan Cheese (recipe in Chapter 9)

Freshly ground black pepper

Thyme-ly Tip

You can use this Caesar dressing on other leafy green salads or pasta salads or as a topping for steamed veggies. Or chill it in the refrigerator until thickened and use it as a dip for raw veggies or potato chips.

1. Preheat the oven to 400°F.

2. For croutons, in a small bowl, combine bread cubes, 1½ teaspoons water, 1½ teaspoons olive oil, Italian seasoning, garlic powder, paprika, and ¼ teaspoon salt. Transfer bread cubes to a large cookie sheet, and spread out into a single layer, and bake for 7 minutes.

3. Remove from the oven, stir with a spatula, spread out into a single layer, and bake for 3 to 7 more minutes or until golden brown and dry. Remove from the oven. Let cool to room temperature.

4. Meanwhile, for dressing, place remaining ⅓ cup water, remaining 3 tablespoons olive oil, lemon juice, garlic cloves, miso, nutritional yeast flakes, Dijon mustard, kelp powder, remaining ½ teaspoon salt, and ¼ teaspoon black pepper into a food processor fitted with an S blade or a blender. Process for 1 or 2 minutes or until completely smooth. Scrape down the sides of the container with a rubber spatula, and process for 15 more seconds.

5. In a large bowl, place lettuce, croutons, dressing, and vegan Parmesan cheese. Season with black pepper, and toss gently to combine. Serve immediately, assembling salad components as individual servings on large plates or in bowls, serving Caesar dressing on the side, or drizzling it over servings as desired.

Variation: For an even creamier version of this dressing, blend ⅓ cup (3 ounces) firm or extra-firm silken tofu along with the other dressing ingredients until completely smooth.

Greek Country Salad

We prefer to use romaine lettuce in this colorful salad made with tomatoes, cucumbers, olives, and feta cheese because it has a crisp and crunchy texture. We also add pepperoncinis to the mix for extra flavor.

1 head romaine lettuce, torn into bite-size pieces	**⅓ cup olive oil**
2 large tomatoes, each cut into 8 wedges	**2 TB. freshly squeezed lemon juice**
1 large cucumber, cut in half lengthwise and sliced	**1 TB. red wine vinegar**
	1 TB. garlic, minced
1 green bell pepper, ribs and seeds removed, and thinly sliced	**1 tsp. dried oregano**
	¼ tsp. sea salt
1 small red onion, thinly sliced	**¼ tsp. freshly ground black pepper**
¾ cup kalamata olives, pitted	**¾ cup Tofu Feta (recipe in Chapter 9)**
⅓ cup jarred pepperoncinis, thinly sliced	

> *Yield: 6 servings*
>
> **Prep time:** 10 to 15 minutes
>
> **Serving size:** 1½ cups

1. In a large bowl, combine lettuce, tomatoes, cucumber, green bell pepper, red onion, olives, and pepperoncinis.

2. For dressing, in a small bowl, whisk together olive oil, lemon juice, vinegar, garlic, oregano, salt, and black pepper.

3. Drizzle dressing over salad, and toss gently until evenly coated. Scatter Tofu Feta over salad and serve.

Variation: For a classic Greek salad, omit the romaine lettuce, and simply toss the cut vegetables and Tofu Feta with the dressing.

> ### Soy What?
>
> One of the most influential vegetarians was the Greek Pythagoras of Samos, who is known as the "father of mathematics" and is best known for his Pythagorean Theorem. Pythagoras was also a philosopher, scientist, social reformer, and educator who developed a large group of loyal followers known as Pythagoreans. In fact, until the nineteenth century, vegetarians were commonly referred to as Pythagoreans.

Chinese Un-Chicken Salad

Chinese Chicken Salad appears on restaurant and fast-food menus from coast to coast, so we eagerly took up the task of concocting this vegan version made with fried tofu and other crisp and crunchy Asian-inspired ingredients.

Yield: 6 servings
Prep time: 15 to 20 minutes
Cook time: 6 to 8 minutes
Serving size: 1½ cups

8 oz. firm or extra-firm tofu

3 TB. tamari

2 TB. toasted sesame oil

½ tsp. garlic granules or garlic powder

½ tsp. ground ginger

1 cup snow peas, cut in half diagonally

3 cups napa cabbage, shredded

3 cups romaine lettuce, shredded

1 cup mung bean sprouts

1 cup carrot, shredded

¼ cup green onions, thinly sliced

¼ cup chopped fresh cilantro

¼ cup brown rice vinegar

2 TB. peanut butter

2 TB. water

1 TB. agave nectar or turbinado sugar

1 TB. fresh ginger, minced

½ tsp. crushed red pepper flakes

½ cup crispy chow mein noodles or crispy rice noodles

⅓ cup roasted peanuts, coarsely chopped

1. For un-chicken, squeeze tofu block over the sink to remove excess water. Cut tofu in thirds lengthwise and then into 1-inch strips. Place strips in a small bowl. Add 1 tablespoon tamari, 1 tablespoon toasted sesame oil, garlic granules, and ground ginger, and stir well to evenly coat tofu.

2. Cook tofu strips in a large nonstick skillet over medium heat, stirring often, for 5 to 7 minutes or until golden brown and crispy. Remove from heat, and set aside to cool.

3. Fill a small saucepan half full with water, and bring to a boil over medium heat. Add snow peas, and cook for 1 or 2 minutes or until bright green. Remove from heat. Drain snow peas in a colander, and run cold water over them until cool.

4. Place napa cabbage, romaine lettuce, mung bean sprouts, carrot, green onions, and cilantro in a large bowl. Add cool snow peas, and toss gently to combine.

5. For dressing, in a small bowl, whisk together vinegar, peanut butter, 2 tablespoons water, remaining 2 tablespoons tamari, remaining 1 tablespoon toasted sesame oil, agave nectar, ginger, and red pepper flakes.

6. Scatter un-chicken, chow mein noodles, and peanuts over salad. Drizzle dressing over salad, and toss gently until evenly coated.

Variation: You can replace the tofu with 8 ounces prepackaged chicken-flavored seitan strips, as well as substitute other varieties of lettuce.

Thyme-ly Tip

Adapt this recipe to make it into a Mandarin Broccoli Salad by skipping the tofu-frying step. Simply cook 2 cups broccoli florets in boiling water for a few minutes or until bright green and cool them off quickly in ice water. Combine the broccoli and 1 (11-ounce) can drained mandarin oranges with the remaining salad ingredients, and toss together with the dressing.

Asian Slaw with Cilantro and Peanuts

This Thai-inspired vegetable slaw has a crisp and crunchy texture when served right away. The leftovers make a great addition to baked tofu sandwiches.

Yield: 6 servings
Prep time: 10 to 15 minutes
Serving size: 1½ cups

4 leaves rainbow Swiss chard, coarsely chopped

3 cups savoy cabbage, shredded

1½ cups green cabbage, shredded

1 cup carrot, shredded

1 red bell pepper, ribs and seeds removed, and diced

2 green onions, thinly sliced

½ cup chopped fresh cilantro

2 TB. toasted sesame oil

2 TB. tamari

4 tsp. freshly squeezed lime juice

½ tsp. crushed red pepper flakes

¼ tsp. sea salt

⅛ tsp. freshly ground black pepper

⅓ cup roasted peanuts, coarsely chopped

1. In a large bowl, combine Swiss chard, savoy cabbage, green cabbage, carrot, red bell pepper, green onions, and cilantro.

2. For dressing, in a small bowl, whisk together toasted sesame oil, tamari, lime juice, red pepper flakes, salt, and black pepper.

3. Drizzle dressing over slaw, and toss gently until evenly coated. Sprinkle peanuts over slaw, and toss again.

Variation: You can also add cubes of baked or fried tofu or tempeh to the slaw, as well as combine it with cooked soba noodles or spaghetti for a one-plate meal.

Thyme-ly Tip _____

To achieve the proper crunchy texture for this vegetable slaw, you must use savoy cabbage. Savoy cabbage's beautiful crinkled leaves help it take hold of dressings and sauces and also retain their shape and texture in raw and cooked dishes better than the average green cabbage.

Sweet Red Cabbage, Apple, and Cranberry Slaw

This colorful slaw can be served as an alternative to the typical deli-style coleslaw at summer picnics, as well as in the autumn and winter months when the flavors of cranberries and pecans are most appreciated.

6 cups red cabbage, shredded

1 large Granny Smith apple, diced

1 large Gala or Fuji apple, diced

⅓ cup dried cranberries

⅓ cup raw pecans, coarsely chopped

¼ cup chopped fresh parsley

1 (6-oz.) pkg. plain or vanilla soy yogurt

½ cup Tofu Mayonnaise (recipe earlier in this chapter, preferably silken tofu variation)

1 TB. apple cider vinegar

1 TB. maple syrup or agave nectar

¼ tsp. ground cinnamon

¼ tsp. ground ginger

¼ tsp. sea salt

⅛ tsp. freshly ground black pepper

Yield: 6 servings
Prep time: 8 to 10 minutes
Serving size: 1 cup

1. In a large bowl, combine red cabbage, Granny Smith apple, Gala apple, dried cranberries, pecans, and parsley.

2. For dressing, in a small bowl, combine soy yogurt, Tofu Mayonnaise, vinegar, maple syrup, cinnamon, ginger, salt, and black pepper.

3. Pour dressing over slaw, and stir well until evenly coated. Chill in the refrigerator for 30 minutes or more to allow the flavors to blend before serving.

Variation: If you prefer a lighter slaw dressing, substitute No-Fat Raspberry–Poppy Seed Dressing (recipe earlier in this chapter).

 Sour Grapes

Most conventionally grown apple orchards are routinely sprayed with organophospate pesticides, and residue from one or more pesticides was found on more than 90 percent of conventionally grown apples tested by the Environmental Working Group. Avoid them by choosing organically grown apples.

Chapter **13**

More Sensational Salads

In This Chapter

- ◆ Fast and easy raw salad creations
- ◆ Pasta salads for any occasion
- ◆ Colorful cooked grain-, bean-, and potato-based salads

By now, you've cast aside bottled salad dressings in favor of your own homemade versions and mastered the art of tossing leafy greens. Now let's delve deeper into salad-making, because when it comes to cooking, vegans like to think outside the box—or in this case, past the lettuce.

Yes, we love our greens, which supply us with a wide range of vitamins (B, C, E, and K) and minerals (iron, calcium, etc.), and even protein, but so many other vegetable families are out there for us to embrace to round out our vegan diet and fill up our plate. Roots like beets and carrots, terrific tubers such as Yukon Gold potatoes, tomatoes and cucumbers that creep on vines, sweet and spicy peppers for color and flavor, and lest we forget, those that often bring a tear to our eyes, the round and thin onions—all these vegetable-based ingredients, and much more, are featured in the sensational salad recipes in this chapter.

As more and more of us are learning, it's best to eat as much of our foods raw and uncooked whenever possible, as cooking often destroys many of foods' vital nutrients and naturally occurring "live" enzymes. Also, diets containing higher amounts of fruits and vegetables reduce risks for many chronic diseases such as heart disease, diabetes, and cancer. So the salads in this chapter contain many raw vegetables, fruits, and fresh herbs as ingredients, which provide a nice, fresh flavor and also a slight crunch to the recipes.

Vegans are sometimes at a disadvantage in terms of food options at potlucks and picnics, as most Americans add animal-based products to nearly every salad they prepare. This chapter is loaded with recipes perfect for potlucks and other get-togethers. You are sure to wow friends and family with any of the cooked salad selections in this chapter.

Autumn Pear and Apple Waldorf

This classic American favorite is usually made with apples, celery, and walnuts combined with a mayonnaise dressing, but this lighter version also features pears, raisins, currants, and a spiced pear dressing.

1 large Bartlett pear or other pear of choice, peeled and diced	**2 large golden delicious apples, cut into ½-in. cubes**
⅓ cup water	**2 large Gala or Fuji apples, cut into ½-in. cubes**
⅓ cup olive oil	**2 TB. freshly squeezed lemon juice**
3 TB. apple cider vinegar	
3 TB. fresh ginger, minced	**1 cup celery, diced**
½ tsp. ground cardamom	**½ cup raw walnuts, coarsely chopped**
¼ tsp. sea salt	**¼ cup raisins**
2 large Bartlett pears or other pear of choice, cut into ½-in. cubes	**¼ cup dried currants**
	¼ cup chopped fresh parsley

> *Yield: 6 servings*
>
> **Prep time:** 10 to 15 minutes
>
> **Serving size:** 1 cup

1. For dressing, place diced pear, water, olive oil, vinegar, ginger, cardamom, and salt in a food processor fitted with an S blade or a blender, and process for 1 or 2 minutes or until completely smooth. Scrape down the sides of the container with a rubber spatula and process for 15 more seconds.

2. In a large bowl, place cubed pears, golden delicious apples, and Gala apples. Drizzle lemon juice over the top, and toss gently to evenly coat to prevent discoloration. Add celery, walnuts, raisins, currants, and parsley, and stir well to combine.

3. Pour dressing over mixture, and stir well until evenly coated. Chill in the refrigerator for 30 minutes or more to allow the flavors to blend before serving.

Variation: For a classic Waldorf salad, replace the dressing with Tofu Mayonnaise (see Chapter 12, preferably the silken tofu variation).

> **Soy What?**
>
> Waldorf salad is named after the Waldorf-Astoria Hotel in New York. It was created for the hotel's private preopening party on March 13, 1893, by maître d'hôtel Oscar Michel Tschirky. The recipe was first shared with the public in 1896, and it consisted of just apples, celery, and mayonnaise.

Sweet Beet Salad

Raw beets are deliciously sweet, and after sampling this raw beet and fruit salad, you're sure to become a certified beet lover.

Yield: 4 servings
Prep time: 8 to 10 minutes
Serving size: 1 cup

1½ lb. red beets, peeled and shredded

3 large Gala or Fuji apples, peeled and shredded

2 oranges, peeled and cut into segments

⅓ cup green onions, thinly sliced

¼ cup chopped fresh parsley

1 TB. fresh ginger, minced

1 TB. water

1 TB. olive oil

1 TB. apple cider vinegar

¾ tsp. ground cinnamon

¾ tsp. sea salt

½ tsp. freshly ground black pepper

Sour Grapes

Beet juice can stain your hands, your clothes, and your kitchen. Try making this salad in a food processor fitted with a shredding disc to avoid messes.

1. In a medium bowl, combine beets and apples. Add oranges, green onions, and parsley, and toss gently to combine.

2. For dressing, in a small bowl, whisk together ginger, water, olive oil, vinegar, cinnamon, salt, and black pepper.

3. Pour dressing over beet mixture, and stir well until evenly coated. Serve immediately.

Variation: You can replace the apples with 3 large shredded carrots. Feel free to serve this salad on top of mixed greens or cooked grains.

Mediterranean Pasta Salad

A slightly cheesy, herb-flavored vinaigrette provides a slight tang to this pasta salad made with Mediterranean-inspired ingredients like artichoke hearts, zucchini, tomatoes, and kalamata olives.

8 oz. *rotini* or other shaped pasta of choice

1 cup canned garbanzo beans, drained and rinsed

¾ cup artichoke hearts packed in water, drained and cut into quarters

¾ cup zucchini, cut into quarters lengthwise and thinly sliced

½ cup cherry tomatoes, cut into quarters

½ cup red onion, diced

¼ cup kalamata olives or other black olives, pitted and coarsely chopped

¼ cup chopped fresh parsley

3 TB. red wine vinegar

3 TB. olive oil

1 TB. nutritional yeast flakes

2 tsp. garlic, minced

2 tsp. Dijon mustard

¾ tsp. dried basil

¾ tsp. dried oregano

½ tsp. crushed red pepper flakes

½ tsp. sea salt

¼ tsp. freshly ground black pepper

Yield: 6 servings
Prep time: 10 to 15 minutes
Cook time: 8 to 18 minutes (depending on pasta)
Serving size: 1½ cups

1. Fill a large saucepan ⅔ full of water, and bring to a boil over medium-high heat. Add rotini and cook, stirring occasionally, according to package directions or until just tender. Drain pasta in a colander, rinse with cold water, and drain well again.

2. Transfer pasta to a large bowl. Add garbanzo beans, artichoke hearts, zucchini, cherry tomatoes, red onion, olives, and parsley, and toss gently to combine.

3. For dressing, in a small bowl, whisk together vinegar, olive oil, nutritional yeast flakes, garlic, mustard, basil, oregano, red pepper flakes, salt, and black pepper.

4. Pour dressing over salad mixture, and toss gently to combine. Serve immediately or chill in the refrigerator for 30 minutes or more to allow the flavors to blend. Serve alone or on mixed greens.

Variation: For an Italian antipasto-style pasta salad, also add ⅓ cup vegan mozzarella cheese cut into ¼-inch cubes; ¼ cup vegetarian pepperoni or salami, coarsely chopped; and ¼ cup jarred pepperoncinis, thinly sliced.

def•i•ni•tion

Rotini is a twisted, spiral-shape pasta that's great for making cold pasta salads, hot pasta dishes, and casseroles. Its shape helps hold on to dressings, sauces, chopped vegetables, and vegan cheeses.

High-Five Bean Salad

This salad is made with an assortment of canned beans, crunchy raw green beans, and other vegetables, all tossed together in a tangy vinaigrette.

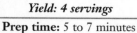

Yield: 4 servings
Prep time: 5 to 7 minutes
Serving size: 1 cup

1 (15-oz.) can mixed salad beans (kidney beans, pinto beans, and garbanzo beans), drained and rinsed

8 oz. fresh green beans, cut into 1½-in. pieces

1 cup canned black-eyed peas, drained and rinsed

½ cup red onion, diced

½ cup celery, diced

½ cup red bell pepper, ribs and seeds removed, and diced

¼ cup chopped fresh parsley

2 TB. red wine vinegar

2 TB. olive oil

½ tsp. dried basil

½ tsp. dried oregano

½ tsp. garlic powder

½ tsp. sea salt

¼ tsp. freshly ground black pepper

Thyme-ly Tip

Make this salad even more colorful and hearty by adding 8 ounces each cut yellow wax beans, 1 cup shelled edamame or lima beans, and 1 finely diced jalapeño pepper to the vegetable mixture.

1. In a medium bowl, combine mixed salad beans, green beans, black-eyed peas, red onion, celery, red bell pepper, and parsley.

2. For dressing, in a small bowl, whisk together vinegar, olive oil, basil, oregano, garlic powder, salt, and black pepper.

3. Pour dressing over bean mixture, and stir well to combine. Serve immediately or chill in the refrigerator for 30 minutes or more to allow the flavors to blend. Serve alone, on mixed greens, or combine with cooked pasta or grains.

Variation: Vary the flavor and color of this salad by substituting other canned bean varieties, such as black beans, white or black soybeans, butter beans, or navy beans, and also adding 2 diced plum tomatoes or 1 large tomato.

Tabouli

This classic Middle Eastern dish made with bulgur and chopped vegetables has a fresh, herb flavor due to the generous addition of fresh parsley and mint, as well as a slight tang, thanks to the lemon zest and juice.

1 cup water

1 cup *bulgur*

Juice and zest of 1 lemon

2 TB. olive oil

2 TB. garlic, minced

½ tsp. ground cumin

½ tsp. sea salt

¼ tsp. freshly ground black pepper

2 large tomatoes, seeds removed, and diced

½ cup green onions, thinly sliced

½ cup chopped fresh parsley

¼ cup chopped fresh mint

Yield: 4 servings
Prep time: 8 to 10 minutes, plus 25 minutes for rehydrating bulgur and 30 minutes for chilling
Cook time: 1 or 2 minutes
Serving size: 1 cup

1. Place water in a small saucepan, and bring to a boil over medium heat.

2. In a medium bowl, place bulgur, lemon juice, lemon zest, olive oil, garlic, cumin, salt, and black pepper. Pour boiling water over bulgur mixture, and stir well to combine. Cover and set aside for 25 to 30 minutes or until all of liquid is absorbed and bulgur is tender. Fluff bulgur with a fork, and set aside to cool for 15 minutes.

3. Add tomatoes, green onions, parsley, and mint, and stir gently to combine.

4. Chill in the refrigerator for 30 minutes or more to allow the flavors to blend. Stir gently again before serving. Serve plain, on top of mixed greens, or use as a filling for pita bread with lettuce and/or Roasted Red Pepper Hummus (recipe in Chapter 7).

Variation: For an even more vibrant green color and herb flavor, use 1 cup sliced green onions, 1 cup chopped parsley (preferably Italian parsley), and ½ cup chopped mint.

def•i•ni•tion

Bulgur is made from steamed or parboiled wheat berries that are then dried and crushed or cracked into small, coarse pieces.

Deli-Style Macaroni Salad

With a little help from our Creamy Agave Dijon Dressing, you can create your own vegan version of the creamy macaroni salad commonly found in most grocery stores and corner delis.

Yield: 6 servings
Prep time: 10 to 15 minutes
Cook time: 8 to 18 minutes (depending on pasta)
Serving size: 1 cup

8 oz. elbow macaroni or other shaped pasta of choice

¾ cup celery, diced

¾ cup red bell pepper, ribs and seeds removed, and diced

½ cup carrot, shredded

½ cup green onions, thinly sliced

¼ cup chopped fresh parsley

1 cup Creamy Agave Dijon Dressing (recipe in Chapter 12)

½ tsp. celery seed

¼ tsp. sea salt

¼ tsp. freshly ground black pepper

Thyme-ly Tip

To help your cooking liquids reach a boil more quickly, cover your saucepan or pot with a lid. This helps trap in the escaping steam and heat, which helps reach the boiling point at a much faster rate.

1. Fill a large saucepan ⅔ full of water, and bring to a boil over medium-high heat. Add macaroni and cook, stirring occasionally, according to package directions or until just tender. Drain pasta in a colander, rinse with cold water, and drain well again.

2. Transfer pasta to a large bowl. Add celery, red bell pepper, carrot, green onions, and parsley, and stir gently to combine.

3. In a small bowl, stir together Creamy Agave Dijon Dressing, celery seed, salt, and black pepper.

4. Pour dressing mixture over pasta mixture, and stir gently until evenly coated. Serve immediately or chill in the refrigerator for 30 minutes or more to allow the flavors to blend.

Variation: For a milder-flavored macaroni salad, replace the Creamy Agave Dijon Dressing with Tofu Mayonnaise (recipe in Chapter 12), add 1 tablespoon each apple cider vinegar and yellow mustard, and season with salt and black pepper.

French Potato Salad

Here, buttery flavored Yukon Gold potatoes are tossed with green onions, fresh herbs, and a simple vinaigrette featuring tarragon, Dijon mustard, and white wine vinegar, and served warm or at room temperature.

3 lb. Yukon Gold potatoes, cut into quarters lengthwise and thinly sliced

3 TB. water or vegetable broth

3 TB. olive oil

2 TB. white wine vinegar

1 TB. Dijon mustard

1 tsp. dried tarragon

¾ tsp. sea salt

¼ tsp. freshly ground black pepper

½ cup green onions, thinly sliced

¼ cup chopped fresh parsley

2 TB. chopped fresh dill

Yield: 6 servings
Prep time: 10 to 15 minutes
Cook time: 8 to 10 minutes
Serving size: 1 cup

1. Place potatoes in a large pot, cover with water, and cook over medium heat for 8 to 10 minutes or until potatoes are just tender and can be pierced easily with a knife. Drain potatoes in a colander, rinse with cold water, and drain well again. Transfer potatoes to a large bowl.

2. For dressing, in a small bowl, whisk together water, olive oil, vinegar, Dijon mustard, tarragon, salt, and black pepper.

3. Pour dressing over warm potatoes, and stir gently until evenly coated. Add green onions, parsley, and dill, and toss gently to combine. Serve immediately or set aside for 15 minutes or more to allow the flavors to blend.

Variation: Fingerling potatoes also work well in this salad, but cook them whole and then cut them into ½-inch-thick slices.

Thyme-ly Tip

To adapt this recipe to make a classic mayonnaise-based potato salad, cut potatoes of choice into cubes, cook, and cool completely. In addition to the green onions, parsley, and dill, add 1 cup diced celery, ½ cup diced red onion, and either 1 cup Tofu Mayonnaise or Creamy Agave Dijon Dressing (recipes in Chapter 12). Stir well to combine, and season to taste.

Thai Cucumbers

The flavors of Thailand are well represented in this spicy salad made with cucumber, red bell pepper, jalapeño pepper, and cilantro, which goes nicely with Cold Sesame Noodles (see recipe later in this chapter), curries, and other spicy dishes.

Yield: 4 servings
Prep time: 8 to 10 minutes
Serving size: 1 cup

1 English cucumber or 2 medium cucumbers, thinly sliced

½ cup red bell pepper, ribs and seeds removed, and finely diced

1 jalapeño pepper, ribs and seeds removed, and finely diced

¼ cup green onions, thinly sliced

¼ cup chopped fresh cilantro

1 TB. raw sesame seeds

4 tsp. toasted sesame oil

1 TB. tamari

1 TB. freshly squeezed lime juice

2 tsp. brown rice vinegar

2 tsp. garlic, minced

2 tsp. fresh ginger, minced

½ tsp. crushed red pepper flakes

¼ tsp. sea salt

⅛ tsp. freshly ground black pepper

1. In a medium bowl, combine cucumber, red bell pepper, jalapeño pepper, green onions, cilantro, and sesame seeds.

2. For dressing, in a small bowl, whisk together toasted sesame oil, tamari, lime juice, vinegar, garlic, ginger, red pepper flakes, salt, and black pepper.

3. Pour dressing over cucumber mixture, and stir gently until evenly coated. Serve immediately or set aside for 15 minutes or more to allow the flavors to blend.

Variation: For an all-raw-ingredient version, replace the toasted sesame oil with raw sesame oil, the tamari with Bragg Liquid Aminos, and the brown rice vinegar with apple cider vinegar.

Thyme-ly Tip

For an easy yet refreshing cold cucumber salad, combine 1 thinly sliced English cucumber (or 2 medium cucumbers), 2 tablespoons chopped mint or dill, 2 tablespoons chopped parsley, the juice and zest of ½ a lemon, and 1 tablespoon olive oil. Season with salt and black pepper.

Cold Sesame Noodles

These Asian-style noodles covered in a sweet, salty, and spicy sesame-flavored sauce will tantalize your taste buds, so grab a pair of chopsticks or a fork, and dig right in!

8 oz. udon noodles, soba noodles, or spaghetti	2 tsp. fresh ginger, minced
2 TB. tamari	1½ tsp. turbinado sugar
4 tsp. raw tahini	½ tsp. crushed red pepper flakes
4 tsp. toasted sesame oil	⅓ cup green onions, thinly sliced
1 TB. brown rice vinegar	⅓ cup chopped fresh cilantro
2 tsp. garlic, minced	2 TB. raw sesame seeds

> **Yield: 4 servings**
>
> **Prep time:** 5 to 7 minutes
>
> **Cook time:** 8 to 18 minutes (depending on pasta)
>
> **Serving size:** 1 cup

1. Fill a large saucepan ²⁄₃ full of water and bring to a boil over medium-high heat. Add noodles and cook, stirring occasionally, according to package directions or until just tender. Drain pasta in a colander, rinse with cold water, and drain well again. Transfer pasta to a large bowl.

2. For dressing, in a small bowl, whisk together tamari, tahini, toasted sesame oil, vinegar, garlic, ginger, sugar, and red pepper flakes.

3. Pour dressing over pasta, and stir gently until evenly coated. Add green onions, cilantro, and sesame seeds, and toss gently to combine. Serve immediately or set aside for 15 minutes or more to allow the flavors to blend.

Variation: For a spicier flavor, replace 1 teaspoon toasted sesame oil with hot pepper sesame oil or chili oil. Vary the flavor of the noodles by replacing the tahini with 2 tablespoons peanut butter or other nut butter of choice.

Soy What?

Soba and udon noodles are available made from wheat and other grains and flavored varieties such as buckwheat, brown and white rice, kamut, spelt, green tea, lotus root, mugwort, and wild yam, just to name a few. You can find soba and udon noodles in most grocery and natural foods stores. Check out Asian specialty markets for a larger selection.

Chapter 14

Satisfying Sandwiches

In This Chapter

- ◆ Vegan versions of your favorite deli sandwiches
- ◆ Soy-based sandwich ingredient alternatives
- ◆ Meatless burgers, sloppy joes, and BLTs

There's something so satisfying about wrapping your hands around a sandwich and sinking your teeth into a large mouthful of whole-grain and veggie goodness. In this chapter, we provide you with tasty recipes to expand your vegan sandwich-making skills. Whether you're in the mood for a hot or cold sandwich, something made with tofu or tempeh, or you're hankering for a totally soy-free meatless burger made just the way you like it, we've got you covered.

If these don't satisfy your cravings, several other hot vegan sandwich options await you in the upcoming pages, so grab some bread and let's make some sandwiches!

Veggie and Tofu Cream Cheese Wraps

These colorful wraps are bursting with fresh lettuce, tomatoes, and sprouts, and they also feature a creamy spread made with lightly seasoned tofu cream cheese, carrot, and red pepper.

Yield: 4 servings
Prep time: 10 to 15 minutes
Serving size: 1 wrap

½ cup (4-oz.) tofu cream cheese

2 TB. soy milk or other nondairy milk of choice

½ tsp. nutritional yeast flakes

¼ tsp. dried basil

⅛ tsp. sea salt

⅛ tsp. freshly ground black pepper

¼ cup carrot, shredded

¼ cup red bell pepper, ribs and seeds removed, and finely diced

1 green onion, thinly sliced

4 (8-in.) flour tortillas of choice

4 leaves leaf lettuce or other lettuce of choice

2 plum tomatoes, thinly sliced

1 cup alfalfa sprouts or other fresh sprouts of choice

Thyme-ly Tip

Use these wrap ingredients to create tortilla pinwheels. Spread cream cheese mixture thinly over the entire surface of 4 (8-inch) tortillas. Apply a thin layer of baby spinach and chopped tomatoes over spread, leaving a 2-inch border on one side. Beginning at filling side, tightly roll tortilla, ending with seam side down. Cut into 1- or 2-inch slices as desired.

1. For cream cheese spread, in a small bowl, combine tofu cream cheese, soy milk, nutritional yeast flakes, basil, salt, and black pepper. Add carrot, red bell pepper, and green onion, and stir well to combine.

2. For easier rolling, warm each tortilla in a large skillet over medium heat for 1 or 2 minutes per side, or warm in a microwave oven for 20 to 30 seconds.

3. To assemble, place 1 tortilla flat on a large cutting board or work surface. Spread ¼ of cream cheese spread over the top half of tortilla, leaving a 1-inch border around the edges. Place 1 lettuce leaf vertically in the center of tortilla so it hangs slightly over top edge. Place ¼ of tomato slices and sprouts on top of lettuce.

4. Fold the bottom of tortilla up to the center, and then fold in each side, one overlapping the other, to enclose vegetables. Secure wrap with a toothpick, threading it through both sides. Serve immediately, or wrap tightly in plastic wrap or place in an airtight container. Stored in the refrigerator, wraps will keep for 2 or 3 days.

Variation: You could also simply spread 2 tablespoons plain tofu cream cheese on tortillas and then layer lettuce, tomatoes, shredded carrots, and sprouts, and roll into wraps as suggested. Also, you can replace the cream cheese spread with Roasted Red Pepper Hummus (recipe in Chapter 7) or your favorite mashed bean spread, or with a little mustard or Tofu Mayonnaise (recipe in Chapter 12).

Tofuna Salad Sandwiches

Previously frozen and thawed tofu is combined with celery, green onions, and our Tofu Mayonnaise to make a veganized version of tuna salad—or "tofuna," as we call it.

8 oz. firm or extra-firm tofu

1 TB. tamari

1½ tsp. freshly squeezed lemon juice

½ tsp. kelp powder

½ cup Tofu Mayonnaise (recipe in Chapter 12)

¼ cup celery, finely diced

2 TB. green onions, thinly sliced

2 TB. chopped fresh parsley

8 slices whole-grain bread of choice

4 leaves leaf lettuce or other lettuce of choice

1 large tomato or 2 plum tomatoes, cut into 4 slices (optional)

Yield: 4 servings
Prep time: 10 to 15 minutes, plus 3 days for freezing and thawing tofu
Serving size: 1 sandwich

Thyme-ly Tip

Freezing tofu changes its texture dramatically, making it firmer and chewier. Freeze whole blocks or partial blocks of tofu in an airtight container or zipper-lock bag. Thaw tofu in the refrigerator overnight, or submerge it in water for 20 minutes or longer, as needed. Be sure to squeeze out the excess moisture prior to using.

1. For tofuna, freeze tofu in an airtight container for at least 2 days and then thaw tofu overnight in the refrigerator. Squeeze tofu block over the sink to remove excess water.

2. Crumble thawed tofu into a medium bowl using your fingers. Add tamari, lemon juice, and kelp powder, and stir well to combine. Add Tofu Mayonnaise, celery, green onions, and parsley, and stir well to combine.

3. Place 4 bread slices on a work surface, and top each with 1 lettuce leaf. Spread ¼ of tofuna mixture on top of lettuce. Place 1 tomato slice (or 2 slices of plum tomato, if using) on tofuna, and then place remaining 4 slices of bread on top. Slice each sandwich in half and serve.

Variation: If desired, toast the whole-grain bread prior to assembling the sandwiches. You can also make tofuna sandwiches using split pita breads, or roll it up in a tortilla for a tasty wrap.

VBLT Sandwiches

Our Tempeh Un-Bacon tastes delicious alongside pancakes, but it can also be used to make an awesome vegan bacon, lettuce, and tomato sandwich, or as we like to call it, a "VBLT."

Yield: 2 sandwiches
Prep time: 5 to 7 minutes
Cook time: 2 or 3 minutes
Serving size: 1 sandwich

6 slices Tempeh Un-Bacon (recipe in Chapter 4)

4 slices whole-grain bread of choice

2 to 4 TB. Tofu Mayonnaise (recipe in Chapter 12)

4 leaves leaf lettuce or other lettuce of choice

1 large tomato or 2 plum tomatoes, cut into 4 slices

1. Reheat Tempeh Un-Bacon in a small nonstick skillet over medium heat for 1 or 2 minutes per side or until heated through; or reheat in the microwave for 30 to 45 seconds.

2. Meanwhile, toast slices of bread and place them on a work surface. Spread Tofu Mayonnaise on each slice of bread. Top 2 slices of bread with 1 lettuce leaf, 3 slices Tempeh Un-Bacon, and 2 tomato slices (or 4 slices of plum tomato). Top with remaining slices of bread. Slice each sandwich in half and serve.

Variation: You can replace the Tempeh Un-Bacon with slices of prepackaged vegetarian Canadian bacon or fake bacon, cooked according to package instructions.

Soy What?

Tempeh, unfermented soybean cakes, originated in Indonesia, where it was developed as an inexpensive, high-protein meat alternative. Although amounts vary from brand to brand, tempeh is a good source of vitamin B_{12}, which is also found in other fermented foods, sea vegetables, and nutritional yeast.

Tempeh Reubens

You'll think you're in a vegan deli after sampling one of these tempeh reubens made with seasoned and sautéed sauerkraut, vegan cheese, and a tangy homemade Russian dressing.

½ cup Tofu Mayonnaise (recipe in Chapter 12)

2 TB. ketchup

1 TB. prepared horseradish

1 TB. onion, grated

1 TB. chopped fresh parsley

½ tsp. chili powder

½ tsp. garlic powder

¼ tsp. tamari or vegetarian Worcestershire sauce

¼ cup onion, finely diced

1½ tsp. plus 1 TB. olive oil

1 cup sauerkraut, drained

¼ tsp. caraway seeds

1 (8-oz.) pkg. tempeh

1 TB. tamari

1 TB. water

4 slices vegan cheese of choice

8 slices rye bread or whole-grain bread of choice

Yield: 4 sandwiches
Prep time: 20 to 25 minutes
Cook time: 10 to 15 minutes
Serving size: 1 sandwich

1. For Russian dressing, in a small bowl, combine Tofu Mayonnaise, ketchup, horseradish, grated onion, parsley, chili powder, garlic powder, and ¼ teaspoon tamari. Chill in the refrigerator while preparing remaining ingredients.

2. Place diced onion and 1½ teaspoons olive oil in a large nonstick skillet over medium heat, and sauté onion, stirring often, for 2 or 3 minutes or until soft. Add sauerkraut and caraway seeds, and sauté for 2 or 3 more minutes or until dry and slightly browned. Transfer sauerkraut to a small plate and set aside.

3. Rinse and dry skillet. Cut tempeh block into quarters lengthwise and slice each piece horizontally to yield 8 pieces. Place tempeh pieces and 1½ teaspoons olive oil in skillet over medium heat, and cook for 3 or 4 minutes or until golden brown. Flip over tempeh pieces with a spatula, add remaining 1½ teaspoons olive oil, and cook for 2 or 3 more minutes or until golden brown.

4. Add 1 tablespoon tamari and water, flip over tempeh pieces to evenly coat, and cook for 1 or 2 minutes or until liquid is absorbed.

Thyme-ly Tip

For vegan Thousand Island dressing: in a small bowl, combine ½ cup Tofu Mayonnaise; 2 tablespoons each of ketchup, water, and finely diced green or red bell pepper; 1 tablespoon each freshly squeezed lemon juice, chopped fresh parsley, pickle relish, and grated onion; 1 minced garlic clove; and 1 pinch cayenne.

5. Group tempeh pieces into pairs, place 1 slice of vegan cheese on top of each pair, and remove the skillet from heat.

6. Toast slices of bread, and place them on a work surface. Spread Russian dressing on each slice of bread. Top 4 bread slices with cheese-covered tempeh pairs, and top tempeh with sauerkraut mixture, dividing it evenly among sandwiches. Top with remaining slices of bread. Slice each sandwich in half and serve.

Variation: For an easier version, replace the tempeh with a few vegetarian deli-style meat slices of choice or slices of avocado, use plain drained sauerkraut (skip cooking step altogether), and also add tomato slices to the reubens.

Sloppy No's

Sloppy joe sandwiches are a classic American comfort food that can be enjoyed as a messy and tasty treat any time, and we affectionately call our vegan version made with pinto beans Sloppy No's because they contain no ground meat.

Yield: 6 sandwiches
Prep time: 5 to 7 minutes
Cook time: 10 to 12 minutes
Serving size: 1 sandwich

¾ cup onion, diced

¾ cup green bell pepper, ribs and seeds removed, and diced

2 tsp. olive oil

1 jalapeño pepper, ribs and seeds removed, and finely diced

1 TB. garlic, minced

1 TB. chili powder

1½ tsp. dried basil

1 tsp. dried oregano

½ tsp. sea salt

¼ tsp. freshly ground black pepper

¼ tsp. cayenne

1 (6-oz.) can tomato paste

⅓ cup water

1 (15-oz.) can pinto beans, drained and rinsed

2 TB. wheat bran or oat bran

1 TB. nutritional yeast flakes (optional)

2 tsp. tamari or Bragg Liquid Aminos

2 tsp. *blackstrap molasses*

6 whole-grain hamburger buns or rolls, split

1. Place onion, green bell pepper, and olive oil in a large nonstick skillet over medium heat and sauté, stirring often, for 3 or 4 minutes or until soft. Add jalapeño pepper, garlic, chili powder, basil, oregano, salt, black pepper, and cayenne, and sauté for 2 more minutes.

2. Add tomato paste and water to the skillet, and stir well to combine.

3. Place pinto beans in a small bowl, and roughly mash with a fork or potato masher. Add pinto beans, wheat bran, nutritional yeast flakes (if using), tamari, and molasses to the skillet, and stir well to combine. Reduce heat to low, and simmer, stirring often, for 5 minutes or until slightly thickened. Remove from heat. Divide mixture evenly among buns, and serve hot.

Variation: These sandwiches also taste delicious topped with slices of vegan cheese or pickle slices. You can also use this mixture as a filling for tortillas or as a topping for cooked grains, pasta, or pieces of Tex-Mex Cornbread (recipe in Chapter 20).

def•i•ni•tion

Blackstrap molasses is one of several varieties of molasses, the dark, thick syrup with a bittersweet flavor that results from the production of sugar. Blackstrap molasses is also quite nutritious compared to other sweeteners, as it contains B vitamins and minerals such as calcium, magnesium, potassium, iron, copper, and manganese.

Filet-o-Tofu Sandwiches

Tofu and kelp powder team up to create a faux fish-flavored dish, this time a breaded and baked tofu filet sandwich. These vegan sandwiches can hold their own against similar sandwiches commonly sold in fish houses and fast-food restaurants.

Yield: 4 sandwiches
Prep time: 15 to 20 minutes, plus 20 minutes for pressing tofu
Cook time: 30 minutes
Serving size: 1 sandwich

1 lb. firm or extra-firm tofu

½ cup soy milk or other nondairy milk of choice

1 tsp. tamari

1¾ tsp. freshly squeezed lemon juice

¼ tsp. plus ½ tsp. kelp powder

¼ cup whole-wheat pastry flour or brown rice flour

⅓ cup cornmeal

⅓ cup rice breadcrumbs or dry breadcrumbs

1 TB. nutritional yeast flakes

½ tsp. garlic powder

½ tsp. onion powder

½ tsp. paprika

¼ tsp. sea salt

¼ tsp. freshly ground black pepper

½ cup Tofu Mayonnaise (recipe in Chapter 12)

3 TB. pickle relish

4 whole-grain hamburger buns or 8 slices whole-grain bread of choice

4 leaves leaf lettuce or other lettuce of choice

4 slices vegan cheddar cheese

1. Squeeze tofu block over the sink to remove excess water. Place tofu in a colander in the sink, cover with a plate, place a 28-ounce can on top of the plate, and leave tofu to press for 20 minutes.

2. Meanwhile, in a small bowl, combine soy milk, tamari, 1 teaspoon lemon juice, and ¹/₄ teaspoon kelp powder. Set aside for 10 minutes to thicken.

3. Place flour on a small plate and set aside.

4. On a large plate, combine cornmeal, breadcrumbs, nutritional yeast flakes, remaining ¹/₂ teaspoon kelp powder, garlic powder, onion powder, paprika, salt, and ¹/₈ teaspoon black pepper.

5. Preheat the oven to 400°F. Lightly oil a large cookie sheet.

6. Cut pressed tofu block vertically into 4 pieces. Working with 1 tofu piece at a time, place tofu into flour, flip over to evenly coat on all sides, and place tofu on a large plate. Stir any remaining flour into cornmeal mixture.

7. Dip each tofu piece into soy milk mixture and then into cornmeal mixture, pressing down slightly and flipping over, as needed, to evenly coat piece on all sides. Place coated pieces on prepared cookie sheet.

8. Bake for 15 minutes. Remove from the oven and flip over tofu with a spatula. Bake for 10 to 15 more minutes or until golden brown and crisp around the edges.

9. Meanwhile, for tartar sauce, in a small bowl, combine Tofu Mayonnaise, pickle relish, remaining $3/4$ teaspoon lemon juice, and remaining $1/8$ teaspoon black pepper. Chill in the refrigerator while preparing remaining ingredients.

10. To assemble sandwiches, place open hamburger buns on a work surface. Spread tartar sauce on each hamburger bun. Top bottom half of each hamburger bun with 1 lettuce leaf, 1 tofu fillet, and 1 slice vegan cheese. Top with hamburger bun tops, and serve hot.

Variation: Alternatively, cook tofu filets in a little olive oil in a large nonstick skillet for 2 or 3 minutes per side or until golden brown and crispy. Or for a mock chicken fillet sandwich, omit the kelp powder from the soy milk mixture and the cornmeal mixture, and serve the baked tofu filets with lettuce leaves, tomato slices, and Tofu Mayonnaise (recipe in Chapter 12) instead of the tartar sauce.

Thyme-ly Tip

Pressing tofu by placing a heavy weight on it for 30 minutes or more removes even more water from the tofu, resulting in a denser texture—beneficial when marinating or cooking it in a sauce. You can press tofu in the sink as a whole block in a colander with a plate and weight (large cans work well) on top.

Breaded Eggplant Sandwiches

We use a 5-step breading procedure to cover thick slices of eggplant, and then oven-bake them until golden brown and crispy instead of frying them in oil. The resulting breaded eggplant sandwiches are similar to the po'boy sandwiches commonly served in the South.

Yield: 4 sandwiches
Prep time: 20 to 25 minutes
Cook time: 15 to 20 minutes
Serving size: 1 sandwich

1 cup soy milk or other nondairy milk of choice

2 tsp. Dijon mustard

1 tsp. freshly squeezed lemon juice

1 cup whole-wheat pastry flour or spelt flour

⅓ cup cornmeal

1 TB. nutritional yeast flakes

1½ tsp. Italian seasoning blend or ½ tsp. each dried basil, oregano, and thyme

½ tsp. chili powder

½ tsp. garlic granules or garlic powder

¼ tsp. freshly ground black pepper

1 large eggplant, cut into 8 round slices

4 Italian rolls or hoagie rolls, split, or 8 slices whole-grain bread

Spinach or lettuce leaves, tomato slices, vegan cheese slices, or other toppings of choice

Creamy Agave Dijon Dressing or Tofu Mayonnaise (recipes in Chapter 12), stone ground mustard, or other condiments of choice

1. Preheat oven to 400°F. Line a cookie sheet with parchment paper.

2. In a shallow bowl, combine soy milk, Dijon mustard, and lemon juice. Set aside for 10 minutes to thicken slightly.

3. On a large plate, combine flour, cornmeal, nutritional yeast flakes, Italian seasoning blend, chili powder, garlic granules, and black pepper.

4. To bread eggplant, coat each eggplant slice on both sides with flour mixture and then dip into soy milk mixture. Place eggplant slice back into flour mixture to evenly coat on both sides, dip eggplant into soy milk mixture again, and place eggplant back into flour mixture to evenly coat on both sides one final time. Place breaded eggplant on the prepared cookie sheet. Repeat breading procedure for remaining eggplant.

5. Bake for 15 to 20 minutes or until golden brown and crisp around the edges. Remove cookie sheet from the oven. Serve 2 pieces of breaded eggplant per sandwich on rolls with your choice of toppings and condiments. Serve hot.

Variation: Alternatively, you can cook breaded eggplant slices in a little olive oil in a large nonstick skillet for 3 to 5 minutes per side or until golden brown and crispy. You can also replace the eggplant slices with thick slices of zucchini, yellow summer squash, tomatoes, or whole portobello mushrooms.

Thyme-ly Tip

You can adapt this recipe to make a breaded eggplant Parmesan sandwich. When eggplant is finished baking, group eggplant slices in pairs, top each pair with slices of vegan mozzarella cheese, and heat in the oven until cheese just begins to melt. Place cheese-covered eggplant slices on split Italian rolls, top with your favorite jarred marinara sauce, and serve.

Grain 'n' Garden Burgers

These gluten-free vegan burgers are made with frozen mixed vegetables, kale, sunflower seeds, and supernutritious millet and quinoa. They're oven-baked instead of fried, to give them a light, crisp texture.

Yield: 4 burger sand-wiches
Prep time: 7 to 10 minutes
Cook time: 45 minutes
Serving size: 1 burger sandwich

¼ cup millet

¼ cup quinoa

1½ cups vegetable broth

¾ cup frozen mixed vegetable blend (carrots, green beans, corn, and peas)

2 TB. raw sunflower seeds

¼ cup green onions, thinly sliced

1 TB. garlic, minced

1 leaf kale, stem removed, and finely chopped

1 TB. nutritional yeast flakes

1 TB. tamari or Bragg Liquid Aminos

2 tsp. toasted sesame oil

1 tsp. Italian seasoning blend

½ tsp. sea salt

¼ tsp. freshly ground black pepper

3 TB. cornmeal

2 whole-grain hamburger buns or rolls, split

Lettuce leaves, tomato slices, vegan cheese slices, pickle slices, pickle relish, or toppings of choice

Tofu Mayonnaise (recipe in Chapter 12), mustard, ketchup, or condiments of choice

1. Place millet and quinoa in a fine mesh strainer and rinse well under running water. Transfer millet and quinoa to a medium saucepan over medium heat. Toast millet and quinoa, stirring often, for 2 or 3 minutes or until it begins to "pop" and some is lightly browned.

2. Remove from heat, add vegetable broth, and bring to a boil. Cover, reduce heat to low, and simmer for 20 minutes or until liquid is absorbed. Remove from heat, and set aside for 5 minutes to allow grains to steam.

3. Meanwhile, in a dry, small nonstick skillet over medium heat, cook frozen mixed vegetables, stirring often, for 2 minutes to thaw. Add sunflower seeds, and cook, stirring often, for 2 minutes.

4. Add green onions and garlic, and cook for 1 or 2 minutes or until sunflower seeds are lightly toasted. Add kale, and cook for 1 minute or until it just begins to wilt. Remove from heat.

5. Add nutritional yeast flakes, tamari, toasted sesame oil, Italian seasoning, salt, and black pepper, and stir well to combine. Add cooked vegetables and cornmeal, and stir well to combine.

6. Preheat the oven to 425°F. Line a cookie sheet with parchment paper.

7. Use a $1/2$ cup measuring cup to portion each burger patty by lightly filling and gently packing burger mixture into the cup with the back of a spoon. Flip over patty onto the prepared cookie sheet, and give the cup a tap to release the patty. Repeat with remaining burger mixture to make 4 patties. Using a burger press or your hands, slightly flatten patties.

8. Bake for 15 to 20 minutes or until patties are lightly browned around the edges. Serve burgers on buns with your choice of toppings and condiments. Serve hot.

Variation: Alternatively, you can chill burgers for 15 minutes, and then cook them in a large nonstick skillet with a little olive oil for 2 or 3 minutes per side or until lightly browned. You can also replace the millet and quinoa with 2 cups other cooked grains, such as rice, couscous, or bulgur.

Thyme-ly Tip

Burger presses, which consist of a large ring and hand-grip plunger, result in perfectly shaped, well-compacted patties.

Onion-Mushroom Cheeseburgers

Portobello mushrooms work exceptionally well as meatless substitutes, and one of the best ways to showcase their rich, meaty texture is by marinating them whole and cooking them like burgers, as in this recipe, which tops the juicy caps with browned onions and vegan cheese.

Yield: 2 cheeseburger sandwiches
Prep time: 10 to 12 minutes
Cook time: 8 to 12 minutes
Serving size: 1 cheeseburger sandwich

2 TB. balsamic vinegar

1 TB. tamari

2 TB. olive oil

1 TB. garlic, minced

1 tsp. Italian seasoning blend

2 large portobello mushrooms

⅔ cup onion or red onion, thinly sliced

2 slices vegan cheese of choice

2 whole-grain hamburger buns or rolls, split

Lettuce leaves, tomato slices, pickle slices, pickle relish, or toppings of choice

Tofu Mayonnaise (recipe in Chapter 12), mustard, ketchup, or condiments of choice

1. In a small bowl, combine vinegar, tamari, 1 tablespoon olive oil, garlic, and Italian seasoning.

2. Remove stems from mushrooms. Place mushrooms on a large plate, pour vinegar mixture over top, flip over mushrooms, and set aside for 10 minutes to marinate.

3. Meanwhile, place onion and remaining 1 tablespoon olive oil in a large nonstick skillet over medium heat, and sauté, stirring often, for 3 to 5 minutes or until lightly browned. Remove from heat, transfer onions to a small plate, and set aside.

4. Return the skillet to medium heat. Remove mushrooms from the plate (save marinade), and place in skillet, top side down, and cook for 3 minutes or until mushrooms begin to soften. Flip over mushrooms with a spatula, pour reserved marinade over mushrooms, and cook for 2 or 3 minutes longer or until mushrooms are tender. Place 1 slice vegan cheese on each mushroom and remove from heat.

5. To assemble burgers, place open hamburger buns on a work surface. Dividing evenly among mushrooms, place reserved onions on top of cheese. Serve mushroom cheeseburgers with your choice of toppings and condiments. Serve hot.

Variation: Alternatively, you can use thick slices of onion, cooking them and the mushrooms on a grill or under the broiler until tender. For Asian-inspired mushroom cheeseburgers, marinate and cook mushrooms in 1/4 cup Teriyaki Stir-Frying and Dipping Sauce (recipe in Chapter 8).

Thyme-ly Tip _____

Transform these cheeseburgers from a simple sandwich into a dinner entrée by serving them open-faced on toasted slices of bread along with mashed potatoes. Top both with Crimini Mushroom Gravy or Roasted Garlic and Shallot Gravy (recipes in Chapter 8). Add a side of steamed vegetables or a mixed-green salad to round out your meal.

Part 5

What's for Dinner?

The chapters in Part 5 cover a vast assortment of main entrée dishes and pasta specialties that offer something for everyone and are sure to appeal to many different tastes. You'll also find many interesting side-dish recipes. In the mood for mashed, fried, roasted, or steamed vegetables of all varieties? Looking for new and creative ways to cook up beans and grains? Look no further! Many of these tasty side dishes also work well for holiday meals, themed dinner parties, and other special occasions.

Marvelous Main Dishes

In This Chapter

◆ Getting creative with homemade seitan

◆ Soy-based suppers

◆ Versatile veggies

After a long, hard day in the trenches, you arrive home tired and hungry. Inevitably, you soon find yourself scratching your head and pondering what to have for supper. You open the cabinets, freezer, and refrigerator and tentatively peer in, in the hope that inspiration will strike for a tasty vegan supper concoction.

Sometimes you may be fortunate to have leftovers you can combine with something else to create a wonderful meal. Other times, you're left thinking that it's not worth the effort and maybe you'll just grab some take-out. But you can easily avoid supper setbacks by keeping your pantry well stocked with staples, as well as a few prepackaged items, for making great vegan meals.

In the freezer sections of some grocery stores and most natural foods stores, you can find several vegan meal options such as burritos, enchiladas, casseroles, pot pies, and even full TV-style dinners. In a pinch, you can use these convenient quick-fixes as a starting point for planning your dinner meal. But no matter how hungry or crunched for time you may be, you shouldn't rely on only pre-made foods, because many convenience foods tend to be high in salt, sugar, calories, and fat.

We included a wide assortment of main dish options in this chapter to appeal to a variety of tastes, in the hope of encouraging you to cook more for yourself and to give you some ideas for what to serve on special occasions and holiday celebrations.

Simmered Seitan

Traditional seitan used to take hours to prepare, but using vital wheat gluten greatly speeds up the process. You can enjoy this seitan as a main dish topped with gravy or used in your favorite recipes.

1½ cups *vital wheat gluten*	1¼ cups water
4 tsp. nutritional yeast flakes	2 TB. plus ¼ cup tamari
2 tsp. onion powder	8 cups vegetable stock
1 tsp. garlic powder	1 bay leaf
¼ tsp. freshly ground black pepper	

> *Yield: 1 pound (approximately 4½ cups)*
>
> **Prep time:** 20 to 25 minutes
>
> **Cook time:** 40 to 45 minutes
>
> **Serving size:** ¾ cup

1. In a medium bowl, combine vital wheat gluten, nutritional yeast flakes, onion powder, garlic powder, and black pepper. Add water and 2 tablespoons tamari, and stir well to combine.

2. Transfer mixture to a clean counter or work surface. Using your hands, knead mixture for 3 to 5 minutes or until it forms a smooth and pliable ball of dough. Divide dough into 2 pieces, and roll each into a log. Let dough logs rest for 15 minutes.

3. Place vegetable broth, remaining ¼ cup tamari, and bay leaf in a large pot. Add seitan pieces, partially cover pot, and bring to a boil over medium heat. Cover pot fully, reduce heat to very low, and gently simmer for 40 to 50 minutes or until seitan is very firm to the touch. Do not allow cooking liquid to boil again or it will affect the final texture of seitan.

4. Remove seitan from cooking liquid and allow to cool slightly before using. Thinly slice seitan and top with Crimini Mushroom Gravy or Roasted Garlic and Shallot Gravy (recipes in Chapter 8), or use in sandwiches. Or cut it into cubes or chop it, and add to soups, stews, stir-fries, or your favorite dishes. Serve hot or cold as desired.

def•i•ni•tion

Vital wheat gluten, also known as *instant gluten flour* or just *gluten flour,* is a powdered form of dehydrated pure wheat gluten. It's often mixed with liquids and seasonings and used to make seitan and its many meat analog variations. Find it in bulk bins or prepackaged in most grocery and natural foods stores.

Variation: For a chickenlike-flavored seitan, add 2 tablespoons nutritional yeast to the dry ingredients along with ¾ teaspoon each dried thyme and sage. For a beeflike-flavored seitan, add an additional 1 tablespoon tamari and 2 tablespoons ketchup to the water mixture, and an additional 2 tablespoons tamari and ¼ cup ketchup to the cooking liquid.

Seitan Piccata

The classic piccata recipe is typically made with meat, but in our vegan version, thin slices of Simmered Seitan are lightly coated with flour, fried until crispy, and topped with a tangy wine, lemon, and caper sauce.

Yield: *8 slices*
Prep time: 5 minutes
Cook time: 5 to 7 minutes
Serving size: 2 slices

½ cup whole-wheat pastry flour or spelt flour

1 TB. Raw Parmesan Cheese (recipe in Chapter 9) or vegan soy Parmesan cheese

8 oz. prepared Simmered Seitan (recipe earlier in this chapter)

2 TB. olive oil

⅔ cup vegetable broth

⅓ cup white wine

2 TB. freshly squeezed lemon juice

4 tsp. capers, drained

2 tsp. garlic, minced

2 tsp. nutritional yeast flakes

¼ cup chopped fresh parsley

4 tsp. nonhydrogenated vegan margarine

½ tsp. sea salt

¼ tsp. freshly ground black pepper

Thyme-ly Tip

You can adapt this recipe to make a delicious seitan scaloppine: prepare the seitan in the same manner and set aside. Replace capers and lemon juice with one or more of the following: 1 cup sliced crimini mushrooms; 1 (14-ounce) can diced tomatoes, drained; ⅔ cup Herbed Tofu Sour Cream (recipe in Chapter 9); or ¼ cup chopped kalamata olives.

1. Combine flour and Raw Parmesan Cheese on a large plate.

2. Cut seitan on the diagonal into 8 thin slices. Coat each seitan slice on both sides with flour mixture and place on a large plate.

3. Place olive oil in a large nonstick skillet over medium-high heat. When olive oil is hot, add seitan and cook for 30 to 60 seconds or until golden brown and crisp. Turn over seitan with tongs, and cook for 30 to 60 seconds or until golden brown. Transfer seitan to a large plate, and set aside while making sauce. (If you can't fit all of seitan in your skillet at one time, cook them in two batches, using only 1 tablespoon olive oil with each batch.)

4. For sauce, add vegetable broth, wine, lemon juice, capers, garlic, and nutritional yeast flakes to the hot skillet, and cook over medium heat for 2 minutes. Add parsley, margarine, salt, and black pepper, and cook for 1 minute or until margarine is melted and sauce is slightly thickened. Remove from heat.

5. Pour sauce over seitan, and serve hot. You can also garnish seitan slices with lemon slices, if desired.

Variation: You can replace the seitan slices with 8 ounces tofu or tempeh, thinly sliced, or substitute prepackaged seitan, thinly sliced.

Barbecued Seitan "Short Ribs"

In our meatless oven-baked barbecue "short ribs" recipe, our Zesty Barbecue Sauce covers and flavors cut strips of homemade seitan made with vital wheat gluten and a few other simple ingredients.

1 cup vital wheat gluten	**¾ cup water or vegetable broth**
3 TB. nutritional yeast flakes	**2 TB. creamy peanut butter or other nut butter of choice**
1½ tsp. chili powder or chipotle chile powder	**1 TB. tamari**
1½ tsp. garlic powder or garlic granules	**1 cup Zesty Barbecue Sauce (recipe in Chapter 8)**
1½ tsp. onion powder	

Yield: 16 seitan strips

Prep time: 5 to 7 minutes
Cook time: 30 to 35 minutes
Serving size: 4 seitan strips

---

1. Preheat the oven to 350°F. Lightly oil a 9-inch-square baking dish.

2. In a medium bowl, combine vital wheat gluten, nutritional yeast flakes, chili powder, garlic powder, and onion powder.

3. In a small bowl, combine water, peanut butter, and tamari.

4. Using your hands, mix wet ingredients into dry ingredients until well combined. Knead mixture lightly in the bowl for 1 or 2 minutes to form a soft dough.

5. Transfer dough to prepared pan, and using your hands, flatten dough to evenly cover bottom of pan. Using a sharp knife, cut dough into 8 strips lengthwise, turn pan ¼ turn, and make 1 cut through the middle, widthwise, to form 16 pieces.

6. Bake for 20 minutes. Remove from the oven. Spread Zesty Barbecue Sauce evenly over seitan. Return pan to the oven, and bake for 10 to 15 more minutes or until seitan is firm to the touch. Let cool slightly, and cut through seitan again before serving. Serve as an appetizer, main dish, on buns as a sandwich, or chop and use to add flavor to soups, stews, grains, and side dishes.

Variation: Alternatively, after baking for 20 minutes, top with ½ of Zesty Barbecue Sauce, remove seitan from baking dish, and cook on a hot grill for 2 or 3 minutes or until lightly browned on the bottom. Flip over seitan, top with remaining sauce, and cook for 2 or 3 minutes or until lightly browned. You can also substitute bottled barbecue sauce, as well as replace the seitan mixture with 1 pound tofu or tempeh cut into strips.

 Sour Grapes

If you suffer from wheat and gluten sensitivities, these seitan "short ribs" and all other seitan recipes are off-limits. Unfortunately, as far as we know, there are no suitable gluten-free flour substitutes for making seitanlike recipes.

TVP Tacos

You can fool almost anyone into thinking they're eating an actual beef taco with these meatless tacos made with a seasoned TVP-based filling and all the traditional taco toppings.

Yield: 12 tacos
Prep time: 10 to 15 minutes
Cook time: 12 to 15 minutes
Serving size: 2 tacos

½ cup onion, finely diced

1½ tsp. olive oil

1 TB. garlic, minced

1½ tsp. chili powder

½ tsp. ground cumin

½ tsp. dried oregano

¼ tsp. freshly ground black pepper

⅛ tsp. cayenne

1 (14-oz.) can crushed tomatoes

¾ cup TVP granules

¼ cup water

1½ tsp. tamari

12 corn taco shells

Shredded lettuce, diced tomatoes (or salsa of choice), shredded vegan cheddar cheese (or other flavor of choice), or other toppings of choice

Thyme-ly Tip

Use the filling and topping ingredients to make taco salads instead. Place shredded lettuce or mixed greens on a plate; spoon a little TVP filling over the lettuce; and top with a few crumbled tortilla chips, shredded vegan cheese, diced tomatoes or salsa, or whatever other toppings you like.

1. In a large nonstick skillet over medium heat, sauté onion and olive oil, stirring often, for 2 minutes. Add garlic, chili powder, cumin, oregano, black pepper, and cayenne, and sauté for 1 minute.

2. Add crushed tomatoes, TVP, water, and tamari, and stir well to combine. Reduce heat to low, and simmer, stirring often, for 10 to 12 minutes or until most of liquid is absorbed and TVP is fully rehydrated. Taste and adjust seasonings as desired. Remove from heat.

3. Meanwhile, bake taco shells according to package instructions. Remove from the oven and set aside.

4. Fill warm taco shells with TVP filling, and top with shredded lettuce, diced tomatoes, shredded vegan cheese, or other toppings as desired. Serve hot.

Variation: You can replace the TVP with 1 cup frozen or refrigerated meatless crumbles or 8 ounces tempeh, crumbled, and only add ¾ cup crushed tomatoes.

Shanghai Tofu

In this dish, slices of tofu are oven-baked in a sweet, sour, and spicy marinade inspired by the flavors prominent in Shanghai cuisine.

2 TB. tamari

2 TB. *brown rice vinegar*

2 TB. freshly squeezed orange juice

1 TB. turbinado sugar

1 TB. toasted sesame oil

1 TB. garlic, minced

1 TB. fresh ginger, minced

2 tsp. raw sesame seeds

¾ tsp. crushed red pepper flakes

¼ tsp. cayenne

¼ cup green onions, thinly sliced

1 lb. firm or extra-firm tofu

Yield: 8 slices
Prep time: 5 to 7 minutes
Cook time: 20 to 25 minutes
Serving size: 2 slices

1. Preheat the oven to 400°F.

2. In a small bowl, combine tamari, vinegar, orange juice, sugar, toasted sesame oil, garlic, ginger, sesame seeds, red pepper flakes, and cayenne. Pour mixture into a 9-inch-square baking dish, and stir in green onions.

3. Squeeze tofu block over the sink to remove excess water. Cut tofu in half lengthwise, turn each half cut side down, and cut each half into 4 slices for a total of 8 slices.

4. Transfer tofu to the baking dish. Flip over tofu to coat on both sides with tamari mixture.

5. Bake for 10 minutes. Remove from the oven and flip over tofu with a spatula. Bake for 10 to 15 more minutes or until all of liquid is absorbed and tofu is golden brown around the edges. Serve hot or cold as desired.

Variation: For a firmer texture, press the tofu block by placing it in a colander in the sink, cover with a plate, place a 28-ounce can on top of plate, and leave tofu to press for 20 minutes.

def•i•ni•tion

Brown rice vinegar is made from fermented brown rice, water, and koji (a beneficial mold), or from un-refined rice wine (sake) and water, and is aged in wooden barrels or crocks. It has a slightly sweet and mild flavor.

Indonesian Tempeh

In Indonesian cuisine, tempeh and peanut-flavored sauces are commonly combined, and with that in mind, we created these marinated cubes of tempeh and steam-fried vegetables covered in a rich, peanuty sauce.

Yield: 4 servings
Prep time: 10 to 15 minutes
Cook time: 10 to 12 minutes
Serving size: 1½ cups

1 (8-oz.) pkg. tempeh, cut into ½-in. cubes

3 TB. tamari

4 tsp. toasted sesame oil

½ cup plus 2 TB. water

2 TB. creamy or crunchy peanut butter

1½ tsp. freshly squeezed lime juice or brown rice vinegar

¼ tsp. crushed red pepper flakes

3 cups broccoli, cut into small florets, or 8-oz. frozen broccoli florets

1 cup carrot, thinly sliced diagonally

1 TB. garlic, minced

1 TB. fresh ginger, minced

3 cups savoy cabbage or green cabbage, shredded

1½ cups red cabbage, shredded

⅓ cup chopped fresh cilantro

1. In a small bowl, combine tempeh, 2 tablespoons tamari, and 2 teaspoons toasted sesame oil. Set aside for 10 minutes to marinate.

2. For sauce, in a separate small bowl, combine ½ cup water, peanut butter, remaining 1 tablespoon tamari, remaining 2 teaspoons toasted sesame oil, lime juice, and red pepper flakes. Set aside.

3. In a wok or a large nonstick skillet over medium-high heat, cook tempeh cubes and marinade, stirring often, for 5 minutes or until lightly browned on all sides. Transfer tempeh to a large plate, and set aside.

4. Add broccoli, carrot, remaining 2 tablespoons water, garlic, and ginger to the skillet, and cook over medium heat, stirring often, for 3 to 5 minutes or until vegetables are crisp-tender.

5. Add savoy cabbage, red cabbage, cilantro, tempeh cubes, and sauce, and cook for 1 or 2 minutes or until cabbage begins to wilt. Serve hot over cooked rice, grains, or pasta.

Sour Grapes

If your block of tempeh has red spots on it, feels slimy, or takes on an unpleasant or strong ammonialike odor, discard it. However, because tempeh is a fermented food (much like cheese), black or gray marbling is perfectly normal and you can still eat it.

Variation: Feel free to add other fresh or frozen vegetables such as bok choy, bell peppers, cauliflower, mushrooms, or eggplant. Or replace tempeh with 8 ounces tofu or seitan.

Thai Tempeh Curry

This mildly hot curry made with red curry paste and coconut milk is chock-full of chunks of tempeh, sweet potato, red pepper, and vegetables.

1 (8-oz.) pkg. tempeh, cut into ½-in. cubes

1 TB. olive oil or safflower oil

⅔ cup onion, diced

1 TB. garlic, minced

1 TB. *red curry paste*

½ tsp. sea salt

1 (16-oz.) pkg. frozen California blend vegetables (broccoli, cauliflower, and carrots)

1 large sweet potato, cut into ½-in. cubes

1½ cups water or vegetable broth

1 cup lite coconut milk

1 cup red bell pepper, ribs and seeds removed, and diced

½ cup frozen peas

¼ cup chopped fresh basil (preferably Thai basil)

2 TB. chopped fresh mint (optional)

Yield: 6 servings
Prep time: 10 to 15 minutes
Cook time: 25 to 30 minutes
Serving size: 1¼ cups

1. In a large pot over medium-high heat, cook tempeh and olive oil, stirring often, for 3 minutes. Add onion, and sauté for 3 minutes or until tempeh is lightly browned on all sides. Add garlic, curry paste, and salt, and sauté for 1 minute.

2. Add California vegetables, sweet potato, water, coconut milk, red bell pepper, and peas. Stir well to combine, and bring to a boil. Cover, reduce heat to low, and simmer for 15 to 20 minutes or until vegetables are tender and sauce is thickened.

3. Add basil and mint (if using), and cook for 2 more minutes. Remove from heat. Serve over cooked rice or grains.

Variation: If you like your curry really hot and spicy, add more red curry paste. Or replace the red curry paste with yellow or green curry paste or curry powder if you prefer.

def•i•ni•tion

Red curry paste is a spicy, thick paste used as a condiment and flavoring for curries, soups, stews, sauces, and stir-fries. It's typically made by grinding red chiles, lemon grass, shallots, garlic, ginger, kaffir lime, oil, salt, and several spices. Be sure to thoroughly read the ingredients, as many brands also contain shrimp paste.

Veggie Stir-Fry

We've included many of our favorite stir-fry vegetables in this recipe flavored with our Teriyaki Stir-Frying and Dipping Sauce, but feel free to use whatever fresh, frozen, or even canned vegetables you have on hand.

Yield: 6 servings
Prep time: 15 to 20 minutes
Cook time: 7 to 10 minutes
Serving size: 1½ cups

4 tsp. peanut oil or safflower oil

½ cup green onions, thinly sliced diagonally

1 TB. garlic, minced

1 TB. fresh ginger, minced

½ tsp. crushed red pepper flakes

1 medium Japanese eggplant, cut in half lengthwise and cut into ½-in. thick slices, or 2½ cups eggplant, cut into 1-in. cubes

3 cups bok choy, cut into 1-in. slices

1½ cups shiitake mushrooms or other mushrooms of choice, sliced

1 cup carrot, thinly sliced diagonally

1 cup red bell pepper, ribs and seeds removed, cut into quarters lengthwise, and thinly sliced

1½ cups mung bean sprouts

1 cup fresh or frozen snap peas or snow peas

½ cup canned water chestnuts or bamboo shoots

2 TB. cold water

2 tsp. cornstarch

⅓ cup Teriyaki Stir-Frying and Dipping Sauce (recipe in Chapter 8)

1. In a wok or large nonstick skillet over medium-high heat, warm peanut oil. When oil is hot, add green onions, garlic, ginger, and red pepper flakes, and stir-fry for 1 minute.

2. Add eggplant and stir-fry for 2 minutes. Add bok choy, mushrooms, carrot, and red bell pepper, and stir-fry for 2 minutes. Add mung bean sprouts, snap peas, and water chestnuts, and stir-fry 1 or 2 minutes or until vegetables are crisp-tender.

3. In a small bowl, combine water and cornstarch until cornstarch is dissolved.

4. Add cornstarch mixture and Teriyaki Stir-Frying and Dipping Sauce to wok, stir well to combine, and cook for 1 or 2 minutes or until sauce is thickened. Serve hot over cooked rice, grains, or pasta.

Variation: For a tofu or tempeh and vegetable stir-fry, add 8 ounces tofu or tempeh, cut into 1-inch cubes, prior to adding the vegetables, and stir-fry cubes for 2 or 3 minutes or until lightly browned.

Thyme-ly Tip

When stir-frying, cut and assemble all your ingredients before you begin cooking. Use a wok or large skillet, and preheat with oil over medium-high heat. Cook aromatic ingredients like onion, garlic, and ginger first. Add ingredients to wok according to length of time needed to cook (longer ones first, quick-cooking last). Constantly stir ingredients with a spatula or spoon, and if food sticks, add a little water or additional oil. And flavor and finish stir-fry with a sauce, tamari, toasted sesame oil, or fresh herbs.

Mushroom and Veggie Fajitas

Here, thick slices of portobello mushrooms, red onions, and green and red bell peppers are marinated and cooked in a tangy lime and balsamic vinaigrette and then folded up in tortillas with our Almond Pepper Jack Cheese.

¼ **cup chopped fresh cilantro**

2 **TB. olive oil**

1 **TB. balsamic vinegar**

1 **TB. tamari**

1 **TB. freshly squeezed lime juice**

1 **TB. garlic, minced**

½ **tsp. chili powder**

½ **tsp. dried oregano**

⅛ **tsp. freshly ground black pepper**

3 **medium portobello mushrooms, cut into ½-in.-thick slices**

2 **medium red onions, cut into half moons**

2 **green bell peppers, ribs and seeds removed, and cut into ½-in.-thick slices**

2 **red or orange bell peppers, ribs and seeds removed, and cut into ½-in.-thick slices**

2 **jalapeño peppers, ribs and seeds removed, and thinly sliced**

6 **(8-in.) flour tortillas of choice**

¾ **cup Almond Pepper Jack Cheese (recipe in Chapter 9), crumbled, or 6 TB. vegan cheese of choice, shredded**

Yield: 6 fajitas
Prep time: 15 to 20 minutes
Cook time: 5 to 7 minutes
Serving size: 1 fajita

1. In a large bowl, combine cilantro, olive oil, vinegar, tamari, lime juice, garlic, chili powder, oregano, and black pepper.

2. Add mushrooms, onions, green bell peppers, red bell peppers, and jalapeño peppers, and toss well to thoroughly coat vegetables with marinade. Set aside for 10 minutes to marinate.

3. Place vegetables in a large nonstick skillet over medium heat and sauté, stirring often, for 5 to 7 minutes or until vegetables are crisp-tender. Remove from heat.

4. Warm each tortilla in a large skillet over medium heat for 1 or 2 minutes per side, or warm them in a microwave for 1 minute.

5. Place 1 tortilla flat on a large plate. Place ³/₄ cup vegetable mixture horizontally in the center of tortilla. Top with 2 tablespoons crumbled Almond Pepper Jack Cheese (or 1 tablespoon shredded vegan cheese). Fold the sides of tortilla toward center to enclose filling. Serve hot.

Variation: Alternatively, cook the vegetable mixture on a large cookie sheet under the broiler for 5 minutes or until vegetables are crisp-tender. Or cook vegetables on a hot grill, but leave portobello mushrooms whole. Cut red onions, bell pepper, and jalapeño peppers in half, turn them as needed until vegetables are crisp-tender, and cut grilled vegetables into thin strips. Or replace portobello mushrooms with 1 pound tempeh, cut into ¹/₄-inch-thick slices.

Sour Grapes

Capsaicin, the compound in the internal ribs and membrane that encapsulates the seeds within peppers, is responsible for the hot flavor, and direct contact may cause burning of the eyes, nose, and mouth, as well as irritate the skin. Remove the ribs and seeds using a knife, or wear rubber or plastic gloves while handling.

Mushroom Stroganoff

Earthy crimini mushrooms take center stage in this hearty meatless stroganoff. White wine, soy milk, and our Herbed Tofu Sour Cream create the creamy sauce backdrop.

1 cup onion, diced

1 cup vegetable broth

2 TB. garlic, minced

12 oz. crimini mushrooms, cut in ½ and thinly sliced

¼ cup white or red wine

2 TB. tamari

1½ cups soy milk or other nondairy milk of choice

¼ cup whole-wheat pastry flour or spelt flour

¾ cup Herbed Tofu Sour Cream (recipe in Chapter 9)

¼ cup chopped fresh parsley

1 tsp. paprika (preferably Hungarian paprika)

1 tsp. dried dill weed

½ tsp. sea salt

¼ tsp. freshly black pepper

Yield: 4 servings
Prep time: 30 to 35 minutes
Cook time: 10 to 15 minutes
Serving size: 1 cup

1. In a medium saucepan over medium heat, cook onion, ¹/₂ cup vegetable broth, and garlic for 3 minutes. Add mushrooms, wine, and tamari. Cover and cook for 3 to 5 minutes or until onions are soft.

2. In a small bowl, whisk together soy milk and flour. Add soy milk mixture and remaining ¹/₂ cup vegetable broth to the saucepan and cook, stirring often, for 3 to 5 minutes or until thickened.

3. Reduce heat to low. Add Herbed Tofu Sour Cream, parsley, paprika, dill weed, salt, and black pepper, and stir well to combine. Cook for 2 minutes, and remove from heat. Taste and adjust seasonings. Serve hot over cooked brown rice or fettuccine pasta.

Variation: If you prefer, instead of simmering them in ¹/₂ cup vegetable broth, sauté onion, mushrooms, and garlic in 1 tablespoon olive oil and then simmer them with wine and tamari for 1 minute.

Soy What?

We avoided adding excess fat by steam-frying the onions and mushrooms in vegetable broth instead of sautéing them in oil. You can use this fat-substitution trick in other recipes, in most instances without impacting the final flavor of your dish.

Stuffed Winter Squash

In this recipe, we filled squash halves with a slightly sweet and savory apple and dried-fruit bread stuffing. It's perfect for Thanksgiving and other holiday get-togethers.

Yield: 4 servings
Prep time: 20 to 25 minutes
Cook time: 45 to 55 minutes
Serving size: ½ squash

4 cups whole-wheat bread, cut into 1-in. cubes

1 Gala or Fuji apple, diced

½ cup onion or red onion, diced

½ cup celery, diced

1½ tsp. olive oil

⅓ cup raw pecans, coarsely chopped

⅓ cup green onions, thinly sliced

1 TB. garlic, minced

1 tsp. dried thyme

½ tsp. ground cinnamon

⅓ cup dried cranberries

¼ cup dried currants or raisins

¼ cup chopped fresh parsley

2 tsp. nutritional yeast flakes

½ tsp. sea salt

¼ tsp. freshly ground black pepper

1 cup water or vegetable broth

2 tsp. tamari or Bragg Liquid Aminos

2 (1-lb.) delicata, sweet dumpling, or acorn squash

1. Place bread cubes in a medium bowl, and set aside to dry out for 15 minutes.

2. Meanwhile, in a large nonstick skillet over medium heat, cook apple, onion, celery, and olive oil, stirring often, for 3 to 5 minutes or until soft. Add pecans, green onions, garlic, thyme, and cinnamon, and sauté for 2 minutes. Remove from heat.

3. Add apple mixture, cranberries, currants, parsley, nutritional yeast flakes, salt, and black pepper to bread cubes, and stir well to combine. Add water and tamari, and gently stir to moisten bread cubes.

4. Preheat the oven to 400°F.

5. Cut off the stems of each squash, cut each in half, and scoop out and discard seeds. Place squash halves cut side up in a large baking dish. Fill squash halves with stuffing mixture, dividing it evenly among them. Cover baking dish with a lid or aluminum foil.

6. Bake for 30 minutes, remove cover, and bake for 10 to 15 minutes longer or until squash halves are tender and stuffing is lightly brown on top. Serve hot.

Variation: For a more savory stuffing, replace the apples with 2 cups crimini mushrooms, coarsely chopped, and omit the dried cranberries and currants.

Soy What?

Unlike zucchini and other summer squashes, winter squashes are harvested at maturity when their skins have hardened, usually at the end of summer or early fall. Winter squashes include acorn, butternut, buttercup, delicata, sweet dumpling, pumpkins, kabocha, spaghetti squash, turban, and Hubbard. Store them at room temperature or in a cool, dry place.

Roasted Ratatouille with Basil Aioli

Here, vegetables are oven-roasted with fresh rosemary, thyme, parsley, and olive oil and accompanied by a creamy garlic and basil–flavored aioli.

Yield: 6 servings
Prep time: 10 to 15 minutes
Cook time: 35 to 40 minutes
Serving size: 1½ cups

1 large eggplant or 2 medium (about 1¼ lb.), cut into 1-in. cubes

2 medium yellow summer squashes, cut in half lengthwise and cut into ½-in.-thick slices

2 medium zucchini, cut in half lengthwise and cut into ½-in.-thick slices

1 green bell pepper, ribs and seeds removed, and cut into 1-in. pieces

1 red bell pepper, ribs and seeds removed, and cut into 1-in. pieces

1 orange or yellow bell pepper, ribs and seeds removed, cut into 1-in. pieces

1 large red onion, cut into half moons ¼-in. thick

¼ cup olive oil

¼ cup chopped fresh parsley

2 TB. garlic, minced

2 TB. chopped fresh rosemary or 2 tsp. dried, crushed a bit with your fingers

1 TB. chopped fresh thyme or 1 tsp. dried

1 tsp. sea salt

½ tsp. freshly ground black pepper

1 cup cherry tomatoes, cut in half, or 2 plum tomatoes, cut into quarters

½ cup loosely packed basil leaves

2 large garlic cloves

⅔ cup Tofu Mayonnaise (recipe in Chapter 12)

1 TB. nutritional yeast flakes

1 tsp. freshly squeezed lemon juice

1. Preheat the oven to 450°F. Lightly oil a large cookie sheet.

2. In a large bowl, combine eggplant, summer squash, zucchini, green bell pepper, red bell pepper, orange bell pepper, red onion, olive oil, parsley, minced garlic, rosemary, thyme, salt, and black pepper. Transfer vegetable mixture to prepared cookie sheet, and spread out into a single layer.

3. Bake for 15 minutes. Remove from the oven, stir vegetable mixture with a spatula, spread out into a single layer, and bake for 15 more minutes. Remove from the oven, stir again, spread into a single layer again, and scatter tomatoes over top. Bake for 5 to 10 minutes or until vegetables are tender and lightly browned around the edges. Remove from the oven.

4. Meanwhile, for basil aioli, place basil and 2 garlic cloves in a food processor fitted with an S blade, and process for 1 minute or until finely chopped. Scrape down the sides of the container. Add Tofu Mayonnaise, nutritional yeast flakes, and lemon juice, and process for 1 minute. Transfer aioli to a glass bowl. Serve ratatouille hot, with aioli on the side.

Variation: You can use the ratatouille and basil aioli as a filling for sandwiches on split rolls or focaccia.

Thyme-ly Tip _____

You can easily adapt these ingredients for a traditional ratatouille: Sauté onion and garlic in olive oil for several minutes. Add remaining vegetables (omit cherry tomatoes), salt, and pepper, and sauté for 5 minutes. Add 1 (28-ounce) can crushed tomatoes, fresh herbs, and ¼ cup chopped fresh basil. Cover and simmer over low heat until vegetables are crisp-tender.

Chapter 16

Perfect Pasta and Polenta

In This Chapter

- Super stove-top pasta and vegetable dishes
- Impressive oven-baked pasta casseroles
- The secret to great polenta

Who doesn't love pasta? It's affordable, quick and easy to prepare, and results in a tasty and filling meal. The recent low-carb craze, which discouraged its consumption, hurt pasta sales for a while, but now that more whole-grain varieties have hit the market, pasta has regained its place in our hearts and on our plates. Pasta is so versatile and can be prepared and flavored in so many different ways. Dry pasta also has a very long shelf life, which makes it convenient to keep on hand in your pantry.

We've also included a few polenta recipes and two hearty sauces that work with either pasta or polenta. Although many people stir and stir their polenta to give it an ultra-creamy texture, we show you a much simpler method for preparing it with the same results. We also provide tips for achieving firm polenta that can be sliced and grilled, or fried until crispy.

Are you ready to get cooking? Well, then, put some water on to boil, cook up some pasta (or polenta) and one of these tasty recipes, and as Ray's great-grandmother would say, "*Mangia!*" (Eat!).

Teriyaki Tofu Rice Noodles

Our sweet and sour, tamari-based Teriyaki Stir-Frying and Dipping Sauce is first used to flavor the fried crumbled tofu and then added again when the tofu is tossed with vegetables and cooked brown rice pasta.

Yield: 6 servings
Prep time: 10 to 15 minutes
Cook time: 18 to 20 minutes
Serving size: 1½ cups

12 oz. *brown rice spaghetti*

8 oz. tofu

1½ tsp. toasted sesame oil

¾ cup Teriyaki Stir-Frying and Dipping Sauce (recipe in Chapter 8)

2 cups spinach, stems removed, and finely chopped

1½ cups red cabbage, shredded

1 cup carrot, shredded

⅓ cup chopped fresh cilantro

⅓ cup chopped fresh parsley

2 TB. raw sesame seeds

def•i•ni•tion

Brown rice spaghetti and other pastas are made from brown rice, and not only are they egg-free and totally vegan, but they're gluten-free as well.

1. Fill a large saucepan two thirds full of water and bring to a boil over medium-high heat. Add spaghetti and cook, stirring occasionally, according to package directions or until just tender. Drain spaghetti in a colander but do not rinse.

2. Meanwhile, crumble tofu into a large nonstick skillet using your fingers. Add toasted sesame oil, and cook over medium heat, stirring often, for 5 to 7 minutes or until lightly browned.

3. Pour ¼ cup Teriyaki Stir-Frying and Dipping Sauce over tofu, and cook for 1 or 2 minutes or until liquid is absorbed. Remove from heat.

4. Add hot spaghetti to tofu, along with remaining ½ cup Teriyaki Stir-Frying and Dipping Sauce, and stir well to combine. Cook over medium heat, stirring often, for 1 or 2 minutes or until sauce is absorbed. Remove from heat.

5. Add spinach, red cabbage, carrot, cilantro, parsley, and sesame seeds, and stir well to combine. Serve hot.

Variation: You can replace the tofu with 1 (8-ounce) package tempeh, crumbled; 1½ cups prepared Simmered Seitan (recipe in Chapter 15) or 1 (8-ounce) package chicken-style seitan, coarsely chopped; or 2 cups mushrooms, coarsely chopped.

Mushroom Fettuccine

This elegant fettuccine dish features two varieties of mushrooms, onion, garlic, and a creamy wine-infused sauce. The wine you choose determines the dish's final flavor.

12 oz. fettuccine or other shaped pasta of choice

1 cup onion, cut into half moons

2 TB. olive oil

8 oz. crimini mushrooms, cut in ½ and thinly sliced

8 oz. shiitake or button mushrooms, cut in ½ and thinly sliced

1 TB. garlic, minced

1 tsp. dried thyme

½ cup vegetable broth or water

½ cup Dairy-Free Creamer (recipe in Chapter 9), or ⅓ cup Herbed Tofu Sour Cream (recipe in Chapter 9)

¼ cup white or red wine

½ tsp. sea salt

¼ tsp. freshly ground black pepper

¼ cup chopped fresh parsley (preferably Italian parsley)

Vegan soy Parmesan cheese or Raw Parmesan Cheese (recipe in Chapter 9)

Yield: 6 servings
Prep time: 10 minutes
Cook time: 10 to 12 minutes (depending on pasta)
Serving size: 1½ cups

1. Fill a large saucepan two thirds full of water and bring to a boil over medium-high heat. Add fettuccine and cook, stirring occasionally, according package directions or until just tender. Drain fettuccine in a colander but do not rinse.

2. Meanwhile, in a large nonstick skillet over medium heat, sauté onion and olive oil, stirring often, for 3 minutes. Add crimini mushrooms, shiitake mushrooms, garlic, and thyme, and sauté for 3 minutes.

3. Add vegetable broth, Dairy-Free Creamer, white wine, salt, and pepper. Reduce heat to low, and simmer for 2 or 3 minutes or until mushrooms are soft.

4. Add hot fettuccine and parsley, and toss well to combine. Taste and adjust seasonings. Remove from heat, and serve hot, garnished with vegan Parmesan cheese.

Variation: For added color and flavor, use spinach-flavored fettuccine. You can also add chopped spinach or Swiss chard or diced vegetarian Canadian bacon.

Soy What?

Shiitake mushrooms have light to dark brown convex caps, and off-white to beige gills, and are commonly used in Asian cuisine. If you purchase them dried, rehydrate them in hot water or broth prior to using.

Pasta Primavera

Our low-fat version of this classic dish contains a colorful mix of fresh and frozen vegetables combined with a light sauce made with vegetable broth, fresh herbs, nutritional yeast flakes, and a little margarine and lemon juice.

Yield: 6 servings
Prep time: 10 to 15 minutes
Cook time: 10 to 12 minutes (depending on pasta)
Serving size: 1½ cups

12 oz. farfalle or other shaped pasta of choice

6 oz. asparagus, thinly sliced diagonally into 1-in. pieces

2 carrots, cut in half lengthwise and thinly sliced diagonally

1 medium yellow summer squash, cut in half lengthwise and thinly sliced diagonally

1 medium zucchini, cut in half lengthwise and thinly sliced diagonally

1 red bell pepper, ribs and seeds removed, and thinly sliced into 1-in. pieces

½ cup plus ⅓ cup vegetable broth

⅓ cup sun-dried tomato pieces

½ cup frozen peas

½ cup frozen shelled fava beans (optional)

½ cup green onions, thinly sliced diagonally

¼ cup chopped fresh parsley (preferably Italian parsley)

¼ cup chopped fresh basil, or 2 TB. chopped fresh dill

3 TB. nutritional yeast flakes

2 TB. nonhydrogenated vegan margarine

1 TB. freshly squeezed lemon juice

¾ tsp. sea salt

½ tsp. freshly ground black pepper

1. Fill a large saucepan two thirds full of water and bring to a boil over medium-high heat. Add farfalle and cook, stirring occasionally, according to package directions or until just tender. Drain farfalle in a colander but do not rinse.

2. Meanwhile, in a large nonstick skillet over medium heat, cook asparagus, carrots, summer squash, zucchini, red bell pepper, ½ cup vegetable broth, and sun-dried tomatoes, stirring often, for 5 minutes or until vegetables are crisp-tender.

3. Add peas, fava beans (if using), and green onions, and cook for 2 minutes.

4. Add hot farfalle, remaining ¹/₃ cup vegetable broth, parsley, basil, nutritional yeast flakes, margarine, lemon juice, salt, and black pepper, and toss well to combine. Taste and adjust seasonings. Remove from heat, and serve hot.

Variation: This pasta dish can also be served cold as a pasta salad.

Thyme-ly Tip

For a more robust flavor, omit the parsley, basil, and lemon juice, and toss the cooked pasta first with ¼ cup Spinach-Walnut Pesto (recipe in Chapter 7), remaining ⅓ cup vegetable broth, and nutritional yeast flakes. Then toss the pesto-covered pasta with the cooked vegetables, taste, and season with salt and black pepper.

Vegan Macaroni and Cheese

You won't believe how creamy and cheesy-tasting this vegan macaroni and cheese is. We took this recipe one step further by topping it with seasoned breadcrumbs and oven-baking it as a casserole.

8 oz. elbow macaroni
½ cup dry breadcrumbs or rice breadcrumbs
1 TB. olive oil
1 TB. chopped fresh parsley
¾ tsp. garlic powder
¾ tsp. paprika
2 cups Béchamel Sauce (recipe in Chapter 8)

¾ cup Vegan Cheese Sauce Mix (recipe in Chapter 9), or ½ cup nutritional yeast flakes

¾ cup vegan cheddar cheese, shredded

½ tsp. dry mustard

Pinch cayenne

Sea salt

Freshly ground black pepper

Yield: 4 servings
Prep time: 10 to 12 minutes
Cook time: 25 to 30 minutes
Serving size: 1¹/₄ cups

1. Fill a large saucepan two thirds full of water and bring to a boil over medium-high heat. Add macaroni and cook, stirring occasionally, for 8 minutes. Drain macaroni in a colander but do not rinse.

2. Meanwhile, for breadcrumb topping, in a small bowl, combine breadcrumbs, olive oil, parsley, $1/4$ teaspoon garlic powder, and $1/4$ teaspoon paprika.

3. Preheat the oven to 375°F. Lightly oil a 9-inch baking dish.

4. Return macaroni to the pot. Add Béchamel Sauce, Vegan Cheese Sauce Mix, shredded vegan cheese, dry mustard, remaining $1/2$ teaspoon garlic powder, remaining $1/2$ teaspoon paprika, and cayenne, and stir well to combine. Taste and season with salt and black pepper.

5. Transfer mixture to prepared pan. Sprinkle breadcrumb topping mixture evenly over top. Bake for 25 to 30 minutes or until topping is golden brown and crisp. Remove from the oven. Let cool for 5 minutes before serving.

Variation: Add other ingredients to the macaroni and cheese, such as peas, sliced mushrooms, diced vegetarian ham or Canadian bacon, sliced meatless hot dogs, or flavored sausages. Or omit the breadcrumb topping mixture, heat the remaining ingredients in a saucepan until shredded vegan cheese is melted, cook elbow macaroni until fully tender, and stir it in cooked Béchamel Sauce mixture.

Thyme-ly Tip

Cook pasta only until it's tender but still chewy, or *al dente*, which literally means "to the tooth." You can test pasta by tasting it during the last few minutes of cooking time as suggested on its packaging. It should still be slightly firm when you bite into it.

Vegan Lasagna Roll-Ups

In this recipe, we use a homemade tofu ricotta substitute and chopped vegetables as a filling for lasagna roll-ups, which are much easier to assemble than a full pan of traditionally layered lasagna.

6 lasagna noodles

1 lb. firm or extra-firm tofu

¼ cup soy milk or other non-dairy milk of choice

¼ cup freshly squeezed lemon juice

¼ cup plus 1 TB. nutritional yeast flakes

3 TB. plus ¼ cup chopped fresh basil

3 TB. plus ¼ cup chopped fresh parsley (preferably Italian parsley)

3 TB. garlic, minced

1 TB. agave nectar or brown rice syrup

1 TB. onion powder

1½ tsp. dried oregano

1½ tsp. sea salt

¾ tsp. freshly ground black pepper

2 cups spinach, coarsely chopped, or ½ (10-oz.) pkg. frozen chopped spinach, thawed and squeezed dry

1 cup broccoli florets, coarsely chopped

½ cup red onion, diced

½ cup carrot, diced

½ cup red bell pepper, ribs and seeds removed, and diced

½ cup zucchini, diced

½ cup onion, diced

1 TB. olive oil

2 TB. red wine (optional)

½ tsp. dried marjoram

1 (28-oz.) can fire-roasted crushed tomatoes

Yield: 6 roll-ups
Prep time: 15 to 20 minutes
Cook time: 35 to 40 minutes
Serving size: 1 roll-up

1. Fill a large saucepan two thirds full of water and bring to a boil over medium-high heat. Add lasagna noodles, and cook, stirring occasionally, according to package directions or until just tender. Drain lasagna noodles in a colander, rinse with cold water, and drain well again.

2. Meanwhile, for filling, crumble tofu into a large bowl using your fingers. Add soy milk, lemon juice, ¼ cup nutritional yeast flakes, 3 tablespoons basil, 3 tablespoons parsley, 2 tablespoons garlic, agave nectar, onion powder, 1 teaspoon oregano, 1 teaspoon salt, and ¼ teaspoon black pepper, and mash with a fork until completely smooth.

3. Add spinach, broccoli, red onion, carrot, red bell pepper, and zucchini, and stir well to combine.

4. For sauce, in a small saucepan over medium heat, sauté onion and olive oil, stirring often, for 3 to 5 minutes or until onion is soft.

5. Add red wine (if using), remaining 1 tablespoon garlic, remaining $\frac{1}{2}$ teaspoon oregano, marjoram, remaining $\frac{1}{2}$ teaspoon salt, and remaining $\frac{1}{2}$ teaspoon black pepper, and sauté for 1 minute.

6. Add crushed tomatoes, remaining 1 tablespoon nutritional yeast flakes, remaining $\frac{1}{4}$ cup basil, and remaining $\frac{1}{4}$ cup parsley. Stir well to combine, reduce heat to low, and cook for 2 minutes. Remove from heat.

7. Preheat the oven to 375°F. Lightly oil a 9×13-inch baking dish.

8. Spoon $\frac{1}{3}$ of sauce in the bottom of the prepared pan.

9. Lay 1 lasagna noodle flat on a work surface. Place $\frac{3}{4}$ cup filling 2 inches from the bottom edge of noodle, fold bottom edge up over filling, and roll up the entire length of noodle to enclose filling. Place roll-up seam side down in the prepared pan. Spoon remaining sauce evenly over each lasagna roll-up.

10. Bake for 20 to 25 minutes. Remove from the oven, let cool for 5 minutes, and serve.

Variation: For a white lasagna roll-up, replace the tomato sauce with Béchamel Sauce (recipe in Chapter 8).

Thyme-ly Tip

If you want to make a pan of layered lasagna, cook 1 pound lasagna noodles and prepare double the amount of the tofu-vegetable filling and tomato sauce. To assemble, place 1½ cups tomato sauce in the bottom of a baking dish, layer 4 lasagna noodles, ⅓ of filling, and top with 1½ cups tomato sauce. Repeat layers two more times, and top with remaining lasagna noodles and tomato sauce. Sprinkle with nutritional yeast or shredded vegan cheese and bake for 30 minutes at 375°F.

Herbed Polenta

The addition of fresh herbs and olive oil provides a savory touch to this soft polenta, which can be served all on its own or topped with tomato sauce or vegetables.

6 cups water

1¼ tsp. sea salt

1½ cups cornmeal (preferably medium-grind or coarse)

¼ cup chopped fresh basil

¼ cup chopped fresh parsley (preferably Italian parsley)

2 TB. olive oil

½ tsp. freshly ground black pepper

Vegan Parmesan cheese or Raw Parmesan Cheese (recipe in Chapter 9)

Yield: 6 servings
Prep time: 3 to 5 minutes
Cook time: 40 to 45 minutes
Serving size: 1 cup

1. In a large pot over high heat, bring water to a boil. Add salt and reduce heat to medium.

2. Slowly add cornmeal, whisking constantly to prevent lumps. Continue to whisk for 1 or 2 minutes until mixture begins to boil again and starts to thicken.

3. Reduce heat to very low. Cover and simmer, stirring every 10 minutes with a long-handled spoon, for 30 to 35 minutes or until very thick and polenta starts to pull away from the sides of the pot.

4. Add basil, parsley, olive oil, and black pepper, and stir well to combine. Remove from heat. Garnish individual servings with vegan Parmesan cheese, and serve hot.

Variation: For extra flavor, replace 2 cups water with vegetable broth, and top polenta with homemade or jarred tomato sauce or cooked vegetables.

Thyme-ly Tip

You can also pour cooked polenta into an oiled loaf pan or large shallow casserole and chill it in the refrigerator for 1 hour or more to give a firmer texture. Then, cut it into slices, squares, triangles, or other shapes and broil, grill, or fry them in oil until crisp.

Polenta with Beans and Garlicky Greens

Beans and greens are a classic combination often served on cooked rice or grains. We find them especially tasty served as a topping for creamy polenta.

Yield: 4 servings
Prep time: 7 to 10 minutes
Cook time: 40 to 45 minutes
Serving size: 1½ cups

4 cups water

1¾ tsp. sea salt

1 cup medium-grind or coarse cornmeal

2 TB. nutritional yeast flakes

1 TB. olive oil or nonhydrogenated vegan margarine

¾ tsp. freshly ground black pepper

1 cup onion or red onion, cut into half moons

2 TB. olive oil

4 large garlic cloves, thinly sliced

1 tsp. dried basil

1 (15-oz.) can cannellini beans or other beans of choice, drained and rinsed

1 bunch or 6 cups rainbow Swiss chard, kale, and/or spinach, stems trimmed and coarsely chopped

½ tsp. crushed red pepper flakes

Sour Grapes

Be especially careful when stirring cooking polenta, because it can easily splatter and burn you. Use a long-handled spoon, pull the polenta slightly off the heat, and lean back a bit when stirring to reduce your chances of being burned.

1. In a large saucepan over high heat, bring water to a boil. Add 1 teaspoon salt, and reduce heat to medium.

2. Slowly add cornmeal, whisking constantly to prevent lumps. Continue to whisk for 1 or 2 minutes until mixture begins to boil again and starts to thicken.

3. Reduce heat to very low. Cover and simmer, stirring every 10 minutes with a long-handled spoon, for 30 to 35 minutes or until very thick and polenta starts to pull away from the sides of the saucepan.

4. Add 1 tablespoon nutritional yeast flakes, 1 tablespoon olive oil, and ¼ teaspoon black pepper, and stir well to combine. Remove from heat.

5. Meanwhile, for vegetable topping, in a large nonstick skillet over medium heat, sauté onion and remaining 2 tablespoons olive oil, stirring often, for 5 minutes or until onions are soft and lightly browned.

6. Add garlic and basil, and sauté for 2 minutes or until garlic is lightly browned. Add beans and sauté for 1 minute. Add Swiss chard, remaining 1 tablespoon nutritional yeast flakes, remaining ¾ teaspoon salt, red pepper flakes, and remaining ½ teaspoon black pepper, and cook for 2 or 3 more minutes or until Swiss chard just begins to wilt. Remove from heat.

7. Place polenta on a large platter or divide into individual servings, and top with vegetable topping mixture. Serve hot.

Variation: Feel free to replace the polenta with Herbed Polenta (see recipe earlier in this chapter), either the soft version or crispy, broiled, or fried version.

Red Lentil Bolognese

Red lentils provide a thick and hearty texture to this spicy, versatile sauce.

1¼ cups onion, diced

1 cup carrot, diced

¾ cup celery, diced

2 TB. olive oil

2 TB. garlic, minced

1 tsp. dried basil

¾ tsp. dried oregano

½ tsp. crushed red pepper flakes

1 (28-oz.) can crushed tomatoes (preferably fire-roasted)

2½ cups water or vegetable broth

¾ cup dried red lentils, sorted and rinsed

3 TB. tomato paste

1 bay leaf

¼ cup chopped fresh parsley (preferably Italian parsley)

2 TB. nutritional yeast flakes

¾ tsp. sea salt

½ tsp. freshly ground black pepper

Yield: 6 cups
Prep time: 10 minutes
Cook time: 30 to 35 minutes
Serving size: 1 cup

1. In a large pot over medium heat, sauté onion, carrot, celery, and olive oil, stirring often, for 5 minutes. Add garlic, basil, and oregano, and sauté for 1 minute.

2. Add crushed tomatoes, water, red lentils, tomato paste, and bay leaf, and stir well to combine. Bring to a boil, cover, reduce heat to low, and simmer for 20 to 25 minutes or until red lentils are tender.

3. Add parsley, nutritional yeast, salt, and black pepper. Stir well to combine, and simmer for 2 more minutes. Remove bay leaf and discard. Taste and adjust seasonings. Remove from heat, and serve hot over cooked pasta or polenta as desired.

Variation: Feel free to replace the red lentils with dried brown lentils, but add an additional $1^1/_2$ to 2 cups water as needed to cook brown lentils until tender.

Soy What?

Bolognese sauce is typically made with beef, onion, carrot, celery, and tomatoes and often includes pancetta or pork. To create a meatless version of this sauce as it's traditionally prepared, replace the red lentils with 8 ounces tempeh or tofu, crumbled, or 1 cup refrigerated or frozen meatless crumbles or TVP.

Tempeh Cacciatore

Here, marinated tempeh cubes mix with onion, bell peppers, and mushrooms in a flavorful, wine-infused tomato sauce.

1 (8-oz.) pkg. tempeh, cut into ½-in. cubes

2 TB. tamari

2 tsp. plus 1 TB. olive oil

1 cup onion, cut into half moons

1½ cups crimini mushrooms or other mushrooms of choice, thinly sliced

⅔ cup green bell pepper, ribs and seeds removed, and cut into 1-in. pieces

⅔ cup red bell pepper, ribs and seeds removed, and cut into 1-in. pieces

1 TB. garlic, minced

1 tsp. Italian seasoning blend, or ½ tsp. each dried basil and dried oregano

1 (14-oz.) can crushed tomatoes (preferably fire-roasted)

1 (14-oz.) can diced tomatoes (preferably fire-roasted)

½ cup red wine

½ tsp. sea salt

¼ tsp. freshly ground black pepper

1 bay leaf

Yield: 6 servings
Prep time: 10 to 15 minutes
Cook time: 25 to 30 minutes
Serving size: 1 cup

1. In a small bowl, combine tempeh, tamari, and 2 teaspoons olive oil. Set aside for 10 minutes to marinate.

2. In a large nonstick skillet over medium-high heat, cook tempeh cubes and marinade, stirring often, for 5 minutes or until lightly browned on all sides. Transfer tempeh cubes to a large plate, and set aside.

3. Add onion and remaining 1 tablespoon olive oil to the skillet, reduce heat to medium, and sauté, stirring often, for 3 minutes. Add mushrooms, green bell pepper, and red bell pepper, and sauté for 3 minutes. Add garlic and Italian seasoning, and sauté for 1 minute.

4. Add tempeh cubes, crushed tomatoes, diced tomatoes, red wine, salt, black pepper, and bay leaf. Stir well to combine, and bring to a boil. Cover, reduce heat to low, and simmer for 10 to 15 minutes or until vegetables are tender and tomatoes have broken down a bit.

Soy What?

Cacciatore is Italian for "hunter's style" and is a peasant dish traditionally made with chicken. Veganize it by hunting down some tempeh, canned tomatoes, a few vegetables, and some red wine.

5. Remove bay leaf and discard. Taste and adjust seasonings. Remove from heat, and serve hot over cooked pasta or polenta as desired.

Variation: You can replace the tempeh with 8 ounces tofu or seitan. Or add a few tablespoons chopped fresh basil or Italian parsley for extra flavor.

Chapter 17

Very Veggie Side Dishes

In This Chapter

- ◆ Simply steamed and sautéed vegetables
- ◆ Oven-roasted vegetable casseroles
- ◆ Spectacular side dishes

Most vegans love vegetables and gladly build most of their meals around them. You can even build an entire meal out of just vegetable side dishes, and many of us vegans have a lot of experience with doing just that, especially when dining out at vegan-unfriendly restaurants and attending family get-togethers.

Many of the recipes in this chapter contain commonly used vegetables like carrots, potatoes, onions, peppers, and squashes, plus a few that may be new to you, like parsnips, turnips, and rutabagas. To encourage you to be adventuresome with your vegetable side dishes, we've presented several different preparation methods that are sure to please, like steam-frying, sautéing, glazing, mashing, and oven-roasting.

Several of these recipes make fantastic side dishes suitable for impressing friends and family at holidays and festive occasions. Vegetable side dishes can be straightforward and simply prepared, or elegant and elaborate; it's all up to you!

Sautéed Squash Italiano

This colorful and flavorful side dish is made by lightly sautéing yellow squash, zucchini, and bell peppers with toasted pine nuts, sun-dried tomatoes, kalamata olives, and fresh herbs added to lend an Italian flair.

Yield: 6 servings
Prep time: 7 to 10 minutes
Cook time: 8 to 12 minutes
Serving size: 1 cup

⅓ cup *sun-dried tomato* strips

⅔ cup water

¼ cup pine nuts

3 cups yellow summer squash, cut in half lengthwise, and thinly sliced

3 cups zucchini, cut in half lengthwise, and thinly sliced

⅔ cup green bell pepper, ribs and seeds removed, and cut into 1-in. pieces

⅔ cup red or orange bell pepper, ribs and seeds removed, and cut into 1-in. pieces

4 tsp. olive oil

2 TB. garlic, minced

⅓ cup kalamata olives or other black olives of choice, pitted and coarsely chopped

¼ cup chopped fresh basil

¼ cup chopped fresh parsley (preferably Italian parsley)

½ tsp. crushed red pepper flakes

½ tsp. sea salt

¼ tsp. freshly ground black pepper

def•i•ni•tion

Sun-dried tomatoes are made from ripe plum tomato halves that have been left to dry in the sun to remove their natural water content and concentrate their flavor. Find sun-dried tomatoes as halves or cut pieces or strips, either sold in packages or from bulk bins. They're also sold in jars packed in oil, often with garlic and herbs added.

1. Place sun-dried tomato pieces in a small bowl. Cover with water, and set aside for 5 to 10 minutes to rehydrate. Drain off and discard any excess water.

2. Meanwhile, in a large nonstick skillet over low heat, cook pine nuts, stirring often, for 3 to 5 minutes or until lightly toasted and fragrant. Transfer toasted pine nuts to a small bowl, and set aside.

3. In a skillet over medium heat, sauté summer squash, zucchini, green bell pepper, red bell pepper, and olive oil, stirring often, for 3 minutes.

4. Add garlic and sauté for 1 or 2 minutes or until vegetables are crisp-tender. Add sun-dried tomatoes, pine nuts, olives, basil, parsley, red pepper flakes, salt, and black pepper, and sauté for 1 minute. Remove from heat, and serve hot.

Variation: If you don't have any fresh basil or parsley, substitute 1½ teaspoons Italian seasoning blend or ¾ teaspoon each dried basil and oregano.

Sesame Kale

Savory kale is quickly steam-fried with onion and garlic and then tossed with sesame seeds, hemp seeds, tamari, and toasted sesame oil to create this delicious, calcium-rich side dish.

⅔ cup onion, diced

½ cup water or vegetable broth

2 tsp. garlic, minced

1 bunch green or purple kale, stems trimmed, and torn into large pieces

1½ tsp. raw sesame seeds

1½ tsp. raw hemp seeds

1 tsp. tamari

1 tsp. toasted sesame oil

Sea salt

Freshly ground black pepper

Yield: 4 servings
Prep time: 3 to 5 minutes
Cook time: 5 to 7 minutes
Serving size: ¾ to 1 cup

1. In a large nonstick skillet over medium heat, steam-fry onion, water, and garlic, stirring often, for 2 or 3 minutes or until onion is soft. Add kale and steam-fry, stirring often, for 3 or 4 minutes or until tender.

2. Add sesame seeds, hemp seeds, tamari, and toasted sesame oil, and stir well to combine. Taste and season with salt and black pepper. Remove from heat, and serve hot.

Variation: Feel free to substitute other greens such as Swiss chard, mustard greens, or collard greens. You can also add red bell pepper or canned pinto or garbanzo beans for extra flavor and texture.

Thyme-ly Tip _____

You can use this same steam-frying technique, and many of the same ingredients, to make a delicious sesame-broccoli side dish. Replace the kale with 1 bunch broccoli, cut into florets, and steam-fry them along with the onion, garlic, and 1 tablespoon fresh minced ginger until crisp-tender. Add the remaining ingredients, and season with salt and pepper.

Glazed Carrots

Maple syrup, fresh ginger, and margarine combine to create a sweet glaze for whole baby carrots, creating a great side dish for holiday meals.

Yield: 4 or 5 servings

Prep time: 5 minutes

Cook time: 10 to 15 minutes

Serving size: ³/₄ cup

---

1 lb. whole baby carrots or 1 lb. carrots, cut diagonally into ½-in.-thick slices

⅓ cup water

¼ cup maple syrup

2 TB. nonhydrogenated vegan margarine

2 tsp. fresh ginger, minced, or ¼ tsp. ground ginger

½ tsp. ground cinnamon

¼ tsp. sea salt

1. In a medium saucepan over medium heat, bring carrots, water, maple syrup, margarine, ginger, cinnamon, and salt to a boil.

2. Cook, stirring often, for 10 to 15 minutes or until carrots are just tender and mixture forms a shiny glaze. Serve hot.

Variation: For orange-glazed carrots, use only 2 tablespoons water, replace maple syrup with 3 tablespoons agave nectar, omit cinnamon, add juice and zest of 1 large orange, and cook until carrots are just tender.

Soy What?

Carrots are rich in beta-carotene, which your body converts to vitamin A, the vitamin important for good eyesight.

Roasted Garlic and Rosemary Mashed Potatoes

Yukon Gold potatoes have a natural buttery flavor, which makes them especially well suited for making delicious mashed potatoes, as in this recipe, which adds roasted garlic and rosemary.

6 to 10 large garlic cloves

1 tsp. plus 1 TB. chopped fresh rosemary, or ¼ tsp. plus 1 tsp. dried rosemary, finely chopped

1½ tsp. olive oil

3 lb. (about 8 cups) Yukon Gold potatoes, peeled and cut into 2-in. cubes

½ cup soy milk or other nondairy milk of choice

2 TB. nonhydrogenated vegan margarine or olive oil (optional)

Sea salt

White pepper

Yield: 6 cups	
Prep time: 10 to 15 minutes	
Cook time: 15 to 20 minutes	
Serving size: 1 cup	

1. Preheat the oven to 375°F.

2. Place garlic cloves in a piece of aluminum foil, sprinkle 1 teaspoon fresh rosemary over garlic, and drizzle olive oil over top. Gather the corners of the aluminum foil, crimp to enclose garlic cloves, and place in a 9-inch-round pie pan. Bake for 10 to 15 minutes or until garlic cloves are soft when gently squeezed. Remove from the oven, and let cool for 5 minutes.

3. Meanwhile, place potatoes in a large pot, cover with water, and cook over medium heat for 15 to 20 minutes or until potatoes are tender. Remove from heat. Reserve 1 or 2 cups cooking liquid. Drain potatoes in a colander, and return potatoes to the pot.

4. In a small bowl, mash garlic cloves with a fork to form a smooth paste.

5. Add mashed garlic cloves and soy milk to potatoes, and either mash with a potato masher or beat with an electric mixer on medium speed for 2 or 3 minutes or until smooth. Add a little reserved cooking liquid as needed to achieve a smooth and creamy consistency.

6. Add remaining 1 tablespoon chopped rosemary and margarine (if using), season with salt and white pepper, and stir well to combine. Taste and adjust seasonings, or add additional cooking liquid or margarine as desired. Serve hot.

 Sour Grapes

Never use a food processor to mash potatoes. Always mash potatoes either by hand with an old-fashioned potato masher, or let them cool slightly and beat them with an electric mixer.

Variation: You can also top individual servings with Roasted Garlic and Shallot Gravy or Crimini Mushroom Gravy (recipes in Chapter 8). Or for extra flavor and color, add $^1/_3$ cup sun-dried tomato pieces and 2 tablespoons nutritional yeast flakes to the potatoes prior to mashing.

≈∽

Au Gratin Potatoes

In this tasty vegan version of the classic casserole, we combine our Béchamel Sauce and Vegan Cheese Sauce Mix, layer it with sliced potatoes, and finish it with a touch of shredded vegan cheddar cheese.

Yield: 1 (9×13-inch) pan
Prep time: 10 to 15 minutes
Cook time: 50 to 60 minutes
Serving size: 1 cup

2 cups Béchamel Sauce (recipe in Chapter 8)

¾ cup Vegan Cheese Sauce Mix (recipe in Chapter 9), or ½ cup nutritional yeast flakes

½ tsp. dry mustard

¾ tsp. paprika

Pinch cayenne

Sea salt

Freshly ground black pepper

3 lb. (about 8 cups) red-skinned or Yukon Gold potatoes, cut in half lengthwise and thinly sliced

$^1/_3$ cup vegan cheddar cheese, shredded

1. Preheat the oven to 375°F. Lightly oil a 9×13-inch baking dish.
2. In a medium bowl, combine Béchamel Sauce, Vegan Cheese Sauce Mix, dry mustard, $^1/_2$ teaspoon paprika, and cayenne. Taste and season with salt and black pepper.
3. Layer $^1/_2$ of potatoes in the bottom of the prepared baking dish. Season with salt and pepper, and pour $^1/_2$ of Béchamel Sauce mixture evenly over potatoes. Repeat layers with remaining potatoes and Béchamel Sauce mixture. Evenly sprinkle vegan cheddar cheese over sauce and remaining $^1/_4$ teaspoon paprika lightly over top.
4. Bake for 50 to 60 minutes or until potatoes are fork-tender and sauce is bubbling. Let cool for 5 minutes before serving.

Variation: To make scalloped potatoes, use plain Béchamel Sauce between the potato layers, sprinkle a little nutritional yeast and paprika over the top, and bake.

Soy What?

Au gratin literally refers to anything that's grated and put on top to form a crust, such as breadcrumbs or cheese. The name derives from the use of shallow, oval- or round-shaped gratin dishes for oven-baking in French cuisine.

Roasted Roots

Oven-roasting root vegetables helps bring out their natural sugars. We also added a little vegetable broth, olive oil, and fresh herbs for extra flavor.

3 lb. (about 8 cups) mixed root vegetables such as beets, carrots, parsnips, turnips, or rutabagas

6 large garlic cloves

⅓ cup vegetable broth

3 TB. olive oil

2 TB. chopped fresh thyme or 2 tsp. dried

1 TB. chopped fresh rosemary or 1 tsp. dried, finely chopped

Sea salt

Freshly ground black pepper

2 to 4 TB. balsamic vinegar

Yield: 6 servings		
Prep time: 10 to 15 minutes		
Cook time: 30 to 40 minutes		
Serving size: 1 cup		

1. Preheat the oven to 400°F. Lightly oil a large cookie sheet.

2. If using parsnips, turnips, or rutabagas, peel them; beets and carrots can be left unpeeled or peeled as desired. Cut root vegetables into 1½-inch cubes, wedges, or thick 2-inch-long french fries, and place them in the prepared cookie sheet. Leave garlic cloves whole or slice into large pieces and scatter over cut vegetables.

3. Drizzle vegetable broth and olive oil evenly over vegetables. Sprinkle thyme and rosemary over vegetables, and season with salt and black pepper. Using your hands, toss vegetable mixture until evenly coated, and spread out to form a single layer.

4. Bake for 20 minutes. Remove from the oven, stir with a spatula, and spread out into a single layer. Bake for 10 to 20 more minutes (depending on how vegetables are cut) or until vegetables are tender and lightly browned around the edges.

5. Remove from the oven. Taste and add additional salt and black pepper. Drizzle 2 tablespoons balsamic vinegar over vegetables, stir well to combine, taste, and add additional vinegar as desired. Serve hot.

Variation: Feel free to sprinkle nutritional yeast flakes over the vegetables prior to roasting to give them a slightly cheesy flavor. Or omit the final balsamic vinegar garnishing at the end, roughly mash the roasted roots with a little vegetable broth and nutritional yeast flakes, and serve them in place of mashed potatoes.

 Thyme-ly Tip

If you have any leftover roasted roots, add them to soups or stews, or combine them with cooked greens.

Brussels Sprouts with Peppers and Almonds

You'll become a lover of brussels sprouts after sampling this colorful side dish, where brussels sprouts are oven-roasted with toasted sesame oil, garlic, bell peppers, and almonds.

Yield: 6 servings
Prep time: 10 minutes
Cook time: 35 to 45 minutes
Serving size: 1 cup

1½ lb. brussels sprouts

4 tsp. toasted sesame oil

2 tsp. olive oil

1 tsp. garlic powder or garlic granules

¾ tsp. sea salt

½ tsp. freshly ground black pepper

½ tsp. crushed red pepper flakes (optional)

1 cup red bell pepper, ribs and seeds removed, cut into 1-in. strips

1 cup orange or yellow bell pepper, ribs and seeds removed, cut into 1-in. strips

½ cup raw sliced almonds

Soy What?

Choose brussels sprouts that feel firm; have tight, shiny-edged leaves; and are 1 or 2 inches in size.

---

1. Preheat the oven to 400°F. Lightly oil a large cookie sheet.

2. Trim ends off brussels sprouts, remove any tough or yellow outer leaves, and cut each in ½ lengthwise. Place brussels sprouts on the prepared cookie sheet.

3. Drizzle toasted sesame oil and olive oil evenly over brussels sprouts. Sprinkle garlic powder, salt, black pepper, and red pepper flakes (if using) over the top. Using your hands, toss brussels sprouts until evenly coated, and spread out to form a single layer.

4. Bake for 20 minutes. Remove from the oven, stir with a spatula, and spread out into a single layer.

5. Scatter red bell pepper and orange bell pepper slices over brussels sprouts. Bake for 15 to 20 more minutes or until brussels sprouts are tender and lightly browned around the edges.

6. Scatter almonds over the top, and bake for 2 or 3 more minutes or until lightly toasted. Remove from the oven, stir vegetable mixture well to combine, and serve hot.

Variation: You can also sauté the brussels sprouts with both oils and seasonings in a large nonstick skillet over medium heat, stirring often, for 5 to 7 minutes or until they just begin to brown in places. Add bell peppers and almonds, and sauté for 2 or 3 minutes or until almonds are lightly toasted.

Lemon-Garlic Asparagus

Here, fresh asparagus is steamed in lemon-flavored water, combined with sautéed garlic and olive oil, and given a final boost of flavor with fresh lemon juice and vegan Parmesan cheese.

2 lb. asparagus	¼ cup chopped fresh parsley
2 TB. olive oil	Sea salt
2 TB. garlic, minced	Freshly ground black pepper
¾ cup water or vegetable broth	Vegan soy Parmesan cheese or Raw Parmesan Cheese (recipe in Chapter 9)
2 lemons	

Yield: 4 servings	
Prep time: 5 to 7 minutes	
Cook time: 8 to 12 minutes	
Serving size: 1 cup	

1. Trim asparagus ends. Either leave asparagus whole or cut in half lengthwise, place on a large plate, and set aside.

2. In a large nonstick skillet over medium heat, sauté olive oil and garlic, stirring often, for 1 or 2 minutes or until garlic is soft. Remove from heat, transfer to a small bowl, and set aside.

3. Place asparagus and water in the skillet.

4. Remove zest from 1 lemon, cut lemon in half, squeeze juice over asparagus, and add lemon halves and zest to the skillet. Cover and cook over medium heat, stirring often, for 7 to 10 minutes or until crisp-tender.

5. Meanwhile, cut remaining lemon into wedges, place in a small bowl, and set aside.

6. Drain off excess water from the skillet. Remove lemon halves and discard. Add garlic mixture and parsley, season with salt and black pepper, and stir gently to combine. Serve hot with lemon wedges and vegan Parmesan cheese, and squeeze fresh lemon juice and cheese over individual servings as desired.

Variation: You can also toss the asparagus with the olive oil and garlic, season with salt and black pepper, and grill or roast the asparagus until tender. Serve with lemon wedges and vegan soy Parmesan cheese.

Soy What?

Asparagus contains several sulfurous amino acid compounds that break down during the digestion process and can cause your urine to have a unique odor. Scientists believe they've found the culprit, mercaptan.

Artichoke, Mushroom, and Spinach Toss

Tender canned artichoke hearts take center stage in this quickly sautéed side dish that contains many Mediterranean-inspired flavors and ingredients, including sun-dried tomatoes, pine nuts, mushrooms, and fresh spinach.

Yield: 4 servings
Prep time: 10 to 15 minutes
Cook time: 10 to 15 minutes
Serving size: 1¼ cups

⅓ cup sun-dried tomato pieces

⅔ cup water

¼ cup pine nuts

1 (14-oz.) can artichoke hearts packed in water, drained

1 medium red onion, cut into half moons

4 tsp. olive oil

1½ cups crimini mushrooms or other mushrooms of choice, cut in half and thinly sliced

4 large garlic cloves, thinly sliced

1 tsp. dried basil

½ tsp. dried oregano

½ tsp. crushed red pepper flakes (optional)

1 bunch spinach, stems removed

1 TB. nutritional yeast flakes

Sea salt

Freshly ground black pepper

1. Place sun-dried tomato pieces in a small bowl. Cover with water, and set aside for 5 to 10 minutes to rehydrate. Drain off and discard any excess water.

2. Meanwhile, in a large nonstick skillet over low heat, cook pine nuts, stirring often, for 3 to 5 minutes or until lightly toasted and fragrant. Transfer toasted pine nuts to a small bowl, and set aside.

3. In a skillet over medium heat, sauté artichokes, red onion, and olive oil, stirring often, for 3 minutes. Add mushrooms and sauté, stirring often, for 2 minutes.

4. Add garlic, basil, oregano, and red pepper flakes (if using), and sauté for 1 or 2 minutes or until vegetables are crisp-tender. Add sun-dried tomatoes, pine nuts, spinach, and nutritional yeast flakes, and sauté for 1 minute. Remove from heat, taste, and season with salt and black pepper. Serve hot.

Variation: For extra flavor, add sliced red bell pepper or kalamata olives.

Thyme-ly Tip

Use this artichoke mixture to make personal pizzas. Spread 1 or 2 tablespoons Black Olive and Sun-Dried Tomato Tapenade (recipe in Chapter 7) on a pita bread. Top with some artichoke mixture and a little nutritional yeast or shredded vegan mozzarella cheese. Bake at 425°F for 5 to 7 minutes or until pita bread is crisp and lightly browned around the edges.

Glazed Sweet Potato, Cranberry, and Pecan Medley

This festive version of a holiday favorite is made with a spiced maple syrup mixture. Dried cranberries and pecans add extra color and flavor.

3 lb. (about 8 cups) sweet potatoes, cut into 1½-in. cubes

½ cup raw pecans, coarsely chopped

⅓ cup dried cranberries

⅓ cup maple syrup

3 TB. nonhydrogenated vegan margarine

2 TB. turbinado sugar or agave nectar

1¼ tsp. ground cinnamon

¾ tsp. ground ginger

½ tsp. sea salt

Yield: 6 servings
Prep time: 5 to 7 minutes
Cook time: 25 to 30 minutes
Serving size: 1 cup

1. Place sweet potatoes in a large pot, cover with water, and cook over medium heat for 15 to 20 minutes or until are tender. Remove from heat, drain potatoes in a colander, and return potatoes to the pot.

2. Meanwhile, in a small saucepan over low heat, cook pecans, stirring often, for 3 to 5 minutes or until lightly toasted and fragrant. Transfer toasted pecans to a small bowl, and set aside.

3. In a small saucepan over low heat, cook dried cranberries, maple syrup, margarine, sugar, cinnamon, ginger, and salt for 5 minutes to soften cranberries. Remove from heat.

4. Add cranberry mixture and pecans to cooked sweet potatoes, and stir well to combine. Serve hot.

Variation: For a roasted sweet potato casserolelike dish, roast the sweet potatoes, covered with a little olive oil, in a large casserole dish at 400°F for 30 minutes or until tender. Pour the cranberry mixture over the top, sprinkle with raw pecans, and bake for 5 to 7 minutes or until pecans are lightly toasted and fragrant.

Soy What?

What's often referred to as a yam in the United States is actually a sweet potato. A true yam is a tropical vegetable popular in African, Caribbean, and Latin cuisine and is seldom found in the States. Sweet potatoes are short, thick-skinned, smooth, moist, and sweet. Yams are long, scaly, rough-skinned, dry, and starchy-tasting.

18

Lively Legumes

In This Chapter

- ◆ Savory and spicy simmered legumes
- ◆ Southern-style bean dishes
- ◆ Classic oven-baked bean casseroles

Legumes, while technically seeds and commonly referred to as beans, come in a full range of colors, shapes, and sizes. They're also nutritional dynamos that provide you with sources of low-fat protein, complex carbohydrates, fiber, iron, zinc, B vitamins, and a wide variety of other vitamins and minerals. You can easily bulk up a dish, as well as boost its nutritional value, by adding in some peas or beans.

You're probably most familiar with legumes such as beans, peas, lentils, soybeans, and peanuts. They're grown practically everywhere and featured prominently in cuisines throughout the world in dips, salads, sandwich fillings, soups and stews, sauces, side dishes, hearty main dishes, and even delectable desserts (think tofu-based mousse and cheesecake).

Legumes are one of the most affordable foods around, so not only can you reap great health benefits by including them more often into your meals, but you can save a buck or two as well.

Fresh, Frozen, Canned, or Dried?

You can purchase legumes fresh, frozen, or dried, and in cans in either plain or flavored varieties.

When you can't get freshly picked beans, frozen are a fine substitute. They usually have better flavor, texture, and appearance than canned peas, green beans, and lima beans. Depending on where you live, you may also have more options for buying certain legumes like fava beans, roman beans, and *edamame* from the freezer section.

def•i•ni•tion

Edamame are fresh green soybeans, not the off-white soybeans found canned or dried. They can be hard to find fresh, but most grocery and natural foods stores sell them frozen in the pods or preshelled. Edamame are typically briefly blanched and lightly salted before serving. Gently squeeze them out of the pod to eat if they're not already shelled. They're a great snack or appetizer.

You can purchase dried legumes from bulk bins or in 1-pound packages or more. Store dried legumes in jars or other airtight containers, or in their original packaging, in a cool, dark place for up to a year. Before cooking dried beans, be sure to sort them, which simply means picking over them to look for dirt, rocks, or other debris. Then rinse them in a colander or fine mesh sieve under running water to remove any dirt or dust.

Principles of Presoaking

Some people like to presoak their dried beans covered in water for several hours or overnight to rehydrate them slightly, which cuts down the cooking time by 30 to 45 minutes. You can also do a quick soak by boiling them in water for several minutes, turning off the heat, and letting them stand in the hot water for an hour or more. This method shortens cooking time by 15 to 30 minutes.

Presoaking beans also removes some of their gas-producing sugars, which helps reduce flatulence and makes them more easily digestible for some people.

If you do presoak, discard the soaking water and cover the soaked beans with fresh water for cooking. Some people prefer to add a bay leaf or two or a piece of kombu (a type of seaweed) to the cooking beans to help improve digestibility and reduce gas. You can also add garlic, ginger, herbs, and spices for extra flavor.

Tips for Cooking Legumes

Whether you presoak or not, use a large pot and a generous amount of water when cooking dried legumes—unless you aren't going to drain them; then use whatever amount of water the recipe recommends.

To speed up the cooking process, bring the cooking water to a boil first, slowly add the dried legumes, cover tightly, reduce heat to low, and simmer gently to avoid bursting open their skins, until they reach desired tenderness.

To check for tenderness, taste one or two legumes. They're done when you can easily bite into them. Firm-cooked beans work best in salads and side dishes. Soft-cooked ones work best in soups, stews, sandwich fillings, and dips. You can drain them for use in recipes and use the cooking liquid in soups, sauces, or for cooking grains, or cook them uncovered for several minutes and serve them in their cooking liquid.

Thyme-ly Tip

Use a slow cooker to cook legumes slowly over several hours, overnight, or while you're at work. Or use a pressure cooker to cook them in record time—most cook in 10 to 30 minutes, depending on the variety.

Cooking legumes can be time-consuming, so we suggest cooking larger amounts of your favorite dried legumes than you need for a meal. They'll keep for several days in the refrigerator, or you can freeze them in individual portions in airtight containers or zipper-lock bags for up to six months.

Mediterranean Garbanzos and Green Beans

The flavors and textures of garbanzo beans and green beans complement each other rather well, especially when seasoned with basil, oregano, and cumin and cloaked with tomatoes, as in this savory dish that also contains zucchini, red bell pepper, and onions.

Yield: 6 servings
Prep time: 5 to 7 minutes
Cook time: 12 to 15 minutes
Serving size: 1 cup

1 cup onion, diced

1 TB. olive oil

1½ cups fresh green beans, cut into 2-in. pieces, or frozen cut green beans

1 medium zucchini, cut in half lengthwise and cut into ½-in.-thick slices

1 cup red bell pepper, ribs and seeds removed, and diced

1 TB. garlic, minced

½ tsp. dried basil

½ tsp. dried oregano

½ tsp. ground cumin

½ tsp. sea salt

¼ tsp. freshly ground black pepper

1 (15-oz.) can garbanzo beans, drained and rinsed

1 (14-oz.) can diced tomatoes

1. In a large saucepan over medium heat, sauté onion and olive oil, stirring often, for 2 minutes. Add green beans, zucchini, and red bell pepper, and sauté, stirring often, for 2 minutes.

2. Add garlic, basil, oregano, cumin, salt, and black pepper, and sauté for 1 minute.

3. Add garbanzo beans and diced tomatoes, and stir well to combine. Cover, reduce heat to low, and simmer for 7 to 10 minutes or until vegetables are tender and tomatoes begin to break down. Remove from heat. Taste and adjust seasonings as desired, and serve hot.

Variation: To give this dish a Moroccan flair, replace the zucchini with 2 cups eggplant, cut into 1-inch cubes, and add ½ teaspoon ground coriander or curry powder. You can also serve this dish over cooked grains or pasta as a main dish.

Soy What?

Garbanzo beans are a low-fat source of protein, carbohydrates, dietary fiber, and an assortment of vitamins and minerals. Whole garbanzo beans make great additions to salads, soups, pasta, and grain dishes.

Curried Lentils

These lentils are boldly seasoned with curry powder, cumin, and cayenne. A little tamari and lacinato kale are added at the end for a savory touch and flavor.

⅔ **cup onion, diced**

⅔ **cup carrot, diced**

⅔ **cup celery, diced**

1 TB. olive oil

1 TB. garlic, minced

1 TB. curry powder

1 tsp. ground cumin

1 tsp. dried thyme

¼ tsp. freshly ground black pepper

¼ tsp. cayenne

1 cup dried brown lentils, sorted and rinsed

3 cups water or vegetable broth

4 cups *lacinato kale* or spinach, stems trimmed and shredded

2 tsp. tamari or Bragg Liquid Aminos

Yield: 4 or 5 servings
Prep time: 5 to 7 minutes
Cook time: 30 to 35 minutes
Serving size: 1 cup

1. In a large saucepan over medium heat, sauté onion, carrot, celery, and olive oil, stirring often, for 5 minutes.

2. Add garlic, curry powder, cumin, thyme, black pepper, and cayenne, and sauté for 1 minute.

3. Add lentils and water, stir well to combine, and bring to a boil. Cover, reduce heat to low, and simmer, stirring occasionally, for 20 minutes.

4. Add kale and tamari, cover, and simmer for 5 to 10 more minutes or until lentils are tender and most of liquid is absorbed. Remove from heat. Taste and adjust seasonings, and serve hot.

Variation: Vary the flavor of the lentils by omitting the curry powder, cumin, and cayenne, and replace them with 1½ teaspoons Italian seasoning blend, and also add 2 vegetarian Italian-style flavored sausages, sliced thinly. You can also serve this dish over cooked grains or pasta as a main dish.

def•i•ni•tion

Lacinato kale has slender, wrinkled leaves that are quite tender. It can be eaten raw in salads or added to soups, stews, stir-fries, and casseroles.

Pintos and Corn Medley

The flavors of Mexico and the Southwest United States are captured in this festive combination of pinto beans, corn, bell peppers, and jalapeño pepper, with a generous amount of spices and fresh cilantro and parsley.

Yield: 6 servings

Prep time: 7 to 10 minutes

Cook time: 8 to 10 minutes

Serving size: 1 cup

---

1 lb. (3 cups) frozen cut corn kernels

1 green bell pepper, ribs and seeds removed, and diced

1 red bell pepper, ribs and seeds removed, and diced

1 jalapeño pepper, ribs and seeds removed, and finely diced

1 TB. olive oil

1 TB. garlic, minced

1 tsp. chili powder

¾ tsp. dried oregano

½ tsp. ground cumin

½ tsp. sea salt

¼ tsp. freshly ground black pepper

¼ tsp. cayenne

1 (15-oz.) can pinto beans, drained and rinsed

½ cup green onions, thinly sliced

¼ cup chopped fresh cilantro

¼ cup chopped fresh parsley

1 TB. nutritional yeast flakes

1. In a large nonstick skillet over medium heat, sauté corn, green bell pepper, red bell pepper, jalapeño pepper, and olive oil, stirring often, for 3 to 5 minutes or until vegetables are crisp-tender.

2. Add garlic, chili powder, oregano, cumin, salt, black pepper, and cayenne, and sauté for 1 minute.

3. Add pinto beans, green onions, cilantro, parsley, and nutritional yeast flakes, and sauté for 1 or 2 minutes or until beans are heated through. Remove from heat. Taste and adjust seasonings, and serve hot.

Variation: Add 1 diced tomato or ½ cup salsa for extra flavor, or toss in ¼ cup raw pumpkin seeds for a slight crunch. You can also combine this dish with cooked quinoa or brown rice and serve as a hearty side or main dish.

Thyme-ly Tip

Transform this side dish into a filling for enchiladas by adding 1 cup tomato sauce or prepared salsa. Roll up ⅓ cup medley in 6-inch corn tortillas and place them in an oiled baking dish. Top with Salsa Verde (recipe in Chapter 8) or canned enchilada sauce, sprinkle shredded vegan cheddar cheese over the top, and bake at 375°F for 20 minutes.

Red Beans with Soyrizo

Inspired by the way red beans are prepared down in New Orleans, we used spicy soyrizo to add a little extra something to this pot of well-seasoned red beans.

1 (12-oz.) pkg. soyrizo, removed from casing

1 TB. olive oil

4½ cups water

1½ cups dried red beans, sorted and rinsed

1½ cups onion, diced

1 cup green bell pepper, ribs and seeds removed, and diced

1 cup celery, diced

1 jalapeño pepper, ribs and seeds removed, and finely diced

2 TB. garlic, minced

1 bay leaf

2 tsp. chili powder

1 tsp. dried oregano

1 tsp. dried thyme

¼ tsp. cayenne

½ tsp. sea salt

¼ tsp. freshly ground black pepper

Hot pepper sauce

Yield: 4 or 5 servings
Prep time: 5 to 7 minutes
Cook time: 65 to 95 minutes
Serving size: 1 cup

1. In a medium nonstick skillet over medium heat, sauté soyrizo and olive oil, stirring often, for 3 to 5 minutes or until crispy.

2. Add water, red beans, onion, green bell pepper, celery, jalapeño pepper, garlic, bay leaf, chili powder, oregano, thyme, and cayenne, and bring to a boil. Cover, reduce heat to low, and simmer, stirring occasionally, for 1 to 1½ hours or until red beans are tender.

3. Add salt, black pepper, and hot pepper sauce. Taste and adjust seasonings. Remove bay leaf and discard. Remove from the heat, and serve hot with additional hot pepper sauce as desired.

Variation: You can replace the dried red beans with dried pinto or kidney beans, and the soyrizo with 1 cup TVP granules. You can also serve this dish over cooked brown rice or grains as a main dish.

Thyme-ly Tip

Adding salt and acidic ingredients like tomatoes or vinegar hardens legume skins and can lengthen cooking time, so it's best to add salt to the pot after the legumes are tender. However, when cooking legumes like lentils or lima beans that have softer skins, or when you want their skins to remain intact, add salt at the beginning.

Butter Beans with Sweet Potatoes and Greens

Creamy butter beans blend beautifully with the delicately sweet flavor of sweet potatoes, and tender and colorful rainbow Swiss chard adds color and a subtle savory flavor to this quick-cooking side dish.

Yield: 4 servings
Prep time: 7 to 10 minutes
Cook time: 7 to 10 minutes
Serving size: 1 cup

1 large sweet potato, cut into quarters lengthwise and thinly sliced

1 cup red onion, cut into half moons

1 TB. olive oil

1 TB. garlic, minced

½ tsp. dried thyme

½ tsp. crushed red pepper flakes

½ cup water or vegetable broth

1 bunch rainbow Swiss chard, stems and leaves thinly sliced

1 (15-oz.) can butter beans, drained and rinsed

2 tsp. nutritional yeast flakes (optional)

1 tsp. tamari or Bragg Liquid Aminos

¼ tsp. sea salt

¼ tsp. freshly ground black pepper

1. In a large nonstick skillet over medium heat, sauté sweet potato, red onion, and olive oil, stirring often, for 3 minutes.

2. Add garlic, thyme, and red pepper flakes, and sauté for 1 minute. Add water, reduce heat to low, and simmer for 3 to 5 minutes or until sweet potato is tender.

3. Add Swiss chard, butter beans, nutritional yeast flakes (if using), tamari, salt, and black pepper, and simmer for 2 or 3 minutes or until beans are heated through and Swiss chard begins to wilt. Taste and add additional tamari, salt, or black pepper as desired. Remove from heat, and serve hot.

Variation: You can replace the sweet potato with 1 pound delicata squash or other winter squash, cut into 1-inch cubes.

Soy What?

Butter beans are often referred to as lima beans, but they are really two different beans. They do have a similar, flat, kidney shape, but butter beans are off-white to light beige in color, while limas are green. Cooked butter beans also have a much creamier texture compared to lima beans.

Cuban Black Beans

Cubans are famous for their black beans, which they typically serve over rice. That's exactly how we suggest serving these beans.

5 cups water

1½ cups dried black beans, sorted and rinsed

1 bay leaf, or 1 (6-in.) piece *kombu*

¾ cup onion, diced

¾ cup green bell pepper, ribs and seeds removed, and diced

1 jalapeño pepper, ribs and seeds removed, and finely diced

1 TB. olive oil

2 TB. garlic, minced

2 TB. fresh ginger, minced

1½ tsp. chili powder

1½ tsp. ground cumin

1½ tsp. dried oregano

¾ tsp. sea salt

½ tsp. freshly ground black pepper

1 TB. red wine vinegar

Hot pepper sauce

Yield: 4 or 5 servings
Prep time: 5 minutes
Cook time: 70 to 95 minutes
Serving size: 1 cup

1. In a large pot over high heat, bring water, black beans, and bay leaf to a boil. Cover, reduce heat to low, and simmer, stirring occasionally, for 1 to 1½ hours or until black beans are tender. Remove and discard bay leaf (or kombu).

2. Meanwhile, in a small nonstick skillet, sauté onion, green bell pepper, jalapeño pepper, and olive oil, stirring often, for 3 to 5 minutes or until onion is soft.

3. Add garlic, ginger, chili powder, cumin, oregano, salt, and black pepper, and sauté for 2 minutes. Remove from heat.

4. When black beans are tender, add onion mixture and vinegar, stir well to combine, and simmer for 5 minutes to allow flavors to blend. Taste and adjust seasonings as desired. Remove from heat, and serve hot with hot pepper sauce if desired.

Variation: You can also serve this dish over cooked brown rice or grains as a main dish. To transform this recipe into Cuban black bean soup, add ¾ cup each diced carrot and celery to the sautéed vegetable mixture, and add an additional 2 cups water to the simmering beans.

def•i•ni•tion

Kombu is edible kelp that contains many beneficial vitamins and nutrients. It's sold in thick, dark-colored (nearly black), 5- or 6-inch pieces. Kombu is commonly used in Asian cuisine, especially in making soups and dashi soup stock.

Vegetarian Baked Beans

This recipe for vegetarian baked beans is made the old-fashioned way, using three different dried beans that are first boiled and then oven-baked, with sautéed vegetables and several seasonings and flavoring agents.

Yield: 8 to 10 servings
Prep time: 10 minutes plus 1 hour for soaking beans
Cook time: 2½ to 3 hours
Serving size: 1 cup

¾ **cup dried navy beans, sorted and rinsed**

¾ **cup dried baby butter beans, sorted and rinsed**

¾ **cup dried red beans or pinto beans, sorted and rinsed**

6 cups water

1 bay leaf, or 1 (6-in.) piece kombu

1⅔ **cups onion, diced**

⅔ **cup carrot, diced**

1 TB. olive oil or safflower oil

1 TB. garlic, minced

1 TB. chili powder

¼ **cup turbinado sugar or maple syrup**

¼ **cup ketchup**

2 TB. blackstrap molasses

2 TB. apple cider vinegar

2 TB. Dijon mustard, or 2 tsp. dry mustard

1 TB. tamari or Bragg Liquid Aminos

1 tsp. sea salt

½ **tsp. freshly ground black pepper**

1. Place navy beans, butter beans, and red beans in a large pot, and add enough water to cover. Bring to a boil over medium-high heat, and continue to boil for 2 minutes. Cover, remove from heat, and allow beans to soak in hot water for 1 hour. Drain beans in a colander, and discard soaking liquid.

2. Return beans to the pot. Add 6 cups water and bay leaf, and bring to a boil over medium-high heat. Cover, reduce heat to low, and simmer, stirring occasionally, for 1 to 1½ hours or until beans are tender. Remove and discard bay leaf (or kombu).

3. Meanwhile, in a small nonstick skillet over medium heat, sauté onion, carrot, and olive oil, stirring often, for 3 minutes. Add garlic and chili powder, and sauté for 2 minutes. Remove from heat.

4. Preheat the oven to 300°F.

5. Transfer cooked beans and remaining cooking liquid to a 2½-quart casserole dish. Add onion mixture, sugar, ketchup, molasses, vinegar, Dijon mustard, tamari, salt, and black pepper, and stir well to combine. Cover baking dish with a lid or aluminum foil, and bake for 1 hour. Remove lid or aluminum foil, and bake for 30 more minutes. Serve hot or cold as desired.

Variation: For extra flavor, add 4 slices vegetarian ham or Canadian bacon, diced, or 4 vegetarian hot dogs, thinly sliced, to the bean mixture prior to baking.

Thyme-ly Tip

For quick calico baked beans, use canned beans: in a 2½-quart casserole dish, combine 2 (28-ounce) cans vegetarian baked beans; 1 (15-ounce) can each black beans, butter beans, and kidney beans; ⅓ cup turbinado sugar; 2 tablespoons blackstrap molasses; 1 tablespoon dry mustard; and salt and black pepper. Cover and bake at 350°F for 30 minutes or until bubbling.

Hoppin' John

This is our spicy version of the down-home favorite, made with black-eyed peas, brown rice, and assorted vegetables and seasonings.

Yield: 6 to 8 servings
Prep time: 10 minutes
Cook time: 70 to 75 minutes
Serving size: 1¼ cups

6 cups water

2 cups dried black-eyed peas, sorted and rinsed

1 bay leaf, or 1 (6-in.) piece kombu

1 tsp. chili powder

1 tsp. dried oregano

1 tsp. dried thyme

1 cup long-grain brown rice

1½ cups onion, diced

2 TB. olive oil

1½ cups green bell pepper, ribs and seeds removed, and diced

1½ cups celery, diced

2 jalapeño peppers, ribs and seeds removed, and finely diced

½ cup green onions, thinly sliced

2 TB. garlic, minced

⅓ cup chopped fresh parsley

1 tsp. sea salt

½ tsp. freshly ground black pepper

½ tsp. liquid smoke flavoring (optional)

Hot pepper sauce

Sliced green onions, diced tomatoes, shredded vegan cheese, or toppings of choice

1. In a large pot over high heat, bring water, black-eyed peas, bay leaf (or kombu), chili powder, oregano, and thyme to a boil. Cover, reduce heat to low, and simmer for 30 minutes.

2. Add brown rice, cover, and simmer for 40 to 45 more minutes or until black-eyed peas and brown rice are tender. Remove bay leaf (or kombu) and discard.

3. Meanwhile, in a large nonstick skillet over medium heat, sauté onion and olive oil, stirring often, for 3 minutes. Add green bell pepper, celery, and jalapeño peppers, and sauté for 3 to 5 minutes or until vegetables are soft. Add green onions and garlic, and sauté for 2 minutes. Remove from heat.

4. To black-eyed peas and rice, add onion mixture, parsley, salt, black pepper, liquid smoke (if using), and hot pepper sauce, and stir well to combine. Taste and adjust seasonings as desired. Remove from heat, and serve hot, individual servings garnished with additional hot pepper sauce and toppings of choice.

Soy What?

In the South, it's a custom to serve Hoppin' John as the first thing eaten on New Year's Day. Doing so, it's believed, will bring good luck in the coming year. Some families even hide a coin in their batch of Hoppin' John, and whoever finds it is said to have the best luck of all.

Variation: For a spicier flavor, cook 1 (12-ounce) package soyrizo with 1 tablespoon olive oil in the skillet prior to cooking the other vegetables.

Green Bean Casserole

Traditionally, this popular oven-baked side dish is made with canned soup and a generous amount of crunchy, canned french-fried onions. Here's our updated, vegan version.

1½ lb. fresh green beans, cut into 2-in. pieces

Sea salt

1½ whole-grain bread slices

1 TB. nonhydrogenated vegan margarine

3 tsp. nutritional yeast flakes

⅛ tsp. sea salt

1 (2.8-oz.) can french-fried onions

1½ cups Crimini Mushroom Gravy or Roasted Garlic and Shallot Gravy (recipes in Chapter 8)

1 cup soy milk or other non-dairy milk of choice

Freshly ground black pepper

Yield: 6 servings
Prep time: 5 to 10 minutes
Cook time: 20 to 25 minutes
Serving size: 1 cup

1. Preheat the oven to 400°F. Lightly oil a 9×13-inch baking pan or a 2-quart casserole dish.

2. Place green beans in a large saucepan, cover with water, season with salt, and bring to a boil over high heat. Cover, reduce heat to medium, and cook for 6 to 8 minutes or until beans are crisp-tender. Drain in a colander, rinse with cold water, and drain well again.

3. Meanwhile, for topping, tear bread slices into small pieces and place in a food processor fitted with an S blade. Add margarine, 1 teaspoon nutritional yeast flakes, and ⅛ teaspoon salt, and pulse several times until mixture is crumbly. Transfer mixture to a small bowl. Add french-fried onions, and stir well to combine.

4. Return beans to the pot. Add Crimini Mushroom Gravy, soy milk, and remaining 2 teaspoons nutritional yeast flakes, and stir well to combine. Taste and season with salt and black pepper. Transfer mixture to the prepared pan. Sprinkle topping evenly over green bean mixture.

5. Bake for 15 to 20 minutes or until bubbling and golden brown on top. Remove from the oven, and serve hot.

Variation: Steam the green beans until crisp-tender or replace them with 1½ pounds (5½) cups) frozen cut green beans.

Soy What?
French-fried onions are sold in various-size cans and packages in most grocery stores. Use these crisp and crunchy onion pieces on salads, soups, grain dishes, and casseroles, but use them sparingly—they're high in fat and sodium.

19

Great Grains

In This Chapter

- ◆ Preparing pilafs with grains and rice
- ◆ The secret to making vegan risotto
- ◆ Enhancing grains with vegetables and seasonings

Grains is a general term referring to any foods made from wheat, oats, rice, cornmeal, barley, or any other cereal. *Whole grains* refer to grains that contain the complete grain kernel—the bran, the germ, and the endosperm—which is meant to support new plant growth. Whole grains are great sources of complex carbohydrates; fiber; protein; iron; and the B vitamins thiamin, riboflavin, niacin, folate, and pantothenic acid. It's no wonder grains and rices have been a staple in the human diet for centuries.

Grains can be served at any meal. In this chapter, grains and rices are used to make great-tasting side dishes; using them to occupy a half or third of your plate fills you up without fattening you up. Think of grains and rices as a blank canvas on which you can freely express your culinary creativity. Serve them simply prepared, with just a light sprinkle of sea salt, black pepper, or tamari, or heavily seasoned for a quick and easy side dish. Or add some chopped vegetables, beans, nuts or seeds, and some fresh herbs, and take them to a higher level of gastronomic excellency.

You can find a wide variety of grains and rices in bulk bins or 1- or more pound packages in most stores. Store whole and refined grains in airtight containers because they can attract bugs. Refined grains can last indefinitely in your pantry stored this way; however, the oil-rich bran in whole grains can become rancid, especially during warm weather, so store them in the refrigerator or freezer to preserve freshness. If you have to store them in your cabinets, purchase smaller amounts so you can use them before they go bad.

Bulgur Pilaf with Dried Fruit

Toasted sesame oil and pine nuts give this bulgur dish a lightly smoky flavor, while the dates and currants add a touch of sweetness.

3 TB. raw pine nuts

1 medium leek (white and pale green part only), cut in half lengthwise and thinly sliced

2 TB. plus 2 cups vegetable broth or water

3 tsp. toasted sesame oil

1½ cups bulgur

½ tsp. sea salt

¼ tsp. freshly ground black pepper

¼ cup date pieces

¼ cup dried currants

¼ cup chopped fresh parsley, or 2 TB. chopped fresh mint

1 TB. freshly squeezed lemon juice

Yield: 5 or 6 servings
Prep time: 5 minutes
Cook time: 20 to 25 minutes plus 10 to 15 minutes for rehydrating bulgur
Serving size: ³/₄ cup

1. In a large saucepan over low heat, cook pine nuts, stirring often, for 3 to 5 minutes or until lightly toasted and fragrant. Transfer toasted pine nuts to a small bowl, and set aside.

2. Place leek, 2 tablespoons vegetable broth, and 1¹/₂ teaspoons toasted sesame oil in saucepan, and stir well to combine. Cover and cook over low heat, stirring occasionally, for 6 to 8 minutes or until leek is soft and lightly browned. Add remaining 2 cups vegetable broth, and bring to a boil.

3. Place bulgur in a very fine-mesh strainer and rinse well under running water. Add bulgur to the saucepan, along with salt and black pepper. Cover, reduce heat to medium, and simmer for 10 minutes.

4. Add date pieces and currants. Remove from heat, cover, and set aside for 10 to 15 minutes or until bulgur is tender and all liquid is absorbed. Fluff bulgur with a fork to loosen grains.

5. Add parsley, toasted pine nuts, lemon juice, and remaining 1¹/₂ teaspoons toasted sesame oil, and mix lightly to combine. Serve hot, cold, or at room temperature.

Variation: If leeks aren't available, substitute 1¹/₂ cups green onions, thinly sliced.

Thyme-ly Tip

Leeks' many layers seem to capture dirt, so be sure to thoroughly wash them. Cut them as desired, place the cut pieces in a bowl of water, vigorously move them around, and lift them out into a colander. Repeat as needed (using clean water each time) until no more dirt appears in the bottom of the bowl.

Mixed-Grain Pilaf

In this versatile and savory pilaf, we've combined sautéed vegetables with several hearty grains.

Yield: 6 or 7 servings
Prep time: 7 to 10 minutes
Cook time: 50 to 55 minutes
Serving size: ¾ cup

⅔ **cup onion, diced**

⅔ **cup carrot, diced**

⅔ **cup celery, diced**

2 TB. olive oil

¼ **cup green onions**

2 TB. garlic, minced

1½ **tsp. dried thyme**

1 tsp. rubbed sage

¾ **cup mixed rice and wild rice blend**

¼ **cup pearled barley or buck-wheat groats (or kasha)**

¼ **cup spelt berries or kamut berries**

3 cups water or vegetable broth

1 bay leaf

1 tsp. sea salt

¼ **tsp. freshly ground black pepper**

⅓ **cup chopped fresh parsley**

1½ **tsp. tamari**

Thyme-ly Tip

Lundberg (www. lundberg.com) grows and sells several varieties of rice and rice blends no other company sells. Our favorite is their Wild Blend (long-grain brown, sweet brown, wild rice bits, Wehani, and Black Japonica rices).

1. In a large saucepan over medium heat, sauté onion, carrot, celery, and olive oil, stirring often, for 5 minutes or until soft. Add green onions, garlic, thyme, and sage, and sauté for 2 minutes.

2. Place mixed rice and wild rice blend, pearled barley, and spelt berries in a fine-mesh strainer, and rinse well under running water. Add grains to the saucepan, stir well to combine, and sauté, stirring often, for 2 or 3 minutes or until grains are lightly toasted and fragrant.

3. Add water, bay leaf, salt, and black pepper, and bring to a boil. Cover, reduce heat to low, and simmer for 40 to 45 minutes or until grains are tender and all liquid is absorbed.

4. Remove from heat. Remove and discard bay leaf. Fluff grains with a fork, add parsley and tamari, and mix lightly to combine. Serve hot.

Variation: If you can't find spelt berries or kamut berries, add an additional ¼ cup pearled barley (or buckwheat groats). If you prefer to make an all-rice pilaf, use 1¹/₂ cups mixed rice and wild rice blend.

Special Fried Rice

This vegan version of fried rice uses turmeric-tinted crumbled tofu as an egg replacement and features brown rice, zesty fresh ginger and garlic, and a colorful assortment of diced vegetables.

2¼ cups water

1 cup long-grain brown rice

8 oz. firm or extra-firm tofu

½ tsp. garlic powder

½ tsp. onion powder

⅛ tsp. turmeric

1½ tsp. plus 1 TB. olive oil or peanut oil

⅔ cup carrot, finely diced

⅔ cup celery, finely diced

⅔ cup red bell pepper, ribs and seeds removed, and finely diced

⅔ cup frozen peas

2 TB. garlic, minced

2 TB. fresh ginger, minced

⅔ cup green onions, thinly sliced

3 TB. tamari

4 tsp. toasted sesame oil

¾ tsp. crushed red pepper flakes

1½ cups green cabbage, shredded

2 TB. raw sesame seeds

Sea salt

Freshly ground black pepper

Yield: 4 or 5 servings
Prep time: 15 to 20 minutes
Cook time: 50 to 60 minutes
Serving size: 1 cup

1. In a medium saucepan over high heat, bring water to a boil.

2. In a fine-mesh strainer, rinse brown rice well under running water. Add rice to the saucepan, cover, reduce heat to low, and simmer for 40 to 45 minutes or until water is absorbed. Remove from heat, and set aside for 5 minutes to steam.

3. While rice is steaming, crumble tofu into a small bowl using your fingers. Add garlic powder, onion powder, and turmeric, and stir well to combine. Set aside for 5 minutes.

4. In a large nonstick skillet over medium heat, sauté tofu and 1½ teaspoons olive oil, stirring often, for 3 to 5 minutes or until lightly browned. Transfer tofu to a small bowl, and set aside.

5. Place carrot, celery, red bell pepper, and remaining 1 tablespoon olive oil in the skillet, and sauté over medium heat, stirring often, for 2 minutes. Add cooked rice, frozen peas, garlic, and ginger, and sauté, stirring often, for 2 minutes. Add green onions, tamari, toasted sesame oil, and red pepper flakes, and sauté, stirring often, for 2 minutes.

Thyme-ly Tip

Create your own Chinese feast by combining Special Fried Rice with Veggie Spring Rolls (recipe in Chapter 6), Asian Slaw with Cilantro and Peanuts (recipe in Chapter 12), and either Shanghai Tofu or Veggie Stir-Fry (recipes in Chapter 15).

6. Add cabbage, reserved tofu, and sesame seeds, and sauté for 1 or 2 minutes or until cabbage begins to wilt. Remove from heat. Taste, season with salt and black pepper, and serve hot.

Variation: For a faster preparation, use 3 cups leftover cooked brown rice or other grains of choice.

Risotto Milanese

This is our vegan version of the classic and creamy Italian risotto featuring arborio rice flavored with onion, garlic, white wine, fresh herbs, saffron, and vegan Parmesan cheese, which adds a slightly cheesy flavor and extra richness.

> *Yield: 3 or 4 servings*
>
> **Prep time:** 5 to 7 minutes
> **Cook time:** 30 to 35 minutes
> **Serving size:** 1 cup as a side dish or 1½ cups as a main dish

3 cups vegetable broth

1 cup water

1¼ cups onion, finely diced

2 TB. olive oil

1 TB. garlic, minced

1½ cups *arborio rice* (do not rinse)

1 tsp. dried thyme

¼ tsp. saffron threads or turmeric (optional)

½ cup white wine

¼ cup vegan soy Parmesan cheese or Raw Parmesan Cheese (recipe in Chapter 9)

¼ cup chopped fresh parsley (preferably Italian parsley)

4 tsp. nonhydrogenated vegan margarine

Sea salt

Freshly ground black pepper

1. In a small saucepan over low heat, bring vegetable broth and water, covered, to a simmer.

2. In a medium saucepan over medium heat, sauté onion and olive oil, stirring often, for 3 to 5 minutes or until soft. Add garlic and sauté for 1 minute. Add arborio rice, thyme, and saffron threads (if using). Stir well to evenly coat rice, and sauté, stirring constantly, for 2 minutes.

3. Add wine and cook, stirring constantly, until wine is almost completely absorbed. Add ½ cup vegetable broth mixture, and cook, stirring constantly, until completely absorbed.

4. Continue stirring and adding vegetable broth mixture $1/2$ cup at a time, allowing each addition to be fully absorbed before adding the next, for 15 to 20 minutes or until rice is tender and creamy-looking but still slightly firm. Start tasting rice after cooking for 15 minutes. Some vegetable broth mixture may be left over.

5. Reduce heat to low. Add vegan Parmesan cheese, parsley, and margarine, and season with salt and black pepper. Continue to cook and stir for 1 to 3 more minutes or until very creamy but not runny. Remove from heat, and serve hot.

Variation: Vary the risotto's flavor and color by omitting the saffron and adding vegetables and other ingredients, such as fresh lemon juice and zest, asparagus, mushrooms, sun-dried tomatoes, fresh tomatoes, beans, winter squash, red bell pepper, and spinach or other greens.

def•i•ni•tion

Arborio rice is a short-grain, highly glutinous white rice grown in Italy. Its outer layers contain a high concentration of starch, which is released when cooking it with large quantities of liquid, as when making risotto. This creates a thick and creamy sauce, while the rice's center remains firm and chewy.

Harvest Barley

Here, cooked hulled barley is combined with frozen mixed vegetables, purple kale, dill weed, and thyme—all of which complement the flavor of barley very well.

<table>
<tr><td>

Yield: 4 or 5 servings

Prep time: 5 to 7 minutes

Cook time: 45 to 50 minutes

Serving size: 1 cup

</td></tr>
</table>

1¼ cup hulled barley

4 cups water or vegetable broth

1 tsp. sea salt

½ tsp. freshly ground black pepper

1 cup frozen mixed vegetable blend (carrots, green beans, corn, and peas)

2 leaves purple kale, stems removed, and coarsely chopped

½ cup green onions, thinly sliced

1 TB. nutritional yeast flakes

1½ tsp. dill weed

1 tsp. dried thyme

1 tsp. garlic powder

1. Place barley in a fine-mesh strainer and rinse well under running water.

2. In a large saucepan over high heat, bring water, barley, salt, and black pepper to a boil. Cover, reduce heat to low, and simmer for 45 to 50 minutes or until barley is almost tender and liquid is absorbed. Remove from heat.

3. Remove lid and fluff barley with a fork to loosen grains. Add frozen mixed vegetables, purple kale, and green onions, and stir well to combine. Cover and set aside for 10 minutes.

4. Add nutritional yeast flakes, dill weed, thyme, and garlic powder, and stir well to combine. Taste, adjust seasonings, and serve hot.

Variation: If you prefer, use pearled barley instead of hulled, but only use 3½ cups water, and only cook barley for 35 to 40 minutes.

Thyme-ly Tip

To make a mushroom barley side dish, omit the frozen mixed vegetables and purple kale. In a large nonstick skillet, sauté 2 cups crimini or button mushrooms, cut in half and thinly sliced; and 1 cup each onion, carrot, and celery, diced; in 1 tablespoon olive oil or toasted sesame oil for 3 to 5 minutes or until soft. Stir mixture into the cooked barley along with 1 teaspoon tamari.

Curried Couscous

Curry powder pairs perfectly with rice, grains, and pastas and imparts a spicy, earthy flavor as well as a golden hue. In this fast and easy side dish, whole-wheat couscous is bejeweled with red bell pepper, peas, and pistachios.

3 cups water

1 TB. curry powder

1 tsp. sea salt

½ tsp. freshly ground black pepper

½ tsp. ground cumin

1½ cups whole-wheat couscous (do not rinse)

½ cup red bell pepper, ribs and seeds removed, and finely diced

½ cup frozen peas

⅓ cup pistachios, coarsely chopped

Yield: 4 or 5 servings
Prep time: 5 minutes
Cook time: 5 to 7 minutes
Serving size: 1 cup

1. In a medium saucepan over high heat, bring water, curry powder, salt, black pepper, and cumin to a boil. Add couscous, stir well to combine, and cook for 1 minute. Cover, remove from heat, and set side for 5 to 7 minutes or until all liquid is absorbed.

2. Fluff couscous with a fork. Add red bell pepper, frozen peas, and pistachios, and stir in gently with a fork. Cover and let sit for 3 minutes to allow peas to thaw before serving. Taste and adjust seasonings as desired. Serve hot, cold, or at room temperature.

Variation: You can replace the pistachios with cashews or sliced almonds, and replace the red bell pepper with ¼ cup dried currants.

Soy What?

Couscous is a dry pasta product, but it's usually only boiled very briefly and then covered and left to finish cooking off the heat for 5 minutes or so. It's then fluffed with a fork prior to serving. It's often classified with grains, and can be used interchangeably in recipes.

Mish-Mash Millet

We could call this millet and cauliflower side dish Mock Mashed Potatoes. It's amazing how this humble grain and vegetable are easily transformed into something that has such a similar taste and consistency to mashed spuds.

Yield: 5 or 6 servings
Prep time: 5 to 7 minutes
Cook time: 30 to 35 minutes
Serving size: 1 cup

1½ cups *millet*

1 cup onion, finely diced

1 tsp. olive oil

3½ cups water or vegetable broth

1 medium head cauliflower, cut into small florets (about 4½ cups), or 1 (16-oz.) pkg. frozen cauliflower florets

1 tsp. sea salt

¼ tsp. white pepper or freshly ground black pepper

2 TB. nutritional yeast flakes

1 or 2 TB. nonhydrogenated vegan margarine

def•i•ni•tion

Millet is a tall-growing, annual grass comprised of several small-seeded species of grains or cereal crops. It's rich in fiber, protein, vitamins, and minerals; has a mildly sweet, nutty flavor; and is believed to be one of the first cultivated grain crops.

1. Place millet in a very fine-mesh strainer and rinse well under running water.

2. In a large saucepan over medium heat, toast millet, stirring often, for 2 or 3 minutes or until it begins to "pop" and some appear lightly browned. Transfer toasted millet to a small bowl, and set aside.

3. In the saucepan over medium heat, sauté onion and olive oil, stirring often, for 3 minutes. Add water, cauliflower, toasted millet, salt, and white pepper, and bring to a boil. Cover, reduce heat to low, and simmer for 25 to 30 minutes or until millet is tender and liquid is absorbed. Remove from heat.

4. Mash millet mixture with a potato masher, or beat with an electric mixer, as smooth or chunky as desired. If needed, add a little water to achieve desired consistency.

5. Add nutritional yeast flakes and margarine, and stir well to combine. Taste, adjust seasonings, and serve hot, either plain or topped with gravy.

Variation: To make a colorful mashed millet side dish, add 1 medium carrot or small beet, coarsely chopped, to the millet mixture prior to simmering.

Quinoa with Corn and Pumpkin Seeds

Quinoa is native to Central and South America, and it tastes especially delicious when combined with corn, cilantro, and pumpkin seeds, like in this easy-to-prepare dish.

1½ cups *quinoa*	2 tsp. olive oil
3 cups water or vegetable broth	½ cup green onions, thinly sliced
½ tsp. sea salt	2 tsp. garlic, minced
¼ tsp. freshly ground black pepper	¾ tsp. dried oregano
⅓ cup raw pumpkin seeds	½ tsp. crushed red pepper flakes
1 cup fresh or frozen cut corn kernels	¼ cup chopped fresh cilantro or parsley

> *Yield: 4 or 5 servings*
>
> **Prep time:** 5 minutes
> **Cook time:** 15 to 20 minutes
> **Serving size:** 1 cup

1. Place quinoa in a very fine-mesh strainer, and rinse well under running water for 1 minute.

2. In a medium saucepan over high heat, bring water, quinoa, salt, and black pepper to a boil. Cover, reduce heat to low, and simmer for 10 to 15 minutes or until quinoa is tender and all liquid is absorbed. Remove from heat.

3. Meanwhile, in a medium nonstick skillet over low heat, cook pumpkin seeds, stirring often, for 3 to 5 minutes or until lightly toasted and fragrant. Transfer toasted pumpkin seeds to a small bowl, and set aside.

4. Place corn and olive oil in the skillet, and sauté over medium heat, stirring often, for 2 minutes. Add green onions, garlic, oregano, and red pepper flakes, and sauté for 1 or 2 minutes or until green onions soften. Remove from heat.

5. Fluff quinoa with a fork to loosen grains. Add corn mixture, toasted pumpkin seeds, and cilantro, and stir gently with a fork to combine. Taste, adjust seasonings, and serve hot, cold, or at room temperature.

Variation: For extra color and to bulk up the dish, you can also add some of your favorite canned beans, chopped bell peppers, chopped jalapeño peppers, or chopped black olives.

def•i•ni•tion

> Quinoa (pronounced *KEEN*-wa) is a very tiny grain, roughly the same size as sesame seeds, first used by the Aztecs and Incas. This "supergrain" is a good source of protein (contains almost 50 percent more protein than wheat), carbohydrates, fiber, and many vitamins and minerals, including calcium.

Part 6

Sweet Endings

If you're tired of leaving your local bake shop empty-handed because you can't find anything vegan, welcome to Part 6, where you learn how to make your own sweet treats, with only the ingredients you want to use. So gather your baking supplies and get ready to learn how to bake up a batch of cookies and brownies without ever cracking an egg or reaching into the dairy case. You'll be happily surprised that your baked goods taste delicious without them.

Speaking of doing without, you can create a sweet treat without turning on your oven at all. Instead, just crank up the burners on your stove to stir up some homemade vegan fudge or gelled dessert, or press some buttons on your blender to whirl up some creamy chocolate mousse or fruity delight. The sweets in Part 6 are decadent, delicious, and, of course, totally vegan!

Chapter 20

Cookies, Bars, and Brownies

In This Chapter

- ◆ Rolled sugar cookies for any occasion
- ◆ Scooped and baked cookies
- ◆ Tasty, nutty blondies and brownies

Most of us never outgrow our love of cookies. Whether they're tiny ball-shaped morsels, thin and crisp, or soft and oversized, it's hard to resist a cookie, especially when it's vegan, home-baked, and warm from the oven.

You can easily pop these sweet, handheld treats into your mouth in one or two bites, nibble on them slowly, or dunk them into your coffee or a glass of soy milk. Cookies are great for enjoying on their own, but they can also dress up other simple desserts like puddings, fruit salads, or compotes. And be sure to try them crumbled into a bowlful of sorbet or nondairy ice cream!

Many cookie recipes rely heavily on butter and eggs. Vegan cookies rely more on leaveners like *baking powder* and baking soda to help them rise. When adapting traditional cookie recipes, you can easily swap butter for vegan margarine, or use safflower, olive, corn, or other mild vegetable oil instead. However, if you substitute oil, use 1 to 2 tablespoons less per cup than the butter called for in recipes; otherwise, your cookies will spread out

def•i•ni•tion

Baking powder is a dry leavening agent used in baking. It usually contains an alkali, like sodium bicarbonate (a mined mineral also known as baking soda), an acid like salt crystals, and a starch. Some baking powders contain aluminum salts, which may have detrimental health effects, so look for aluminum-free baking powders like Rumsford.

more when baking than you want them to. Refer to Chapter 2 for suitable vegan substitutions for sugar and eggs if you need help veganizing one of your favorite cookie recipes.

Store your finished cookies and bars in containers. For cookies that you want to remain crisp and crunchy, choose metal tins because they tend to have looser lids. To retain the moisture in soft cookies and bars, use plastic airtight containers. If you want to freeze your baked cookies or bars, be sure they're cooled completely, place them in plastic airtight containers or zipper-lock bags, and thaw them as needed at room temperature.

Sugar Cookies

Use this versatile sugar cookie dough to make crisp or soft cut-out cookies, rolled ball cookies, logs, crescents, or other shapes.

¾ cup nonhydrogenated vegan margarine

½ cup unbleached cane sugar or beet sugar

3 TB. water

1 tsp. pure vanilla extract

2¼ cups whole-wheat pastry flour

⅓ cup tapioca flour

¼ tsp. sea salt

> *Yield: 2½ to 3 dozen cookies*
>
> **Prep time:** 10 to 15 minutes plus 1 hour chilling time
>
> **Cook time:** 8 to 10 minutes
>
> **Serving size:** 2 cookies

1. In a large bowl, combine margarine, sugar, water, and vanilla extract until light and creamy. Add whole-wheat pastry flour, tapioca flour, and salt, and stir well until a smooth dough forms. Cover with plastic wrap and place in the refrigerator to chill for 1 hour or until firm.

2. Preheat the oven to 350°F. Line with parchment paper (or lightly oil) 2 large cookie sheets.

3. Turn out dough onto a lightly floured work surface. Divide dough in half, work with one half at a time, and keep remaining dough covered. Using a rolling pin, roll dough out to desired thickness (⅛-inch for crispy cookies or ¼-inch for soft). Cut into shapes with a knife or cookie cutters as desired.

4. With a spatula, carefully transfer cookies to the prepared cookie sheets, spacing them about 1 inch apart. Leave cookies plain, sprinkle with a little additional unbleached cane sugar or colored sprinkles before baking, or decorate with frosting after baking.

5. Bake for 8 to 10 minutes or until lightly browned around the edges. Remove from the oven. Let cool slightly before transferring to a rack to cool completely.

6. Repeat rolling out and cutting procedure for remaining cookie dough. Store cookies in an airtight container at room temperature.

Variation: To make chocolate-flavored dough, add ¼ cup cocoa powder and 2 tablespoons additional water. To make lemon- or orange-flavored dough, omit vanilla extract and add 1 teaspoon zest and 2 tablespoons freshly squeezed juice. To make nut-flavored dough, replace ½ cup whole-wheat pastry flour with ½ cup finely ground almonds, walnuts, hazelnuts, or pecans and ¼ teaspoon almond extract.

Thyme-ly Tip

Here's a simple frosting recipe you can use for decorating baked sugar cookies: combine 1 cup vegan powdered sugar and ½ teaspoon pure vanilla extract, and add 2 to 4 teaspoons soy milk or other non-dairy milk of choice, 1 teaspoon at a time until desired consistency is achieved. Spread on cookies with a knife or spatula, or use a pastry bag to pipe it on. You can also tint the frosting with natural food coloring.

Cranberry-Walnut-Oatmeal Cookies

Maple syrup, ground ginger, and cinnamon add the perfect blend of sweetness and spice to these chewy cookies made with fiber-rich oatmeal, tart dried cranberries, and chopped walnuts.

Yield: 1 to 1¹/₂ dozen cookies

Prep time: 20 to 25 minutes

Cook time: 15 to 20 minutes

Serving size: 2 cookies

¾ **cup dried cranberries**

½ **cup warm water**

2 **cups rolled oats**

1½ **cups whole-wheat pastry flour**

2 **tsp. aluminum-free baking powder**

¾ **tsp. ground cinnamon**

½ **tsp. ground ginger**

½ **tsp. sea salt**

½ **cup maple syrup or agave nectar**

⅓ **cup safflower oil or olive oil**

1 **tsp. pure vanilla extract**

¼ **tsp. pure almond extract (optional)**

⅔ **cup raw walnuts, coarsely chopped**

Soy What?

Dried cranberries work well as a replacement for raisins in recipes and are a good, healthful, sweet snack. They make a colorful and flavorful addition to trail mixes, cookies, quick breads, cakes, and other baked goods. They're also good sprinkled over fruit salads or hot cereals or added to cooked grain dishes.

---

1. In a small bowl, cover dried cranberries with warm water. Set aside for 15 minutes to rehydrate and soften.

2. Preheat the oven to 375°F. Line with parchment paper (or lightly oil) 2 large cookie sheets.

3. In a medium bowl, combine oats, flour, baking powder, cinnamon, ginger, and salt. Add maple syrup, safflower oil, vanilla extract, and almond extract (if using) and stir well to combine. Stir in dried cranberries mixture and walnuts and stir just until combined.

4. Portion cookie dough using a 2-inch scoop or by heaping 2 tablespoonfuls onto the prepared cookie sheets, spacing them 2 inches apart. Flatten each cookie slightly with wet fingers.

5. Bake for 15 to 20 minutes or until golden brown on the bottom and around the edges. Remove from the oven. Let cool slightly before transferring to a rack to cool completely. Store the cookies in an airtight container at room temperature.

Variation: Feel free to replace the dried cranberries with dried cherries, raisins, or currants, and replace the walnuts with an equal amount of chopped pecans or sunflower seeds.

Mochaccino-Chip Cookies

These chocolate cookies taste similar to a mochaccino specialty coffee drink. They also contain a surprising ingredient—prune purée—but you wouldn't know it, because they're rich, chocolaty, and totally decadent.

7 pitted prunes

½ cup hot coffee

1⅓ cups Sucanat or unbleached cane sugar

¼ cup soy milk or other non-dairy milk of choice

1 tsp. pure vanilla extract

½ tsp. pure almond extract or coffee extract

1⅔ cups whole-wheat pastry flour

⅓ cup cocoa powder

1½ tsp. ground cinnamon

1 tsp. baking soda

½ tsp. sea salt

1 cup vegan chocolate chips or espresso-flavored vegan chocolate chips

½ cup raw sliced almonds

Yield: 1½ dozen cookies

Prep time: 20 to 25 minutes

Cook time: 10 minutes

Serving size: 2 cookies

---

1. In a small bowl, cover prunes with hot coffee. Set aside for 15 minutes to rehydrate and soften.

2. Preheat the oven to 350°F. Line with parchment paper (or lightly oil) 2 large cookie sheets.

3. Transfer prune mixture to a blender or food processor, and process for 1 or 2 minutes or until completely smooth. Add Sucanat, soy milk, vanilla extract, and almond extract, and process for 1 minute.

4. In a large bowl, sift together flour, cocoa powder, cinnamon, baking soda, and salt. Add wet ingredients to dry ingredients, and stir well to combine. Add chocolate chips and almonds, and stir just until combined.

5. Portion cookie dough using a 2-inch scoop or by heaping 2 tablespoonfuls onto the prepared cookie sheets, spacing them 2 inches apart. Bake for 10 to 12 minutes or until set but still soft to the touch. Remove from the oven. Let cool slightly before transferring to a rack to cool completely. Store cookies in an airtight container at room temperature.

Variation: For even more flavor, replace all or part of the vegan chocolate chips with vegan dark chocolate–covered espresso beans or a vegan espresso chocolate bar, coarsely chopped.

Thyme-ly Tip

You can use prune purée made from pitted prunes as a replacement for oil and for eggs in recipes. It adds moisture as well as a little extra sweetness to baked goods and helps bring out the flavor of chocolate, vanilla, and spices.

Coconut-Almond Macaroons

These decadent, egg-free macaroons contain shredded coconut, coconut milk, and almond meal and bake up crisp and golden brown on the outside while the center stays soft and moist.

Yield: 1 to 1¹/₂ dozen macaroons
Prep time: 5 to 7 minutes
Cook time: 18 to 20 minutes
Serving size: 1 macaroon

2½ cups unsweetened shredded coconut

½ cup *almond meal* or whole-wheat pastry flour

¼ tsp. sea salt

⅓ cup lite coconut milk

¼ cup brown rice syrup

¼ cup agave nectar or maple syrup

1 tsp. pure almond extract

¼ tsp. pure coconut extract (optional)

1. Preheat the oven to 350°F. Line with parchment paper (or lightly oil) a large cookie sheet.

2. In a medium bowl, combine shredded coconut, almond meal, and salt. Add coconut milk, brown rice syrup, agave nectar, almond extract, and coconut extract (if using), and stir well to combine. (Dough will be sticky.)

3. Portion cookie dough using a 2-inch scoop or by heaping 2 tablespoonfuls onto the prepared cookie sheets, spacing them 2 inches apart. Bake for 18 to 20 minutes or until golden brown. Remove from the oven. Let cool completely on cookie sheet. Store in an airtight container at room temperature.

Variation: These macaroons are also delicious with ²/₃ cup chocolate or carob chips added to the dough. You can also replace 3 tablespoons almond meal with cocoa powder or carob powder.

def•i•ni•tion

Almond meal, or *almond flour,* is made from either raw almonds or blanched almonds that are finely ground to a powderlike consistency. It's sold in most grocery and natural foods stores. You can also make your own by finely grinding almonds in a food processor or coffee grinder.

Dried Fruit Energy Bars

These slightly sweet, crispy, and crunchy bars are packed with fiber-rich rolled oats, crispy brown rice cereal, and an assortment of raw nuts, seeds, and dried fruits.

1 cup brown rice syrup	**1 cup rolled oats**
¼ cup turbinado sugar	**½ cup oat bran or wheat bran**
1 tsp. pure vanilla extract	**⅓ cup raw sliced almonds**
½ tsp. pure almond extract (optional)	**⅓ cup raw pumpkin seeds**
½ tsp. sea salt	**⅓ cup raw sunflower seeds**
½ tsp. ground cinnamon	**⅓ cup raisins or *goji berries***
2 cups crispy brown rice cereal	**⅓ cup date pieces coated in oat flour**
	⅓ cup dried cranberries

> *Yield: 8 bars*
>
> **Prep time:** 5 to 7 minutes plus 30 minutes chilling time
>
> **Serving size:** 1 bar

1. Lightly oil a 9-inch baking pan.

2. In a small saucepan over medium heat, cook brown rice syrup and sugar for 3 or 4 minutes or until mixture begins to boil. Remove from heat. Add vanilla extract, almond extract (if using), salt, and cinnamon, and stir well to combine.

3. Meanwhile, in a large bowl, combine rice cereal, rolled oats, oat bran, sliced almonds, pumpkin seeds, sunflower seeds, raisins, date pieces, and dried cranberries.

4. Pour brown rice syrup mixture over cereal mixture, and stir well to evenly combine. Transfer cereal mixture to the prepared pan, and press evenly into pan using wet hands. Chill pan in the refrigerator for 30 minutes or until firm.

5. Using a sharp knife, cut into 8 bars. Store bars in an airtight container at room temperature.

Variation: For thinner bars, press cereal mixture into an oiled 9×13-inch baking pan.

def•i•ni•tion

Goji berries (also known as *wolfberries* or *lycii berries*) are native to Asia. These extremely nutritious berries have a dark red color and are roughly the same size as raisins, with a somewhat tart flavor similar to cranberries and cherries.

Macadamia Nut Blondies

Blondies are the light-colored cousins of brownies with a similar chewy texture. These blondies have a slightly butterscotch flavor, thanks to the combination of several buttery-tasting ingredients.

Yield: 1 (9×13-inch) pan	
Prep time: 5 to 7 minutes	
Cook time: 25 to 30 minutes	
Serving size: 1 blondie	

6 oz. (about ¾ cup) firm or extra-firm silken tofu	1¾ cups turbinado sugar or Sucanat
⅓ cup soy milk or other non-dairy milk of choice	1 cup barley flour
¼ cup safflower oil	1 tsp. aluminum-free baking powder
1½ tsp. pure vanilla extract	1 tsp. baking soda
¾ tsp. pure almond extract	½ tsp. sea salt
1¾ cups whole-wheat pastry flour	1 cup raw macadamia nuts, coarsely chopped

1. Preheat the oven to 350°F. Lightly oil a 9×13-inch baking pan.

2. Place silken tofu, soy milk, safflower oil, vanilla extract, and almond extract in a blender or food processor fitted with an S blade, and process for 1 or 2 minutes or until completely smooth. Scrape down the sides of the container with a rubber spatula, and process for 15 more seconds.

3. In a medium bowl, combine whole-wheat pastry flour, sugar, barley flour, baking powder, baking soda, and salt, and stir well to combine.

4. Add silken tofu mixture, and stir well to combine. Add macadamia nuts, and stir just until blended. Transfer batter to the prepared pan, and spread evenly.

5. Bake for 25 to 30 minutes or until a toothpick inserted in the center comes out clean. Remove from the oven. Let cool completely before cutting into 12 pieces. Store blondies in an airtight container at room temperature.

Variation: For a nuttier flavor, use Raw ABC Nut Milk (recipe in Chapter 9) or other nut milk of choice in the batter.

Soy What?

Macadamia nuts have a rich and buttery taste both humans and macaw parrots appreciate. Yes, parrots. They're one of the few animals who have the ability to crack open the macadamia nuts' hard shells. Avoid feeding macadamia nuts to dogs, though, because the nuts are toxic to them.

Chocolate–Peanut Butter Brownies

These rich and indulgent brownies are made by layering a peanut butter–flavored brownie batter and homemade vegan chocolate ganache and then swirling them together to create a beautiful marbled effect.

¼ cup soy milk or other nondairy milk of choice

2 TB. plus ⅓ cup nonhydro-genated vegan margarine

1 cup vegan chocolate chips

6 oz. (about ¾ cup) firm or extra-firm silken tofu

⅓ cup smooth or crunchy peanut butter

¼ cup cornstarch

1 tsp. pure vanilla extract

2 cups whole-wheat pastry flour

1⅓ cups turbinado sugar or Sucanat

2 tsp. aluminum-free baking powder

¼ tsp. sea salt

½ cup raw peanuts, coarsely chopped

Yield: 1 (9×13-inch) pan	
Prep time: 10 to 15 minutes	
Cook time: 35 to 40 minutes	
Serving size: 1 brownie	

1. For chocolate ganache, in a small saucepan over medium heat, cook soy milk and 2 tablespoons margarine for 1 or 2 minutes until margarine melts and soy milk is hot. Add chocolate chips, and stir until melted. Remove from the heat. Or place soy milk, margarine, and chocolate chips in a glass bowl; microwave for 1 or 2 minutes or until chocolate chips just begin to soften; and stir mixture until smooth. Let cool slightly for 10 minutes.

2. Preheat the oven to 350°F. Lightly oil a 9×13-inch baking pan.

3. Place silken tofu, peanut butter, remaining ⅓ cup margarine, cornstarch, and vanilla extract in a food processor fitted with an S blade, and process for 1 or 2 minutes or until completely smooth. Scrape down the sides of the container with a rubber spatula, and process for 15 more seconds.

4. In a medium bowl, combine whole-wheat pastry flour, sugar, baking powder, and salt. Add silken tofu mixture, and stir well to combine.

Thyme-ly Tip

You can make the chocolate ganache used in this recipe in larger amounts and use it as a glaze or drizzled sauce for cakes, cookies, quick breads, and other desserts, as well as sorbet and nondairy ice cream. It's also great as a dip for fresh fruit.

5. Transfer ½ of batter to the prepared pan, and spread evenly. Spread cooled chocolate ganache over the top. Spoon brownie batter over chocolate ganache. Use a knife to swirl the layers to make a marbled effect. Sprinkle chopped peanuts evenly over the top.

6. Bake for 35 to 40 minutes or until lightly browned and center is set. Remove from the oven. Let cool for 1 hour or more before cutting into 16 pieces. Store brownies in an airtight container at room temperature.

Variation: If you avoid peanut butter, you can substitute other nut butters and chopped nuts, such as cashew, hazelnut, or pecan.

Hemp, Hemp, Hooray Brownies

These brownies are incredibly rich and chocolaty, and the hemp seeds and walnuts are also rich in omega essential fatty acids.

Yield: 1 (9×13-inch) pan
Prep time: 10 to 15 minutes
Cook time: 30 to 35 minutes
Serving size: 1 piece

2 cups vegan chocolate chips

3 TB. safflower oil or olive oil

1¼ cups whole-wheat pastry flour

1 cup unbleached cane sugar

½ cup cocoa powder

½ tsp. aluminum-free baking powder

½ tsp. sea salt

1 cup applesauce

1 tsp. pure vanilla extract

¼ cup plus 3 TB. raw walnuts, finely chopped

4 TB. raw *hemp seeds*

3 TB. unsweetened shredded coconut, toasted

1. In a small saucepan over medium heat, cook 1½ cups chocolate chips and safflower oil for 1 or 2 minutes, stirring often, until chocolate chips melt. Remove from heat. Or place chocolate chips and safflower oil in a small glass bowl, microwave for 1 or 2 minutes or until chocolate chips just begin to soften, and stir mixture until smooth. Let cool slightly for 10 minutes.

2. Preheat the oven to 350°F. Lightly oil a 9×13-inch baking pan.

3. In a medium bowl, sift together flour, sugar, cocoa powder, baking powder, and salt. Add chocolate-chip mixture, applesauce, and vanilla extract, and stir well to combine.

4. Add ¼ cup walnuts and 3 tablespoons hemp seeds, and stir just until blended. Transfer batter to the prepared pan, and spread evenly.

5. Bake for 30 to 35 minutes or until lightly browned and center is set. Remove from the oven.

6. For brownie topping, immediately sprinkle remaining ½ cup chocolate chips evenly over hot brownies. Let sit for 3 minutes or until chocolate chips melt, and spread them evenly with a knife to cover the top. Evenly sprinkle remaining 3 tablespoons walnuts, toasted coconut, and remaining 1 tablespoon hemp seeds over the top. Let cool for 1 hour or more before cutting into 16 pieces. Store brownies in an airtight container at room temperature.

Variation: Feel free to substitute other raw nuts and seeds inside and on top of these brownies. Pecans, hazelnuts, almonds, or sunflower seeds all work well.

def•i•ni•tion

Hemp seeds, also called *hemp nuts,* are the shelled edible seeds of the hemp plant. They have a mild, nutty flavor similar to sunflower seeds and are rich in dietary fiber, protein, essential fatty acids, and some vitamins and minerals. Purchase hemp seeds in most grocery and natural foods stores.

No-Bake Treats

In This Chapter

- ◆ Bite-size delights
- ◆ Creamy and dreamy desserts
- ◆ Blended toppings and treats

No-bake treats? Why would you need such recipes in your vegan bag of tricks? And what options fall under this distinction?

Let's start with why. How about to avoid turning on your oven and heating up your kitchen, especially in warmer climates or during hot summer months? You do have your stovetop and other kitchen appliances at your disposal for whipping up a dessert or treat, and after all, making vegan food is all about thinking outside the box, or in this case, beyond your oven.

Smooth and Creamy Sweets

When you're craving something sweet but want something more than just a piece of fresh fruit or candy or something that came out of a box, what are you to do? Well, if you're in the mood for something luscious and creamy (and maybe a little lazy), simply pull out your blender or food processor. In this chapter, we show you how these handy machines can transform fresh or frozen fruit into an all-natural, puddinglike treat. Then you can garnish it with additional fruit, or alternately layer them to make a stunning parfait.

Soy What?

Most grocery and natural foods stores stock several varieties of vegan candy bars, candies, and flavored mints perfect for nibbling, garnishing, or adding to your desserts and baked goods. But vegan confections like truffles and fudge are harder to come by except through online or mail-order sources (see Appendix B). We offer vegan recipes for both in this chapter.

Always try to keep some aseptic packages of silken tofu on hand so you can blend it with some sweetener, vegan chocolate chips, or fruit or berries to make a guilt-free mousse in minutes. Once it's chilled, you can also use this mixture as a topping for fruit or other desserts.

Stove-Top Sensations

It wasn't long ago that when people wanted to make a creamy pudding, filling, or gelled dessert, they didn't open up a box and dump out a powder. Oh no, they used their stove top to make them, and so shall you. All you need is a saucepan or two, a whisk, a few pantry staples, and a little chilling time.

In this chapter, you also learn how to make a fruit-flavored gelled dessert using agar-agar flakes rather than animal-based gelatin, just like they've been doing in Asia for ages. You will also tackle comfort-food classics like vanilla custard, rice pudding, and banana cream pudding layered with cookies, each one presented with a slightly new twist on flavorings, ingredients used, and presentation. These rich and creamy puddings are made with nondairy milk and are thickened with flour, starch, and rice rather than eggs.

You can make these types of no-bake sweets and treats ahead of time, and they'll last for several days in the refrigerator. They're great for potlucks and packed lunches, and you're sure to have people asking for the recipe after they get a taste. See, you can enjoy a delicious vegan dessert without ever turning on your oven!

Vegan Truffles

Here, vegan chocolate chips, powdered sugar, cocoa powder, and tofu cream cheese blend together to make creamy, dark-chocolate–tasting vegan truffles that literally melt in your mouth.

¾ **cup vegan chocolate chips**

½ **cup (4 oz.) tofu cream cheese**

1¼ **cups** *vegan powdered sugar*

¼ **cup cocoa powder**

1 **tsp. pure vanilla extract**

Cocoa powder, powdered sugar, finely ground nuts, or toasted unsweetened shredded coconut

Yield: 18 to 20 truffles
Prep time: 10 to 15 minutes plus 1 hour chilling time
Cook time: 2 minutes
Serving size: 2 truffles

1. In the top of a double boiler over medium heat, cook chocolate chips for 1 or 2 minutes or until melted. Or place chocolate chips in a small glass bowl, microwave for 1 or 2 minutes or until chocolate chips just begin to soften, and stir until smooth. Let cool slightly.

2. Place tofu cream cheese and powdered sugar in a food processor fitted with an S blade, and process for 1 minute or until completely smooth. Add melted chocolate chips, cocoa powder, and vanilla extract, and process for 1 minute or until thoroughly blended. Scrape down the sides of the container with a rubber spatula, and process for 15 seconds longer.

3. Transfer mixture to a glass bowl, cover, and place in the refrigerator to chill for 1 hour.

4. Using your hands, shape chilled mixture into 2-inch balls, or use a 2-inch scoop. Place balls on a large plate, and chill in the refrigerator for 15 minutes.

5. Roll chilled balls in your cocoa powder, powdered sugar, ground nuts, or coconut as desired until thoroughly coated on all sides. Store truffles in an airtight container in the refrigerator or freezer.

Variation: You can also add ¹⁄₄ teaspoon coconut or peppermint extract or 1 or 2 teaspoons (or more as desired) rum, brandy, amaretto, raspberry, coffee, or your favorite liqueur or liquor to the truffle mixture. Or divide the truffle mixture to make assorted flavors.

def•i•ni•tion

Vegan powdered sugar is made from either beet sugar or cane sugar (that hasn't been refined with bone char–based charcoal) that is processed with a starch, such as cornstarch, to prevent caking. Find it in most grocery and natural foods stores; some manufacturers even label the packages as vegan.

Creamy Almond Fudge

This almond-studded vegan fudge is made the old-fashioned way, by boiling sugar and beating it until thick and creamy. It's flavored and studded with almonds.

Yield: 1 (9-inch) pan

Prep time: 15 to 20 minutes

Cook time: 10 to 15 minutes

Serving size: 1 piece

Thyme-ly Tip

When making candies and confections, use a candy thermometer to ensure the mixture has the proper consistency after cooking. Most candy thermometers include both degree readings and references, such as soft or hard ball, or light or hard crack.

½ cup raw sliced almonds

3 cups unbleached cane sugar

2 cups soy milk or other non-dairy milk of choice

½ cup nonhydrogenated vegan margarine

2 tsp. pure vanilla extract

1 tsp. pure almond extract

1. Lightly oil a 9-inch baking pan. Line the bottom and sides of the pan with parchment paper, allowing for several inches of overhang for easy removal from the pan.

2. In a 3-quart saucepan over medium heat, cook almonds, stirring often, for 3 to 5 minutes or until lightly toasted and fragrant. Transfer toasted almonds to a small bowl, and set aside.

3. In the saucepan over medium heat, bring sugar, soy milk, and margarine to a boil. Continue to boil until mixture reaches 240°F on a candy thermometer. Remove from heat, add toasted almonds, vanilla extract, and almond extract, and stir gently to combine.

4. Fill a deep casserole dish ¼ full of cold water. Place the saucepan containing fudge into the cold water (do not allow water to come in contact with fudge). Stir fudge mixture for 3 to 5 minutes or until it thickens and turns a creamy, off-white color. Or beat fudge mixture with an electric mixer on low speed.

5. Transfer fudge to the prepared pan, and smooth the top. Chill overnight to fully harden.

6. Using the parchment paper, pull and lift hardened fudge out of the pan. Use a sharp knife to cut fudge into 2-inch squares. Store fudge in an airtight container in the refrigerator.

Variation: For chocolate-flavored fudge, stir ¾ cup vegan chocolate chips into the sugar until melted, just prior to adding the toasted almonds and extracts.

Raw Fruity Delight

This lusciously smooth purée of peaches and papaya is topped with fresh fruit and a little shredded coconut and sliced almonds.

½ **cup dried dates, pitted**

½ **cup freshly squeezed orange juice**

1 papaya

1 lb. fresh or frozen peaches, sliced (thawed if necessary)

½ **cup strawberries, thinly sliced**

½ **cup blueberries or raspberries**

2 kiwi, peeled, cut in half lengthwise, and thinly sliced

2 TB. unsweetened shredded coconut

2 TB. raw sliced almonds

Yield: 4 or 5 servings
Prep time: 15 to 20 minutes
Serving size: ¾ cup

1. Place dates and orange juice in a small bowl, and set aside for 10 minutes to soften dates.

2. Peel papaya, cut in half lengthwise, scoop out seeds into a small bowl, and cut papaya into 1-inch pieces.

3. Place date mixture, ½ of cut papaya, and peaches into a blender, and blend for 1 or 2 minutes or until completely smooth. Scrape down the sides of the container with a rubber spatula, and process for 1 minute longer to make it very light and creamy.

4. Transfer mixture to a glass bowl. Top with remaining cut papaya, strawberries, blueberries, kiwi, shredded coconut, and sliced almonds. Serve immediately or chill for 30 minutes or longer.

Variation: Create beautiful parfaits by alternately layering the peach and papaya purée, and fresh fruit and berries, with the shredded coconut and sliced almonds.

Soy What?

This dessert recipe deliciously illustrates the binding and thickening capabilities of pectin, a natural dietary fiber found in many fruits and vegetables. Pulverizing, mashing, cooking, and soaking can help fruits and vegetables release their natural pectin and begin this thickening action.

Kanten

One might call this vegan Jell-O because it has a similar jiggly texture. Fruit juice is gelled with agar-agar flakes and then combined with assorted fruit to make a tasty, fat-free, and low-calorie dessert.

Yield: 4 or 5 servings
Prep time: 5 minutes plus 1 or 2 hours chilling time
Cook time: 11 to 17 minutes
Serving size: ³/₄ cup

1 qt. apple juice or apple-raspberry juice

¹/₃ cup *agar-agar* flakes

¹/₈ tsp. sea salt

¹/₄ cup water

1 TB. arrowroot

1 tsp. pure vanilla extract

2 cups fresh or frozen sliced fruit (bananas, berries, kiwi, mango, etc.)

1. In a medium saucepan over medium-high heat, bring apple juice, agar-agar flakes, and salt to a boil. Reduce heat to low, and simmer, stirring occasionally, for 10 to 15 minutes or until agar-agar flakes are fully dissolved.

2. In a small bowl, combine water and arrowroot. Add arrowroot mixture and vanilla extract to apple juice mixture, stir well to combine, and simmer for 1 or 2 minutes or until slightly thickened. Remove from heat.

3. Place fruit in the bottom of a 9-inch baking pan. Pour apple juice mixture over fruit, and let cool at room temperature for 20 minutes. Place in the refrigerator to chill for 1 or 2 hours or until set. Serve cold or at room temperature.

Variation: Feel free to substitute other flavors of fruit juice, such as cranberry, grape, or raspberry. Note that citrus fruits and pineapple sometime react adversely with agar-agar flakes and must be combined with other types of fruit or juices to ensure proper gelling.

def•i•ni•tion

Agar-agar, also known as *agar* or *kanten,* is an odorless and tasteless seaweed derivative used as a vegan alternative to animal-based gelatin to gel and thicken. Use it in vegan jellies, sauces, nondairy cheeses and ice creams, puddings, and gelled desserts. Agar-agar is sold in sticks, flakes, and as a powder.

Nut Whipped Topping

Use this irresistibly rich and creamy nondairy topping made with raw cashews and oil, with a little agave nectar added for sweetness, as a topping for all your favorite desserts and even fresh fruit.

1 cup raw cashews

¾ cup water

¼ cup agave nectar

1 tsp. pure vanilla extract

½ tsp. pure almond extract (optional)

¼ cup safflower oil or sunflower oil

Yield: 1³/₄ to 2 cups	
Prep time: 5 to 7 minutes	
Serving size: 2 tablespoons	

1. Place cashews in a blender or food processor fitted with an S blade, and process for 1 or 2 minutes or until finely ground. Add water, agave nectar, vanilla extract, and almond extract (if using), and process for 1 minute.

2. Scrape down the sides of the container with a rubber spatula. While the machine is running, slowly drizzle in safflower oil, and process for 2 minutes or until mixture is very thick and resembles whipped cream.

3. Transfer to an airtight container and place in the refrigerator to chill for 30 minutes or more before serving. Use as a garnish for cakes, pies, and other desserts.

Variation: To vary the flavor, season with ground cinnamon, cardamom, or ginger, or replace part of the water with the juice of 1 orange or 1 or 2 tablespoons juice squeezed from freshly grated ginger.

Soy What?

Soyatoo makes vegan alternatives to traditional whipped cream and nondairy whipped topping. Soy Whip Whipped Soy Topping comes in a spray-nozzle can and is ready for topping and decorating your favorite desserts. Soya Topping Cream comes in an aseptic container; you need to whip it up yourself.

Coconut Rice Pudding

Creamy rice pudding is pure comfort food for some people, and making it with coconut milk and some toasted coconut and pistachios gives it a rich, exotic flavor.

Yield: 4 or 5 servings
Prep time: 5 minutes
Cook time: 30 to 40 minutes
Serving size: ²/₃ cup

⅓ cup raw pistachios, coarsely chopped

½ cup unsweetened shredded coconut

1 (14-oz.) can lite coconut milk

1½ cups soy milk or other nondairy milk of choice

1 cup water

½ cup jasmine rice

Pinch salt

¼ cup agave nectar or brown rice syrup

1 tsp. pure vanilla extract

¼ tsp. pure coconut extract (optional)

½ tsp. ground cinnamon

¼ tsp. ground cardamom or freshly grated nutmeg

Soy What?

A can of regular coconut milk can contain more than 50 grams of fat, most of which is saturated fat. Lite coconut milk usually contains 70 percent less fat than regular coconut milk, but still has a rich coconut flavor. You can use lite coconut milk interchangeably for regular coconut milk in most beverages and sweet and savory recipes.

1. In a 2-quart saucepan over medium heat, cook pistachios, stirring often, for 3 to 5 minutes or until lightly toasted and fragrant. Transfer toasted almonds to a small bowl, and set aside.

2. Place shredded coconut in the saucepan, and cook over medium heat, stirring often, for 3 to 5 minutes or until lightly toasted and fragrant. Transfer toasted coconut to another small bowl, and set aside.

3. Place coconut milk, 1 cup soy milk, water, jasmine rice, and salt in the saucepan, and bring to a boil. Reduce heat to low, and simmer, stirring often, for 20 to 25 minutes or until rice is fully cooked.

4. Add remaining ½ cup soy milk, reserved toasted coconut, agave nectar, vanilla extract, coconut extract (if using), cinnamon, and cardamom, and cook, stirring often, for 3 more minutes. Remove from heat. Serve warm or cold, and garnish with toasted pistachios.

Variation: For a more tropical version, add ½ cup diced mango or crushed pineapple to the finished rice pudding.

Tofu Chocolate Mousse

The dark chocolate flavor and ultra-creamy consistency of this tofu-based mousse rivals any traditional dairy chocolate mousse.

1 (12-oz.) pkg. vegan chocolate chips

2 (12-oz.) pkg. firm or extra-
firm silken tofu

⅓ cup cocoa powder

⅓ cup maple syrup

1 tsp. pure vanilla extract

Yield: 4 or 5 servings
Prep time: 5 to 7 minutes
Cook time: 2 minutes
Serving size: ⅔ cup

1. In the top of a double boiler over medium heat, cook chocolate chips for 1 or 2 minutes or until melted. Or place chocolate chips in a small glass bowl, microwave for 1 or 2 minutes or until chocolate chips just begin to soften, and stir until smooth. Let cool slightly.

2. Place tofu in a food processor fitted with an S blade, and process for 1 minute or until completely smooth. Add melted chocolate chips, cocoa powder, maple syrup, and vanilla extract, and process for 1 minute or until thoroughly blended. Scrape down the sides of the container with a rubber spatula, and process for 15 more seconds.

3. Transfer mixture to a glass bowl, cover, and place in the refrigerator to chill for 1 hour. Serve cold or at room temperature, plain or garnished as desired with Nut Whipped Topping (see recipe earlier in this chapter), fresh berries, toasted shredded coconut, or chopped nuts or chocolate.

Variation: You can make fruit-flavored tofu mousse by replacing the vegan chocolate chips and cocoa powder with 2 cups fresh or frozen sliced fruit or berries.

Thyme-ly Tip

You can also use this tofu chocolate mousse as a pie filling. Pour it into a prebaked piecrust or store-bought or homemade vegan graham cracker crust or chocolate cookie crust. Chill for several hours and then decorate the top with berries, sliced bananas, toasted coconut, chopped nuts, or chocolate.

Banana Cream Vanilla Wafer Dessert

This is a vegan alternative to the classic banana-pudding dessert recipe that many of us grew up on, which features homemade vanilla pudding layered with vanilla wafer cookies and bananas.

Yield: 1 (9-inch) pan
Prep time: 20 to 25 minutes
Cook time: 2 or 3 minutes
Serving size: 1 piece

½ cup unbleached cane sugar or beet sugar

3 TB. cornstarch

3 cups vanilla soymilk or other nondairy milk of choice

1½ tsp. pure vanilla extract

5 oz. (25 to 30) vegan vanilla wafer cookies

3 medium bananas, peeled and sliced ¼-in. thick

1. For pudding, in a medium saucepan, whisk together sugar and cornstarch. Add soy milk, and cook over medium heat, whisking often, for 2 or 3 minutes or until thickened.

2. Remove from heat, and whisk in vanilla extract. Let cool for 5 minutes, whisking occasionally to allow steam to escape, and place in the refrigerator to chill for 10 minutes.

3. Place ⅓ of pudding in the bottom of a 9-inch baking dish. Top with ⅓ of vanilla wafer cookies, followed by ⅓ of banana slices. Repeat layers, and pour remaining pudding on top.

4. Tuck remaining vanilla wafers in around the outer edge of the baking dish, and decoratively garnish top with remaining banana slices. Serve immediately or place in the refrigerator to chill for 30 minutes or longer. Top individual servings with dollops of Nut Whipped Topping (see recipe earlier in this chapter) or store-bought vegan nondairy topping as desired.

Variation: For a peanut butter–banana pudding, add ⅓ cup peanut butter or other nut butter to the pudding and top the finished recipe with chopped peanuts or other nuts.

Thyme-ly Tip

Make the pudding used in this recipe into other flavors simply by substituting other flavors of nondairy milk, like chocolate, carob, strawberry, or even eggnog. You might need to add extra sugar. You can also make chocolate- or carob-flavored pudding by whisking ⅓ cup cocoa or carob powder along with the sugar and cornstarch.

Chapter 22

Decadent Desserts

In This Chapter

◆ Crowd-pleasing pies

◆ Fabulous frosted cupcakes and cakes

◆ Rich and creamy creations

We saved the best for last! In this chapter, you will find a wide variety of vegan dessert recipes, including pies, cakes, and even cheesecake, to appeal to all tastes and appetites.

Some recipes are simple to prepare and can be in the oven in less than 15 minutes, so you can serve up a tasty dessert even on a weeknight. Others are a bit more involved or require more time and effort on your part, and thus are more suitable for making on special occasions.

Delicious Dessert Tips

Your success as a vegan baker is often based on chemical reactions between leaveners and other ingredients, so you're about to get another leavening lesson. You'll notice that most of the cake recipes call for apple cider vinegar, which may sound strange, but it reacts with the baking soda and/or baking powder used in the recipe to give your vegan cakes lift. Don't worry,

Thyme-ly Tip

Baking powder is often used in vegan baked goods, but if an acidic ingredient like soy yogurt, citrus, or vinegar is present in your dough or batter, use less baking powder and add a little baking soda as well. If you have problems with flat baked goods, try adding ¼ to ½ teaspoon additional baking powder per cup of flour in your recipe.

it won't make your cake taste sour; its flavor blends in with the other ingredients nicely.

You'll want to store most of these desserts in the refrigerator, especially those with creamy fillings and frostings. You can't freeze any of the tofu-based desserts in this chapter, because their texture will change as a result of freezing and thawing. However, the shortcakes and unfrosted cupcakes and cakes can be frozen in airtight containers or zipper-lock bags, or wrapped tightly in plastic wrap and then aluminum foil for later use, and thawed in the refrigerator.

Strawberry Shortcake

This vegan take on the classic American summertime dessert features freshly baked sweetened biscuits layered with macerated fresh strawberries and topped with Nut Whipped Topping or nondairy ice cream or sorbet.

1 qt. strawberries, thinly sliced

½ cup plus 2 tsp. unbleached cane sugar or beet sugar

1⅓ cups vanilla soy milk or other nondairy milk of choice

4 tsp. apple cider vinegar or freshly squeezed lemon juice

3 cups whole-wheat pastry flour

1 TB. baking powder

2 tsp. baking soda

½ tsp. sea salt

¼ cup nonhydrogenated vegan margarine

1 tsp. pure vanilla extract

1 cup prepared Nut Whipped Topping (recipe in Chapter 21) or store-bought vegan nondairy whipped topping

Yield: 8 servings
Prep time: 30 to 40 minutes
Cook time: 12 to 15 minutes
Serving size: 1 shortcake, ½ cup strawberries, and 2 tablespoons topping

1. In a medium bowl, gently combine strawberries and ¼ cup sugar. Set aside to macerate for 30 minutes or more at room temperature.

2. Preheat the oven to 425°F. Line a large cookie sheet with parchment paper.

3. While strawberries are macerating, for shortcakes, combine soy milk and apple cider vinegar in a small bowl, and set aside for 5 minutes to thicken.

4. In a medium bowl, combine flour, ¼ cup sugar, baking powder, baking soda, and salt. Using a fork, work margarine into dry ingredients until mixture resembles coarse crumbs. Reserve 1 tablespoon soy milk mixture for tops of shortcakes. Add remaining soy milk mixture and vanilla extract, and stir until mixture just comes together to form a soft dough.

5. Transfer dough to a lightly floured work surface. Knead for 1 minute, pat into a 1-inch-thick 6×12-inch rectangle. Using a sharp knife, cut rectangle into 8 (3-inch) squares. Place shortcakes on the prepared baking sheet, spacing them 2 inches apart. Brush tops of shortcake with reserved soy milk mixture and sprinkle with remaining 2 teaspoons sugar.

Thyme-ly Tip

To make one large shortcake, shape dough into an 8-inch circle on the cookie sheet, brush with reserved soy milk mixture, and sprinkle with sugar. Bake for 18 to 20 minutes. Let cool slightly and then split and layer short-cake and strawberries on a large plate. Dust top with a little vegan powdered sugar, and cut into 8 wedges for serving.

6. Bake for 12 to 15 minutes or until lightly browned on the bottom and around the edges. Remove from the oven. To serve, split shortcake in half place the bottom $\frac{1}{2}$ in a bowl or on a plate, spoon $\frac{1}{2}$ cup macerated strawberries over the top, replace the top $\frac{1}{2}$ of shortcake, and finish with a 2 tablespoon dollop of Nut Whipped Topping. You can also top individual servings with nondairy ice cream or sorbet.

Variation: Feel free to substitute other varieties of fresh fruit, such as blueberries, blackberries, raspberries, peaches, plums, or a combination.

Free-Form Fruit Pie

Free-form-style pies, also known as galettes, are made by partially folding rolled-out pastry dough over the filling, so no fancy fluting is necessary. For this one, juicy fresh plums are combined with fragrant cinnamon and cardamom and lightly sweetened with turbinado sugar.

Yield: 8 servings
Prep time: 15 to 20 minutes
Cook time: 25 to 30 minutes
Serving size: 1 piece

1 cup whole spelt flour

$\frac{2}{3}$ cup plus 2 TB. white spelt flour

2 TB. plus $\frac{1}{4}$ cup *turbinado sugar*

$\frac{1}{2}$ tsp. aluminum-free baking powder

$\frac{1}{4}$ tsp. sea salt

$\frac{1}{3}$ cup soy milk or other non-dairy milk of choice

$\frac{1}{3}$ cup safflower oil or sunflower oil

$\frac{1}{2}$ tsp. pure vanilla extract

$1\frac{1}{2}$ lb. plums (about 3 cups), cut into eighths

1 tsp. ground cinnamon

$\frac{1}{2}$ tsp. cardamom or ground ginger

Vegan powdered sugar

1. Preheat the oven to 350°F. Line a large cookie sheet with parchment paper.

2. For pastry dough, in a medium bowl, combine whole spelt flour, $\frac{2}{3}$ cup white spelt flour, 2 tablespoons turbinado sugar, baking powder, and salt. Add soy milk, safflower oil, and vanilla extract, and stir until mixture just comes together to form a soft dough.

3. Shape pastry dough into a disc. Lightly flour bottom and top of disc, place between 2 (12-inch) sheets of parchment paper, and roll into a 12-inch circle. Place on a large cookie sheet. Remove and discard top sheet of parchment paper.

4. For filling, in a medium bowl, gently combine plums, remaining $1/4$ cup turbinado sugar, remaining 2 tablespoons white spelt flour, cinnamon, and cardamom. Mound filling in center of pastry circle. Fold up edges of pastry slightly to create a 3- or 4-inch-wide pastry border around filling, crimping and pleating to maintain circular shape.

5. Bake for 25 to 30 minutes. Remove from the oven. Let cool for 15 minutes or more. Transfer to a large plate. Sprinkle a light dusting of powdered sugar over the top, and cut it into 8 wedges.

Variation: Vary the flavor by using other seasonally available fruit like peaches, berries, cherries, apples, pears, figs, or a combination.

def•i•ni•tion

Turbinado sugar is made with pure, raw sugar-cane juice that's spun in a cylinder or turbine, which inspired the name. You'll often see it labeled as "raw cane sugar." It has a golden caramel color, a light molasses flavor, and a coarse, crystalline texture. It's great on fresh fruit, as a replacement for brown sugar in sweet and savory recipes, or used to decoratively sprinkle on baked goods.

Vegan Pumpkin Pie

There's no need to go without pumpkin pie at Thanksgiving just because you shun eggs and dairy, as this pumpkin pie flavored with maple syrup, vanilla, and a fragrant blend of cinnamon, ginger, nutmeg, and cloves deliciously illustrates.

Yield: 1 (9-inch) pie

Prep time: 15 minutes plus 30 minutes chilling time

Cook time: 50 to 55 minutes

Serving size: 1 piece

1½ cups whole-wheat pastry flour

½ tsp. sea salt

⅓ cup nonhydrogenated vegan margarine

⅓ cup cold water

1 (15-oz.) can pumpkin purée

¾ cup maple syrup

¾ cup soy milk or other non-dairy milk of choice

¼ cup arrowroot or corn-starch

1½ tsp. pure vanilla extract

1½ tsp. ground cinnamon

¾ tsp. ground ginger

½ tsp. freshly ground nutmeg

¼ tsp. ground cloves or all-spice

1. In a medium bowl, for piecrust, combine flour and salt. Using a fork, work margarine into dry ingredients until mixture resembles coarse crumbs. Add water and stir until mixture just comes together to form a soft dough. Gather dough into a ball, and flatten into a disc. Wrap disc in plastic wrap, and place in the refrigerator to chill for 30 minutes or more.

2. Lightly flour bottom and top of chilled disc, place between 2 (12-inch) sheets of parchment paper, and roll into a 12-inch circle. Remove and discard top sheet of parchment paper. Flip pastry into a 9-inch pie pan, and remove and discard remaining parchment paper. Gently press against bottom and sides of pan. Trim overhanging edge of piecrust about 1 inch from the edge of the pie plate. Tuck excess piecrust underneath, and flute edges as desired.

3. Preheat the oven to 350°F.

4. For filling, place pumpkin purée, maple syrup, soy milk, arrowroot, vanilla extract, cinnamon, ginger, nutmeg, and cloves in a blender or food processor fitted with an S blade, and process for 1 or 2 minutes or until well combined. Scrape down the sides of the container with a rubber spatula, and process for 15 more seconds.

5. Spread pumpkin filling mixture into prepared piecrust. Bake for 50 to 55 minutes or until crust is lightly browned and filling is set. Remove from the oven. Let cool to room temperature and then place in the refrigerator to chill completely. Cut into 8 wedges, and serve chilled or at room temperature. Garnish individual servings with a dollop of Nut Whipped Topping (recipe in Chapter 21) as desired.

Variation: You can make this pie using tofu—just replace the soy milk and arrowroot with 1 (12-ounce) package firm or extra-firm silken tofu.

Thyme-ly Tip

Piecrust recipes often say "flute edges," and this can be done in several ways for visual appeal. After trimming and folding under any excess pastry, the easiest flute finish is to simply press the tines of a fork all the way around the outer edge. For a pinched fluted edge, push the outer edge of pastry in with the thumb and index finger of one hand, while pressing toward it with the index finger of your other hand.

Coconut Cream Tart

No one would ever suspect that this tart is made with tofu. All they'll taste is coconut, because coconut milk, shredded coconut, and coconut extract, along with agave nectar, are used to sweeten and flavor its light and creamy filling.

Yield: 1 (9-inch) tart
Prep time: 15 to 20 minutes
Cook time: 45 to 50 minutes
Serving size: 1 piece

2 cups whole-wheat pastry flour

½ tsp. aluminum-free baking powder

¼ tsp. sea salt

¼ cup safflower oil

2 TB. plus ⅔ cup agave nectar

2 TB. cold water

⅔ cup lite coconut milk

3 TB. arrowroot or corn-starch

2 (12-oz.) pkg. firm or extra-firm silken tofu

1½ tsp. pure vanilla extract

½ tsp. pure coconut extract

¾ cup unsweetened shredded coconut

1. Preheat the oven to 350°F. Lightly oil a 9-inch tart pan with a removable bottom.

2. For piecrust, in a medium bowl, combine flour, baking powder, and salt. Add safflower oil, 2 tablespoons agave nectar, and water, and stir until mixture just comes together to form a soft dough.

3. Transfer crust mixture to the prepared pan. Using your hands, firmly press crust mixture to cover the bottom and sides of the tart pan. Place the tart pan on a large cookie sheet.

4. For filling, in a small saucepan over medium heat, cook coconut milk, remaining ⅔ cup agave nectar, and arrowroot, whisking often, for 2 or 3 minutes or until thickened. Remove from heat.

5. Place coconut milk mixture, tofu, vanilla extract, and coconut extract in a blender or food processor fitted with an S blade, and process for 2 minutes or until completely smooth. Scrape down the sides of the container with a rubber spatula, add ½ cup shredded coconut, and process for 30 more seconds.

6. Spread filling mixture into the prepared tart crust. Bake for 25 minutes. Remove from the oven. Sprinkle remaining $1/4$ cup shredded coconut evenly over the top, and bake for 15 more minutes or until filling is set and coconut is golden brown. Remove from the oven. Let cool completely before removing outer rim. Cut into 8 wedges, and serve.

Variation: The filling can also be baked in a store-bought or homemade piecrust, vegan graham cracker crust, or cookie crust.

Soy What?

Store-bought dried or desiccated coconut, either unsweetened or sweetened, comes finely grated or flaked, in medium- or longer-length shreds, as well as in large thick curls or chipped. For more visual appeal, try using coconut chips when decorating the tops of baked goods, cakes, and pies.

Frosted Cupcakes

These golden, vanilla-flavored cupcakes are covered in a fluffy buttercream-style frosting and made with all-vegan ingredients to create the perfect cupcake.

Yield: 12 cupcakes
Prep time: 15 to 20 minutes
Cook time: 20 to 22 minutes
Serving size: 1 cupcake

½ cup plus 2 TB. vanilla soy milk or other nondairy milk of choice

1 tsp. apple cider vinegar or freshly squeezed lemon juice

½ cup water

¼ cup safflower oil or olive oil

2½ tsp. pure vanilla extract

1½ cups whole-wheat pastry flour

¾ cup unbleached cane sugar or beet sugar

¾ tsp. baking powder

½ tsp. baking soda

¼ tsp. sea salt

⅓ cup nonhydrogenated vegan margarine

2½ cups vegan powdered sugar

Toasted shredded coconut, chopped nuts, sprinkles, vegan chocolate shavings, or vegan candies

1. Preheat the oven to 350°F. Line a 12-cup muffin tin with paper liners or lightly oil.

2. For cupcake batter, in a medium bowl, combine ½ cup soy milk and vinegar, and set aside for 5 minutes to thicken.

3. Add water, safflower oil, and 2 teaspoons vanilla extract, and beat with an electric mixer on medium speed or a whisk for 1 minute or until well combined. Add flour, sugar, baking powder, baking soda, and salt, and beat or whisk well to combine.

4. Fill the prepared muffin cups ¾ full. Bake for 20 to 22 minutes or until a toothpick inserted in the center comes out clean. Remove from the oven. Let cool in muffin tins for 15 minutes, and transfer to a rack to cool completely.

5. For frosting, place margarine in a medium bowl, and beat with an electric mixer on medium speed or a whisk for 1 minute. Add powdered sugar, remaining 2 tablespoons soy milk, and remaining $1/2$ teaspoon vanilla extract, and beat or whisk well for 2 or 3 minutes or until light and fluffy. If you want to tint frosting (see Thyme-ly Tip), add small amount of tint and beat well to thoroughly blend color.

6. Using a small spatula or knife, spread frosting on top of cooled cupcakes. Leave them simply frosted or garnish tops with shredded coconut, chopped nuts, sprinkles, chocolate shavings, vegan candies, or your choice of garnishes. Store cupcakes in an airtight container.

Variation: To make white cupcakes, replace the whole-wheat pastry flour with unbleached all-purpose flour. You can also use the cupcake batter to make a 9-inch-round or -square cake, or double the recipe to make two 9-inch cakes or a 9×13-inch cake.

Thyme-ly Tip

To naturally tint your frosting, add a very small amount of turmeric for a yellow tint, beet powder (available in natural foods stores) for a pink tint, or spirulina powder for a green tint. For other natural tints, add a little mashed or puréed fruit like blueberries or strawberries.

Chocolate Lover's Cake

This cake is for all you vegan chocoholics. A combination of baking soda and apple cider vinegar gives this moist, dark chocolaty cake great height, and it's covered in a fluffy chocolate frosting and garnished with a chopped dark chocolate bar.

Yield: 1 (9×13-inch) cake
Prep time: 15 to 20 minutes
Cook time: 20 to 25 minutes
Serving size: 1 piece

2¾ cups whole-wheat pastry flour

2 cups unbleached cane sugar or beet sugar

¾ cup plus ⅓ cup cocoa powder

2 tsp. baking soda

½ tsp. sea salt

2¼ cups water

⅓ cup safflower oil or olive oil

2 TB. apple cider vinegar

2 tsp. pure vanilla extract

⅓ cup nonhydrogenated vegan margarine

2½ cups vegan powdered sugar

3 TB. chocolate soy milk or other nondairy milk of choice

1 (1.4-oz.) vegan dark chocolate bar, coarsely chopped

1. Preheat the oven to 350°F. Lightly oil a 9×13-inch baking pan.

2. For batter, in a large bowl, sift together flour, sugar, ³/₄ cup cocoa powder, baking soda, and salt.

3. In a small bowl, whisk water, safflower oil, vinegar, and 1¹/₂ teaspoons vanilla extract. Add wet ingredients to dry ingredients, and whisk well to combine.

4. Pour batter into the prepared pan, and smooth top with a rubber spatula. Bake for 20 to 25 minutes or until a toothpick inserted in the center comes out clean. Remove from the oven. Let cool completely before frosting cake.

5. For frosting, in a medium bowl, beat margarine with an electric mixer on medium speed or a whisk for 1 minute. Add powdered sugar, remaining ¹/₃ cup cocoa powder, soy milk, and remaining ¹/₂ teaspoon vanilla extract, and beat or whisk well for 2 or 3 minutes or until light and fluffy.

6. Using a small spatula or knife, spread frosting on top of cooled chocolate cake. Sprinkle chopped chocolate bar evenly over top. Cut into 12 pieces and serve. Cover extra chocolate cake with plastic wrap, and store in the refrigerator.

Variation: Vary the flavor of the cake batter by adding other flavoring extracts, such as peppermint, orange, coconut, or coffee. Or stir in some chocolate chips, raspberries, or cherries into the batter prior to baking.

Soy What?

If you're trying for healthier baking, use cocoa powder when making chocolate-flavored baked goods, rather than chocolate chips, baking chocolate, or chocolate bars. It's lower in both fat and calories, and you don't need to chop, grate, or melt it prior to adding to your batter or frosting.

Carrot Cake with Vegan Cream Cheese Frosting

Two layers of this cake are packed with carrots, walnuts, raisins, shredded coconut, and a generous blend of spices, with fresh orange juice and zest added to brighten up the flavor.

Yield: 1 (9-inch) 2-layer cake

Prep time: 20 to 25 minutes plus 30 minutes chilling time

Cook time: 30 to 35 minutes

Serving size: 1 piece

½ cup raisins or dried currants

½ cup freshly squeezed orange juice

1 cup soy milk

¾ cup agave nectar

⅓ cup applesauce

¼ cup safflower oil or olive oil

2 TB. orange zest

1 TB. apple cider vinegar

3½ tsp. pure vanilla extract

3 cups whole-wheat pastry flour

2 tsp. aluminum-free baking powder

2 tsp. baking soda

2 tsp. ground cinnamon

1½ tsp. ground ginger or cardamom

¾ tsp. freshly ground nutmeg

¾ tsp. allspice or ground cloves

½ tsp. sea salt

2½ cups shredded carrots, firmly packed

⅔ cup raw walnuts or pecans, finely chopped

⅓ cup unsweetened shredded coconut

1 (8-oz.) pkg. tofu cream cheese, softened

⅓ cup nonhydrogenated vegan margarine

3 cups vegan powdered sugar

1. Preheat the oven to 350°F. Lightly oil 2 (9-inch-round) cake pans.

2. For batter, in a small bowl, combine raisins and orange juice, and set aside for 10 minutes to rehydrate.

3. Drain orange juice into a medium bowl, and set raisins aside. Add soy milk, agave nectar, applesauce, safflower oil, orange zest, apple cider vinegar, and 2 teaspoons vanilla extract, and whisk well to combine.

4. In a large bowl, sift together flour, baking powder, baking soda, cinnamon, ginger, nutmeg, allspice, and salt. Add wet ingredients to dry ingredients, and whisk well to combine. Add reserved raisins, shredded carrots, walnuts, and shredded coconut, and stir well with a spatula to combine.

5. Divide cake batter evenly between the prepared pans, and smooth tops with a rubber spatula. Bake for 30 to 35 minutes or until a toothpick inserted in the center comes out clean. Remove from the oven. Let cool for 5 minutes in pans and then invert onto a wire rack to cool completely before frosting cake layers.

6. For frosting, place tofu cream cheese and margarine in a medium bowl, and beat with an electric mixer on medium speed or a whisk for 1 minute. Add powdered sugar and remaining $1^1/_2$ teaspoons vanilla extract, and beat or whisk well for 2 or 3 minutes or until light and fluffy.

7. Place one cake layer on a large plate. Using a small spatula or knife, spread $^1/_4$ of frosting on top of first cake layer within $^1/_2$-inch of outer edge. Place remaining cake layer on top. Spread a thin layer of frosting on side of cake to seal in crumbs. Using upward strokes, spread $^2/_3$ of remaining frosting on side of cake to make a thicker layer. Spread remaining frosting on top of cake, either spreading smoothly or swirling, as desired.

8. Place frosted cake in the refrigerator to chill for 30 minutes or longer before cutting. Cut into 12 pieces and serve. Place carrot cake in a lidded cake carrier or cover with plastic wrap, and store in the refrigerator.

Variation: Feel free to omit the raisins, chopped nuts, and shredded coconut for a plainer carrot cake, or replace $^1/_2$ of the shredded carrots with crushed pineapple, as desired.

 Sour Grapes _____

Sugary-sweet frostings can dress up your vegan baked goods, but the ingredients used to make them—namely margarine, soy milk, and/or tofu cream cheese—can spoil at room temperature. Store frosted cupcakes and cakes in the refrigerator. Baked goods do taste better when they aren't ice cold, so pull them out of the refrigerator 10 minutes prior to serving. They can be left out for up to 1 hour.

Hot Fudge Pudding Cake

While baking, this easy-to-prepare dessert transforms from a dumped-in mess of ingredients to a dark chocolate cake resting on a pool of warm chocolate sauce. The chocolate and walnut combination of this rich and gooey cake will remind you of a fudgy brownie.

Yield: 1 (9-inch) pan

Prep time: 10 minutes
Cook time: 35 minutes
Serving size: ²⁄₃ cup

---

1 cup whole-wheat pastry flour

¾ cup unbleached cane sugar

9 TB. cocoa powder

1½ tsp. baking powder

½ tsp. baking soda

½ tsp. ground cinnamon

¼ tsp. sea salt

½ cup soy milk or other nondairy milk of choice

2 TB. safflower oil or olive oil

1 tsp. pure vanilla extract

⅓ cup raw walnuts, coarsely chopped

½ cup packed light or dark brown sugar

1¾ cups boiling water

1. Preheat the oven to 350°F. Lightly oil a 9-inch baking pan.

2. In a medium bowl, combine flour, unbleached cane sugar, 5 tablespoons cocoa powder, baking powder, baking soda, cinnamon, and salt. Add soy milk, safflower oil, and vanilla extract, and stir well to combine.

3. Add walnuts and stir just until mixed. Batter will be thick. Spread batter evenly into the prepared pan.

4. In a small bowl, combine brown sugar and remaining 4 tablespoons cocoa powder. Sprinkle evenly over batter. Pour boiling water over the top. Do not stir.

5. Bake for 35 minutes or until top springs back slightly when pressed. Do not test for doneness with a toothpick. Let cool slightly and serve warm, either plain or with scoops of nondairy ice cream or sorbet as desired.

Variation: For even more flavor, use chocolate soy milk, or add $1/2$ teaspoon flavoring extract, such as coffee, peppermint, or coconut.

Soy What?

There are two types of cocoa powder: Dutch-process and natural (recommended for recipes in this book). Reddish-brown Dutch-process cocoa powder is treated with an alkali to neutralize its acid, so it is used in recipes with baking powder only. Deep, dark brown natural cocoa powder has nothing added, and has a slightly bitter flavor. Recipes using it must contain baking soda with or without baking powder for baked goods to rise properly.

Vegan Cheesecake

This tofu-based cheesecake is flavored with vanilla, lemon juice and zest, and some soy yogurt to provide a slight tang.

1 (7-oz.) pkg. Health Valley Graham Crackers or 1½ cups vegan graham crackers crumbs

1 tsp. ground cinnamon

¼ cup nonhydrogenated vegan margarine

2 lb. firm or extra-firm tofu

1 cup unbleached cane sugar or beet sugar

1 (6-oz.) pkg. plain or vanilla soy yogurt

Juice and zest of 1 lemon

2 TB. pure vanilla extract

Yield: 1 (9-inch) pan
Prep time: 10 minutes plus several hours chilling time
Cook time: 45 minutes
Serving size: 1 piece

1. Preheat the oven to 350°F. Lightly oil a 9-inch springform pan.

2. For crust, place graham crackers and cinnamon in a food processor fitted with an S blade, and process for 1 minute or until crushed to fine crumbs. Add margarine and process for 1 more minute. Using your hands, firmly press crust mixture into the prepared springform pan.

3. Wipe out the food processor with a clean towel.

4. For filling, squeeze tofu blocks over the sink to remove excess water. Crumble tofu into the food processor using your fingers. Add sugar, soy yogurt, lemon zest, lemon juice, and vanilla extract, and process for 3 minutes. Scrape down sides of the container with a rubber spatula, and process for 2 more minutes or until very smooth and creamy.

5. Pour cheesecake filling over crust, and smooth top with a rubber spatula. Bake for 45 minutes. Remove from the oven. Let cool to room temperature, and place in the refrigerator to chill for several hours or preferably overnight.

6. Loosen sides of cheesecake with a knife, and remove ring from the springform pan. Cut into 12 pieces, and serve.

Variation: For a lighter-textured cheesecake, replace 1 pound tofu with 2 (8-ounce) containers tofu cream cheese.

Thyme-ly Tip

Adapt this recipe to make a chocolate tofu cheesecake by blending 2 tablespoons cocoa powder along with the graham cracker crust ingredients. When making the filling, replace the lemon juice and zest with 1½ cups melted vegan chocolate chips. Let cool slightly, and top with the Chocolate Ganache used in the Chocolate–Peanut Butter Brownies (recipe in Chapter 20), leaving a 2-inch border, and chill.

Glossary

agar-agar   Also known as *agar* or *kanten*, agar-agar is an odorless and tasteless seaweed derivative used as a vegan alternative to animal-based gelatin.

agave nectar   Also known as *agave syrup*, agave nectar is a liquid sweetener derived from the Mexican agave cactus, and has a light, delicate flavor sweeter than honey.

almond meal   Also referred to as *almond flour*, almond meal is made from either raw almonds or blanched almonds, finely ground to a powderlike consistency.

arborio rice   A short-grain, highly glutinous white rice grown in Italy. The outer layers contain a high concentration of starch, which is released when cooked.

baking powder   A dry leavening agent used in baking. It usually contains an alkali, like sodium bicarbonate (also known as *baking soda*); an acid, like salt crystals; and a starch.

balsamic vinegar   A special aging process is used to develop the rich, slightly sweet, and highly acidic flavor; dark brown color; and distinctive aroma balsamic vinegar is so famous for.

beet sugar   Sugar made from sugar beets and processed much like cane sugar. Unlike cane sugar, it's never bleached with bone char.

blackstrap molasses   A dark, thick, bittersweet syrup that results from the production of sugar. It contains several B vitamins, calcium, magnesium, potassium, iron, copper, and manganese.

Bragg Liquid Aminos   A liquid protein concentrate, made from soybeans and water, that contains large amounts of dietary essential and nonessential amino acids.

brown rice pasta   A gluten- and egg-free pasta made from brown rice. It can be cooked and used in the same way as wheat or whole-grain pasta in your favorite recipes.

brown rice vinegar   An aged vinegar made from fermented brown rice, water, and koji (a beneficial type of mold), or from unrefined rice wine (sake) and water.

bulgur   Made from steamed or parboiled wheat berries that are dried and crushed or cracked into small, coarse pieces. It can be cooked quickly or simply rehydrated.

cacao nibs   The small, broken pieces of shelled, raw cacao beans used to produce chocolate. They're dark brown with a slightly bittersweet, coffeelike flavor.

chipotle chile powder   Also known as *ground chipotle powder*, this is made from finely ground dried chipotle chiles. It can be used in place of or along with regular chili powder.

chipotle chiles in adobo sauce   Smoked whole jalapeño chiles canned in a red sauce that typically contains tomatoes, onions, garlic, oil, vinegar, herbs and spices, and salt.

edamame   Fresh soybeans that are green in color rather than off-white like the soybeans found canned or dried. Usually sold frozen in grocery and natural foods stores.

Ener-G Egg Replacer   A product made with potato starch, tapioca flour, and leavening agents that can be substituted for eggs in many of your vegan baked goods.

escarole   A member of the endive family that has dark green, broad, flat leaves, and a slightly bitter flavor. Escarole is sometimes used in salads but is most often served cooked.

essential amino acids (EAAs)   These are the necessary protein-building blocks that must be supplied through dietary sources to aid in the synthesis of body proteins.

essential fatty acids (EFAs)   Also known as omega-3 or -6. EFAs are fats required in the diet because the body either does not make, or cannot synthesize, enough for use.

goji berries   Native to Asia, these berries have a dark red color and are roughly the same size as raisins, with a somewhat tart flavor that some compare to cranberries or cherries.

hemp seeds   The shelled edible seeds of the hemp plant that have a mild, nutty flavor similar to sunflower seeds. Rich in dietary fiber, vitamins, minerals, protein, EAAs, and EFAs.

kombu   An edible kelp that contains many beneficial vitamins and nutrients, and is commonly used in Asian cuisine, especially in making soups.

lacinato kale   An Italian heirloom variety of kale also known as *dinosaur kale* because the tender, dark green leaves have a somewhat wrinkled and prehistoric look.

millet   A tall-growing annual grass comprised of several small-seeded species of grains or cereal crops. It is rich in fiber, protein, vitamins, and minerals, and has a mildly sweet, nutty flavor.

miso   A thick paste made from fermenting soybeans with salt and koji (a beneficial type of mold), often along with other ingredients such as beans or grains.

nutritional yeast   An inactive yeast with a nutty, cheeselike flavor. It contains a wide assortment of minerals and B vitamins and can provide a reliable dietary source of B_{12}.

phyllo   Paper-thin sheets of pastry dough, sold in several varieties made from wheat or spelt flours, and used to prepare many Mediterranean and Middle Eastern sweet and savory dishes.

phytochemicals (or phytonutrients)   These naturally occur in fruits, vegetables, and other edible plants, and can help fight and prevent illness and disease, lower cholesterol levels, and balance hormones.

quinoa (*KEEN-wa*)   Commonly referred to as a supergrain, this small and ancient grain is high in protein, essential amino acids, fiber, calcium, and many vitamins and minerals.

red curry paste   A spicy and thick paste, containing chiles and seasonings, used as a condiment and flavoring for curries, soups, stews, sauces, and stir-fries.

rice breadcrumbs   Made from cooked or baked rice, these have a slightly coarser texture than the traditionally used wheat-based fresh and dry breadcrumbs.

rotini   A twisted, spiral-shape pasta great for making cold pasta salads, hot pasta dishes, and casseroles. Its shape helps hold dressings, sauces, chopped vegetables, and vegan cheeses.

roux (*rue*)   A French cooking term that refers to a mixture of fat (such as butter or oil) and flour, which is commonly used as a thickener for sauces, soups, and stews.

sea vegetables   Algae (often referred to as *seaweed*) that grow in both fresh and salt water, and are good sources of lignans, iodine, iron, magnesium, calcium, and several B vitamins.

Sucanat   A brand of sugar made by dehydrating and granulating sugar cane. It has a slightly coarse texture, a dark brown color, and a high concentration of molasses.

sun-dried tomatoes   Made from ripe plum tomato halves that have been left to dry in the sun to remove their natural water content and concentrate their flavor.

tahini   Made from sesame seeds that are ground into a thick paste, tahini has a consistency similar to peanut butter. It is available in both raw and roasted varieties.

toasted sesame oil   Oil that derives its flavor and color from the pressed, toasted sesame seeds used to produce it. It is very aromatic, with a slightly thick consistency and a dark brown color.

tomatillos   These small fruits are often mistaken for green, unripened tomatoes due to their similar appearance, but they have a much firmer texture and a slightly tart flavor.

turbinado sugar   Made with pure raw sugar cane juice and often labeled as *raw cane sugar*. It has a golden caramel color; light molasses flavor; and coarse, crystalline texture.

textured vegetable protein (TVP)   Made from defatted soy flour that's been cooked, extruded, and dried, TVP might also be called *textured soy flour*, *textured soy protein*, or *hydrolyzed vegetable protein*.

vegan powdered sugar   Sugar made from either beet or cane sugar (not refined with bone char–based charcoal) that's processed with a starch, such as cornstarch, to prevent caking.

vital wheat gluten   Also known as *instant gluten flour*, vital wheat gluten is a powdered form of dehydrated pure wheat gluten (protein) used in the production of seitan.

zest   The outer peel of citrus fruit, used to add extra flavor without adding excess moisture to foods. Obtain it from the peel using a fine grater or zester.

Resources

Now that you've begun your journey into vegan cooking, where can you turn for information and support on a wide variety of related issues? Many resources in the form of books and websites provide you with the information you'll need to help maintain your cruelty-free approach to cooking. This appendix helps point you in the right direction for finding all the information you need.

Vegan Cookbooks

Atlas, Nava. *Vegetarian Soups for All Seasons: Bountiful Vegan Soups and Stews for Every Time of Year.* Poughkeepsie, NY: Amberwood Press, 2006.

———. *Vegan Express.* New York: Broadway Books, 2008.

Bennett, Beverly Lynn. *Vegan Bites: Recipes for Singles.* Summertown, TN: Book Publishing Company, 2008.

Bennett, Beverly Lynn, and Ray Sammartano. *The Complete Idiot's Guide to Vegan Living.* Indianapolis: Alpha Books, 2005.

Burton, Dreena. *Eat, Drink, and Be Vegan: Everyday Vegan Recipes Worth Celebrating.* Vancouver: Arsenal Pulp Press, 2007.

Grogan, Bryanna Clark. *The (Almost) No-Fat Cookbook: Everyday Vegetarian Recipes.* Summertown, TN: Book Publishing Company, 1994.

———. *20 Minutes to Dinner: Quick, Low-Fat, Low-Calorie Vegetarian Meals.* Summertown, TN: Book Publishing Company, 1997.

Kramer, Sarah, and Tanya Barnard. *How It All Vegan!: Irresistible Recipes for an Animal-Free Diet.* Vancouver: Arsenal Pulp Press, 1999.

McCarty, Meredith. *Sweet and Natural: More Than 120 Sugar-Free and Dairy-Free Desserts.* New York: St. Martin's Press, 2001.

Moshowitz, Isa Chandra. *Vegan with a Vengeance: Over 150 Delicious, Cheap, Animal-Free Recipes That Rock.* New York: Marlowe and Company, 2005.

Reinfeld, Mark, and Bo Rinaldi. *Vegan World Fusion Cuisine: Healing Recipes and Timeless Wisdom from Our Hearts to Yours.* Thousand Petals Publishing, 2005.

Reinfeld, Mark, Bo Rinaldi, and Jennifer Murray. *The Complete Idiot's Guide to Eating Raw.* Indianapolis: Alpha Books, 2008.

Robertson, Robin. *Vegan Planet: 400 Irresistible Recipes with Fantastic Flavors from Home and Around the World.* Boston: Harvard Common Press, 2003.

Stepaniak, Joanne. *The Ultimate Uncheese Cookbook: Delicious Dairy-Free Cheeses and Classic "Uncheese" Dishes.* Summertown, TN: Book Publishing Company, 2003.

———. *Vegan Vittles: Down-Home Cooking for Everyone.* Summertown, TN: Book Publishing Company, 2007.

Tucker, Eric, and John Westerdahl. *Millennium Cookbook: Extraordinary Vegetarian Cuisine.* Berkeley, CA: Ten Speed Press, 1998.

Vegan Health and Nutrition Books

Barnard, Neal, M.D. *Food for Life: How the New Four Food Groups Can Save Your Life.* New York: Three Rivers Press, 1994.

Campbell, T. Colin, Ph.D., and Thomas M. Campbell II. *The China Study.* Dallas: BenBella Books, 2005.

Davis, Brenda, and Vesanto Melina. *Becoming Vegan: The Complete Guide to Adopting a Healthy Plant-Based Diet.* Summertown, TN: Book Publishing Company, 2000.

Diamond, Harvey, and Marilyn Diamond. *Fit for Life*. New York: Warner Books, 1985.

Klaper, Michael, M.D. *Vegan Nutrition: Pure and Simple*. Maui: Gentle World, 1987.

McDougall, John A., M.D., and Mary McDougall. *The McDougall Program for a Healthy Heart: A Life-Saving Approach to Preventing and Treating Heart Disease*. New York: Penguin Books, 1996.

Ornish, Dean, M.D. *Dr. Dean Ornish's Program for Reversing Heart Disease*. New York: Random House, 1990.

———. *Eat More, Weigh Less*. New York: HarperCollins, 1995.

Saunders, Kerrie K., Ph.D. *The Vegan Diet as Chronic Disease Prevention: Evidence Supporting the New Four Food Groups*. Lantern Books, 2003.

Schlosser, Eric. *Fast Food Nation*. HarperPerennial, 2005.

Books on Vegan Issues

Adams, Carol J. *Living Among Meat Eaters: The Vegetarian's Survival Handbook*. New York: Three Rivers Press, 2001.

Lappé, Frances Moore. *Diet for a Small Planet, 20th Anniversary Edition*. New York: Ballantine Books, 1991.

Lyman, Howard. *Mad Cowboy: Plain Truth from the Cattle Rancher Who Won't Eat Meat*. New York: Touchstone, 1998.

———. *No More Bull! The Mad Cowboy Targets America's Worst Enemy: Our Diet*. New York: Scribner, 2005.

Marcus, Erik. *Vegan: The New Ethics of Eating, Revised Edition*. Ithaca: McBooks Press, 2001.

———. *Meat Market: Animals, Ethics, and Money*. Brio Press, 2005.

Newkirk, Ingrid. *Making Kind Choices: Everyday Ways to Enhance Your Life Through Earth and Animal-Friendly Living*. St. Martin's Griffin, 2005.

Robbins, John. *Diet for a New America: How Your Food Choices Affect Your Health, Happiness and the Future of Life on Earth*. H. J. Kramer, 1998.

———. *The Food Revolution: How Your Diet Can Help Save Your Life and Our World*. Conari Press, 2001.

Vegan Cooking and Nutrition Websites

Beverly Lynn Bennett's "The Vegan Chef"
www.veganchef.com

Nava Atlas
www.vegkitchen.com

Bryanna Clark Grogan
www.bryannaclarkgrogan.com

International Vegetarian Union's Recipes
www.ivu.org/recipes

McDougall Wellness Center
www.drmcdougall.com

Physicians Committee for Responsible Medicine (PCRM)
www.pcrm.org

VeganCooking.com
www.vegancooking.com

VegSource
www.vegsource.com

VegWeb
www.vegweb.com

Vegetarian Resource Group
www.vrg.org

Vegan Food Websites

A Different Daisy
www.differentdaisy.com

Downbound
www.downbound.com

Gold Mine Natural Foods
www.goldminenaturalfoods.com

Mountain Rose Herbs
www.mountainroseherbs.com

Pangea Vegan Products
www.veganstore.com

Vegan Essentials
www.veganessentials.com

Vegan Store (U.K.)
www.veganstore.co.uk

Index

S

X–Y

Z

It's not a diet—
it's a *lifestyle*.

ISBN: 978-1-59257-417-9

Open your mind to the compassionate principles of a vegan lifestyle—and you'll learn about healthful alternatives to strengthen your body and soul. You get:

- Helpful advice on how to transition to a vegan lifestyle.
- The Vegan Food Pyramid—featuring the substitutes that provide you with your daily doses of protein, calcium, and complex carbohydrates.
- Tips on finding animal-free products, including organic shampoos, synthetic brushes, hemp clothing, and products that are not tested on animals.
- Hints for reading ingredient lists and other labels to find "hidden" animal ingredients or byproducts.
- Ways to apply vegan living to all aspects of your life, not just what you eat.

ALPHA

idiotsguides.com